Introducing Second Language Acquisition

Written for students encountering the topic for the first time, this is a clear and practical introduction to Second Language Acquisition (SLA).

It explains in nontechnical language how a second language is acquired; what the second language learner needs to know; and why some learners are more successful than others.

The textbook introduces in a step-by-step fashion a range of fundamental concepts – such as SLA in adults and children, in formal and informal learning contexts, and in diverse sociocultural settings – and takes an interdisciplinary approach, encouraging students to consider SLA from linguistic, psychological, and social perspectives. Each chapter contains a list of key terms, a summary, and a range of graded exercises suitable for self-testing or class discussion. Providing a solid foundation in SLA, this book is set to become the leading introduction to the field for students of linguistics, psychology, education, and trainee language teachers.

MURIEL SAVILLE-TROIKE is Regent's Professor of English at the University of Arizona. She has made significant contributions to the fields of sociolinguistics and applied linguistics, and has previously held posts at Texas A & M University, the University of Texas, Georgetown University, and the University of Illinois. She has previously published *The Ethnography of Communication: An Introduction (Third Edition, 2003), Foundations for Teaching English as a Second Language* (1976), and *A Handbook of Bilingual Education* (with Rudolph C. Troike, 1971).

Cambridge Introductions to Language and Linguistics

This new textbook series provides students and their teachers with accessible introductions to the major subjects encountered within the study of language and linguistics. Assuming no prior knowledge of the subject, each book is written and designed for ease of use in the classroom or seminar, and is ideal for adoption on a modular course as the core recommended textbook. Each book offers the ideal introductory material for each subject, presenting students with an overview of the main topics encountered in their course, and features a glossary of useful terms, chapter previews and summaries, suggestions for further reading, and helpful exercises. Each book is accompanied by a supporting website.

Books published in the series
Introducing Phonology David Odden
Introducing Speech and Language Processing John Coleman
Introducing Phonetic Science John Maidment and Michael Ashby
Introducing Second Language Acquisition Muriel Saville-Troike

Forthcoming:
Introducing Sociolinguistics Miriam Meyerhoff
Introducing Morphology Maggie Tallerman and S. J. Hannahs
Introducing Historical Linguistics Brian Joseph
Introducing Language Bert Vaux

Introducing Second Language Acquisition

MURIEL SAVILLE-TROIKE
University of Arizona

CAMBRIDGE
UNIVERSITY PRESS

CAMBRIDGE UNIVERSITY PRESS
Cambridge, New York, Melbourne, Madrid, Cape Town, Singapore, São Paulo

Cambridge University Press
The Edinburgh Building, Cambridge CB2 2RU, UK

Published in the United States of America by Cambridge University Press, New York

www.cambridge.org
Information on this title: www.cambridge.org/9780521794077

First published 2006

Printed in the United Kingdom at the University Press, Cambridge

A catalogue record for this book is available from the British Library

ISBN-13 978-0-521-79086-4 hardback
ISBN-10 0-521-79086-7 hardback
ISBN-13 978-0-521-79407-7 paperback
ISBN-10 0-521-79407-2 paperback

Contents

About the book

This book is a brief but comprehensive introduction to the field of Second Language Acquisition (SLA). The intended audience is primarily undergraduate students, but it is also suitable for graduate students who have little or no prior knowledge of linguistics.

My goals in writing this book are threefold: (1) to provide a basic level of knowledge about second language learning phenomena to students as part of their general education in humanities, the social sciences, and education; (2) to stimulate interest in second language learning and provide guidance for further reading and study; and (3) to offer practical help to second language learners and future teachers.

Scope and perspective

I have included a broader range of SLA phenomena in this book than is the usual case: those involved in both adult and child second language learning, in both formal (instructed) and informal (natural) contexts of learning, and in diverse sociocultural settings. Since my own professional identity and commitment are interdisciplinary, I emphasize the importance of integrating linguistic, psychological, and social perspectives on SLA even as I recognize the differential nature of their assumptions and contributions. An effort has been made to maintain balance among them in quantity and quality of representation.

The focus of this book is on the acquisition of second language "competence," but this construct is broadly considered from different points of view: as "linguistic competence" (in the sense of underlying grammatical knowledge); as "communicative competence" (adding notions of requisite cultural knowledge and other knowledge which enables appropriate usage); and as knowledge required for participation in communicative activities involving reading, listening, writing, and speaking.

Design

Each chapter of this book considers three basic questions: *What* exactly does the L2 learner come to know? *How* does the learner acquire this knowledge? *Why* are some learners more successful than others? Chapter 1 introduces the most basic terms and concepts, beginning with "What is SLA?" Chapter 2 provides a foundational background, ranging from the nature and distribution of multilingualism in the world to generally accepted notions of contrasts between first and second language acquisition. The chapter concludes with a preview of the different theoretical frameworks of SLA which will be surveyed. Chapters 3 to 5 focus in turn on different disciplinary perspectives: linguistic, psychological, and social. Chapter 6 focuses on the competence required for academic and interpersonal functions, and on the interdependence of content, context, and linguistic knowledge. The final chapter briefly summarizes and integrates answers to the basic *what*, *how*, and *why* questions that are posed throughout the book.

Each chapter includes a preview of its content and a summary. Chapters 1 to 6 conclude with suggested activities for self-checking of understanding and for class discussion or individual exploration. Chapters 2 to 6 include annotated suggestions for further reading on each major topic in that chapter. Important technical concepts are presented sequentially with key terms listed at the beginning of chapters and highlighted with explanations and examples in the text. A comprehensive glossary is provided for student reference, and the subject index allows for integration and reinforcement of concepts across topics and disciplinary perspectives. All terms which appear in the glossary are highlighted in the text, whether or not they are listed as key terms.

Acknowledgments

Any introductory survey of a field is indebted to many sources, and this is no exception (as the relatively long list of references suggests). I am particularly grateful to Karen Barto in the preparation of this work: she developed the suggestions for further reading and chapter activities, and she has contributed significantly to other aspects of conceptualization and development. I am also grateful to colleagues who provided input on earlier drafts (especially Rudy Troike, Peter Ecke, Renate Schulz, and Mary Wildner-Bassett), although they do not bear responsibility for my conclusions. My students at the University of Arizona have been most helpful in providing relevant examples and in indicating where clarification in my presentation was necessary. I could not begin to make an enumeration, but I thank them all.

Every effort has been made to secure necessary permissions to reproduce copyright material in this work, though in some cases it has proved impossible to trace copyright holders. If any omissions are brought to our notice, we will be happy to include appropriate acknowledgments on reprinting or in any subsequent edition.

1 Introducing Second Language Acquisition

CHAPTER PREVIEW

When you were still a very young child, you began acquiring at least one language — what linguists call your **L1** — probably without thinking much about it, and with very little conscious effort or awareness. Since that time, you may have acquired an additional language — your **L2** — possibly also in the natural course of having the language used around you, but more likely with the same conscious effort needed to acquire other domains of knowledge in the process of becoming an "educated" individual. This book is about the phenomenon of adding languages. In this introductory chapter, I will define a few of the key terms that we will use and present the three basic questions that we will explore throughout the book.

What is SLA?

Second Language Acquisition (SLA) refers both to the study of individuals and groups who are learning a language subsequent to learning their first one as young children, and to the process of learning that language. The additional language is called a **second language (L2)**, even though it may actually be the third, fourth, or tenth to be acquired. It is also commonly called a **target language (TL)**, which refers to any language that is the aim or goal of learning. The scope of SLA includes **informal L2 learning** that takes place in naturalistic contexts, **formal L2 learning** that takes place in classrooms, and L2 learning that involves a mixture of these settings and circumstances. For example, "informal learning" happens when a child from Japan is brought to the US and "picks up" English in the course of playing and attending school with native English-speaking children without any specialized language instruction, or when an adult Guatemalan immigrant in Canada learns English as a result of interacting with native English speakers or with co-workers who speak English as a second language. "Formal learning" occurs when a high school student in England takes a class in French, when an undergraduate student in Russia takes a course in Arabic, or when an attorney in Colombia takes a night class in English. A combination of formal and informal learning takes place when a student from the USA takes Chinese language classes in Taipei or Beijing while also using Chinese outside of class for social interaction and daily living experiences, or when an adult immigrant from Ethiopia in Israel learns Hebrew both from attending special classes and from interacting with co-workers and other residents in Hebrew.

In trying to understand the process of second language acquisition, we are seeking to answer three basic questions:

(1) *What* exactly does the L2 learner come to know?
(2) *How* does the learner acquire this knowledge?
(3) *Why* are some learners more successful than others?

There are no simple answers to these questions – in fact, there are probably no answers that all second language researchers would agree on completely. In part this is because SLA is highly complex in nature, and in part because scholars studying SLA come from academic disciplines which differ greatly in theory and research methods. The multidisciplinary approach to studying SLA phenomena which has developed within the last half-century has yielded important insights, but many tantalizing mysteries remain. New findings are appearing every day, making this an exciting period to be studying the subject. The continuing search for answers is not only shedding light on SLA in its own right, but is illuminating related fields. Furthermore, exploring answers to these questions is of potentially great practical value to anyone who learns or teaches additional languages.

SLA has emerged as a field of study primarily from within linguistics and psychology (and their subfields of applied linguistics, psycholinguistics, sociolinguistics, and social psychology), as a result of efforts to answer the

what, *how*, and *why* questions posed above. There are corresponding differences in what is emphasized by researchers who come from each of these
fields:

- Linguists emphasize the characteristics of the differences and
  similarities in the languages that are being learned, and the linguistic
  competence (underlying knowledge) and linguistic performance
  (actual production) of learners at various stages of acquisition.
- Psychologists and psycholinguists emphasize the mental or cognitive
  processes involved in acquisition, and the representation of language(s)
  in the brain.
- Sociolinguists emphasize variability in learner linguistic performance,
  and extend the scope of study to communicative competence
  (underlying knowledge that additionally accounts for language use, or
  pragmatic competence).
- Social psychologists emphasize group-related phenomena, such as
  identity and social motivation, and the interactional and larger social
  contexts of learning.

Applied linguists who specialize in SLA may take any one or more of these
perspectives, but they are also often concerned with the implications of
theory and research for teaching second languages. Each discipline and
subdiscipline uses different methods for gathering and analyzing data in
research on SLA, employs different theoretical frameworks, and reaches its
interpretation of research findings and conclusions in different ways.

It is no surprise, then, that the understandings coming from these different disciplinary perspectives sometimes seem to conflict in ways that
resemble the well-known Asian fable of the three blind men describing an
elephant: one, feeling the tail, says it is like a rope; another, feeling the
side, says it is flat and rubbery; the third, feeling the trunk, describes it as
being like a long rubber hose. While each perception is correct individually, they fail to provide an accurate picture of the total animal because there
is no holistic or integrated perspective. Ultimately, a satisfactory account of
SLA must integrate these multiple perspectives; this book is a step in that
direction. As in the fable of the elephant, three different perspectives are
presented here: linguistic, psychological, and social. I make no presump-
tion that any one perspective among these is 'right' or more privileged, but
believe that all are needed to provide a fuller understanding of the complex phenomena of SLA.

What is a second language?

I have broadly defined the scope of SLA as concerned with any phenomena
involved in learning an L2. Sometimes it is necessary for us to make further
distinctions according to the function the L2 will serve in our lives, since
this may significantly affect *what* we learn. These differences may determine the specific areas of vocabulary knowledge we need, the level of grammatical complexity we have to attain, and whether speaking or reading

skills are more important. The following are distinctions commonly made in the literature:

- A **second language** is typically an official or societally dominant language needed for education, employment, and other basic purposes. It is often acquired by minority group members or immigrants who speak another language natively. In this more restricted sense, the term is contrasted with other terms in this list.
- A **foreign language** is one not widely used in the learners' immediate social context which might be used for future travel or other cross-cultural communication situations, or studied as a curricular requirement or elective in school, but with no immediate or necessary practical application.
- A **library language** is one which functions primarily as a tool for further learning through reading, especially when books or journals in a desired field of study are not commonly published in the learners' native tongue.
- An **auxiliary language** is one which learners need to know for some official functions in their immediate political setting, or will need for purposes of wider communication, although their first language serves most other needs in their lives.

Other restricted or highly specialized functions for 'second' languages are designated **language for specific purposes** (such as *French for Hotel Management*, *English for Aviation Technology*, *Spanish for Agriculture*, and a host of others), and the learning of these typically focuses only on a narrow set of occupation-specific uses and functions. One such prominent area is *English for Academic Purposes* (*EAP*).

What is a first language?

There is also sometimes a need to distinguish among the concepts **first language**, **native language**, **primary language**, and **mother tongue**, although these are usually treated as a roughly synonymous set of terms (generalized as **L1** to oppose the set generalized as **L2**). The distinctions are not always clear-cut. For purposes of SLA concerns, the important features that all shades of L1s share are that they are assumed to be languages which are acquired during early childhood – normally beginning before the age of about three years – and that they are learned as part of growing up among people who speak them. Acquisition of more than one language during early childhood is called **simultaneous multilingualism**, to be distinguished from **sequential multilingualism**, or learning additional languages after L1 has already been established. ('Multilingualism' as used here includes bilingualism.) Simultaneous multilingualism results in more than one "native" language for an individual, though it is undoubtedly much less common than sequential multilingualism. It appears that there are significant differences between the processes and/or results of language acquisition by young children and by older learners, although this is an issue which is still open to debate, and is one of those which we will explore in chapters to follow.

Diversity in learning and learners

As already noted, the circumstances under which SLA takes place sometimes need to be taken into account, although they are perhaps too often taken for granted and ignored. *What* is learned in acquiring a second language, as well as *how* it is learned, is often influenced by whether the situation involves informal exposure to speakers of other languages, immersion in a setting where one needs a new language to meet basic needs, or formal instruction in school, and these learning conditions are often profoundly influenced by powerful social, cultural, and economic factors affecting the status of both languages and learners.

The intriguing question of *why* some L2 learners are more successful than others requires us to unpack the broad label "learners" for some dimensions of discussion. Linguists may distinguish categories of learners defined by the identity and relationship of their L1 and L2; psycholinguists may make distinctions based on individual aptitude for L2 learning, personality factors, types and strength of motivation, and different learning strategies; sociolinguists may distinguish among learners with regard to social, economic, and political differences and learner experiences in negotiated interaction; and social psychologists may categorize learners according to aspects of their group identity and attitudes toward target language speakers or toward L2 learning itself. All of these factors and more will be addressed in turn in the following chapters.

Chapter summary

Second Language Acquisition (SLA) involves a wide range of language learning settings and learner characteristics and circumstances. This book will consider a broad scope of these, examining them from three different disciplinary perspectives: *linguistic*, *psychological*, and *social*. Different approaches to the study of SLA have developed from each of these perspectives in attempts to answer the three basic questions: *What* exactly does the L2 learner come to know? *How* does the learner acquire this knowledge? *Why* are some learners more (or less) successful than others?

Activities

Questions for self-study

1. Match the following terms to their definitions:

1.	target language	a.	has no immediate or necessary practical application, might be used later for travel or be required for school
2.	second language	b.	the aim or goal of language learning
3.	first language	c.	an officially or societally dominant language (not speakers' L1) needed for education, employment or other basic purposes
4.	foreign language	d.	acquired during childhood

2. The underlying knowledge of language is called _____.
3. Actual production of language is called _____.

Active learning

1. List all of the languages that you can use. First classify them as L1(s) and L2(s), and then further classify the L2(s) as "second," "foreign," "library," "auxiliary," or "for special purposes." Finally, distinguish between the ways you learned each of the languages: through informal exposure, formal instruction, or some combination of these.
2. Do you think that you are (or would be) a "good" or a "poor" L2 learner? Why do you think so? Consider whether you believe that your own relative level of success as a language learner is due primarily to linguistic, psychological, or social factors (social may include type of instruction, contexts of learning, or attitudes toward the L1 and L2).

2 Foundations of Second Language Acquisition

CHAPTER PREVIEW

KEY TERMS

Multilingualism/ bilingualism

Monolingualism

Multilingual competence

Monolingual competence

Learner language

Positive transfer

Negative transfer

Fossilization

Poverty-of-the-stimulus

Most of us, especially in countries where English is the majority language, are not aware of the prevalence of multilingualism in the world today, nor the pervasiveness of second language learning. We begin this chapter with an overview of these points, then go on to explore the nature of language learning, some basic similarities and differences between L1 and L2 learning, and "the logical problem of language acquisition." An understanding of these issues is a necessary foundation for our discussion of linguistic, psychological, and social perspectives on SLA in the next chapters. We follow this with a survey of the theoretical frameworks and foci of interest which have been most important for the study of SLA within each of the three perspectives.

The world of second languages

Multilingualism refers to the ability to use two or more languages. (Some linguists and psychologists use **bilingualism** for the ability to use two languages and **multilingualism** for more than two, but we will not make that distinction here.) **Monolingualism** refers to the ability to use only one. No one can say for sure how many people are multilingual, but a reasonable estimate is that at least half of the world's population is in this category. Multilingualism is thus by no means a rare phenomenon, but a normal and common occurrence in most parts of the world. According to François Grosjean, this has been the case as far back as we have any record of language use:

> [B]ilingualism is present in practically every country of the world, in all classes of society, and in all age groups. In fact it is difficult to find a society that is genuinely monolingual. Not only is bilingualism worldwide, it is a phenomenon that has existed since the beginning of language in human history. It is probably true that no language group has ever existed in isolation from other language groups, and the history of languages is replete with examples of language contact leading to some form of bilingualism.
>
> (1982:1)

Reporting on the current situation, G. Richard Tucker concludes that

> there are many more bilingual or multilingual individuals in the world than there are monolingual. In addition, there are many more children throughout the world who have been and continue to be educated through a second or a later-acquired language, at least for some portion of their formal education, than there are children educated exclusively via the first language.
>
> (1999:1)

Given the size and widespread distribution of multilingual populations, it is somewhat surprising that an overwhelming proportion of the scientific attention which has been paid to language acquisition relates only to monolingual conditions and to first language acquisition. While there are interesting similarities between L1 and L2 acquisition, the processes cannot be equated, nor can multilingualism be assumed to involve simply the same knowledge and skills as monolingualism except in more than one language. This point is made most cogently by Vivian Cook, who introduced the concept of **multilingual competence** (his term is "multicompetence") to refer to "the compound state of a mind with two [or more] grammars" (1991:112). This is distinguished from **monolingual competence** (or "monocompetence" in Cook's terminology), which refers to knowledge of only one language.

> L2 users differ from monolinguals in L1 knowledge; advanced L2 users differ from monolinguals in L2 knowledge; L2 users have a different metalinguistic awareness from monolinguals; L2 users have different cognitive processes. These subtle differences consistently suggest that people with multicompetence are not simply equivalent to two monolinguals but are a unique combination.
>
> (Cook 1992:557)

One message from world demographics is that SLA phenomena are immensely important for social and practical reasons, as well as for academic ones. Approximately 6,000 languages are spoken in the world, with widely varying distribution, and almost all of them have been learned as second languages by some portion of their speakers. The four most commonly used languages are Chinese, English, Spanish, and Hindi, which are acquired by over 2 billion as L1s and almost 1.7 billion as L2s, as shown in 2.1 (based on Zhu 2001 and Crystal 1997b):

2.1 Estimated L1/L2 distribution of numerically dominant languages		
	L1 speakers (in millions)	L2 speakers (in millions)
Chinese	1,200	15
English	427	950
Spanish	266	350
Hindi	182	350

Even just among these four numerically dominant languages, there is great variance. Chinese is an L1 for many more people than any other language, and English is by far the most common L2. In China alone, a recent estimate of numbers of people studying English exceeds 155 million: 10 million in elementary school, 80 million in high school, at least 5 million in universities, and 60 million adults in other instructional contexts. Many more millions will soon be added to these estimates as China implements mandatory English instruction at the primary level. Demographic change is also illustrated by the fact that there are now perhaps 15 million speakers of Chinese L2 (this number is far from certain), but the increasing involvement and influence of China in international economic and political spheres is being accompanied by an increase in the election or need for people elsewhere to learn Mandarin Chinese, the official national language (different varieties, such as Cantonese and Taiwanese, are as different as German and Swedish). An indicator of this trend in the USA is that by 1998, the Modern Language Association reported that Chinese had become the sixth most commonly taught foreign language in US colleges and universities, and numbers are steadily growing.

While multilingualism occurs in every country, for a variety of social reasons the distribution of multiple language use is quite unequal. In some countries, e.g. Iceland, very few people speak other than the national language on a regular basis, while in other countries, such as parts of west Africa, close to 100 percent of the speakers of the national language also speak another language. English L1 speakers often expect to be able to "get along" in English anywhere in the world they may travel for tourism, business, or diplomatic purposes, and may be less likely to become fluent in other languages in part for this reason.

Those who grow up in a multilingual environment acquire multilingual competence in the natural course of using two or more languages from childhood with the people around them, and tend to regard it as perfectly normal to do so. Adding second languages at an older age often takes considerable effort, however, and thus requires motivation. This motivation may arise from a variety of conditions, including the following:

- Invasion or conquest of one's country by speakers of another language;
- A need or desire to contact speakers of other languages in economic or other specific domains;
- Immigration to a country where use of a language other than one's L1 is required;
- Adoption of religious beliefs and practices which involve use of another language;
- A need or desire to pursue educational experiences where access requires proficiency in another language;
- A desire for occupational or social advancement which is furthered by knowledge of another language;
- An interest in knowing more about peoples of other cultures and having access to their technologies or literatures.   (Crystal 1997b)

The numbers of L1 and L2 speakers of different languages can only be estimated. Reasons for uncertainty in reporting language data include some which have social and political significance, and some which merely reflect imprecise or ambiguous terminology. For example:

1. Linguistic information is often not officially collected

Census forms in many countries do not include questions on language background, presumably because there is no particular interest in this information, because it is impractical to gather, or because it is considered to be of a sensitive nature. In cases where responses concerning language would essentially identify minority group members, sensitivities can be either personal or political: personal sensitivities can arise if identification might lead to undesired consequences; political sensitivities can be at issue if the government does not wish to recognize how many speakers of minority languages there are in order to downplay the political importance of a group, or in order to emphasize cultural/linguistic homogeneity and cohesion by not according recognition to cultural/linguistic diversity.

2. Answers to questions seeking linguistic information may not be reliable

Respondents may not want to be identified as speakers of a minority language. For instance, this was the case for a survey which was conducted several years ago for a rural school district in California. The survey was of parents with preschool children, asking them about the language(s) used at home in order to anticipate future English L2 instructional program needs. Many Hispanic parents insisted that they spoke primarily English at home even when they could only understand and respond to the interviewers when questions were asked in Spanish. Their linguistic "misrepresentation" was likely motivated by fear that lack of English would trigger further questions about their US citizenship (a reasonable concern on their part, although not the school's intent). In other cases, respondents may say that they use the dominant language more than they actually do because they reject or are ashamed of their ethnic heritage and wish to assimilate, or because they are afraid of government oppression or social stigmatization. Others may similarly over-report dominant language use because they feel this is the appropriate answer to give official representatives, or in order to qualify for civil privileges, such as being allowed to vote.

On the other hand, respondents may over-report use of minority and ancestral languages because of pride in their heritage. There may also be over-reporting of minority language use in order to obtain more recognition, resources, or services for the groups with which they identify.

How questions are worded also commonly contributes to the unreliability and non-comparability of language data. For example, the following questions might all be intended to elicit the identity of speakers' L1, but the same speakers might respond differently depending on which question is asked:

- What is your native language?
- What is your mother tongue?
- What language did you learn first as a child?
- What language was usually spoken in your home when you were a child?
- What language are you most likely to use with family and friends?
- What is your strongest language?

3. There is lack of agreement on definition of terms and on criteria for identification

It may be difficult for someone to answer the common census question, "What is your native language?" for example, if they acquired multilingual competence simultaneously in two languages. In this case, both are L1s, and either or both might be considered a "native language." Such a question is also problematic for individuals whose language dominance (or relative fluency) has shifted from their L1 to a language learned later.

Another issue is the degree of multilingualism. What level of proficiency is needed before one claims to have multilingual competence, or to "know" a second language? Does reading knowledge alone count, or must one also be able to carry on a conversation? What about languages that have been learned only in relation to limited domains or for special purposes? Do claims of multilingualism require near-balance in ability to function in multiple languages, or does multilingual competence include even early stages of L2 learning (the view in much SLA research)?

Perhaps the most basic definitional basis for unreliability in statistics lies in the meaning of "language" itself, for what counts as a separate language involves social and political (as well as linguistic) criteria. For instance, religious differences and the use of different writing systems result in Hindi and Urdu being counted as distinct languages in India, although most varieties are mutually intelligible; on the other hand, mutually unintelligible "dialects" of Chinese (such as Mandarin and Cantonese) are counted as the same language when emphasis on national cohesion is desired. Similar examples arise when languages are reclassified, a process which may accompany political change. For instance, the demise of Yugoslavia as a political entity led to the official distinction as separate languages of Bosnian and Montenegrin, which had been categorized within former Serbo-Croatian (itself a single language divided into national varieties distinguished by different alphabets because of religious differences). Social status or prestige may also play a role, as in whether Haitian Creole is to be considered a separate language or a variety of French. The creole originated as a contact language between slaves who spoke African languages and French-speaking slave traders and colonists, evolving its own systematic grammar while incorporating vocabulary from French. Linguists classify the creole as a separate language because its grammar and usage are quite distinct from French. In contrast, some people disparage the creole as not a "real" language, but merely an inferior variety of French. Recognition of this and other creoles as full-fledged languages goes beyond linguistic consideration because such recognition strengthens the social identity and status of the people who speak them. There are also potentially important educational implications. For instance, when teachers recognize that native speakers of Haitian Creole are really learning a second language in acquiring French, they are likely to use different instructional methods. Thus teachers no longer view their task as "correcting" or "cleaning up" their students' "bad French," and are more likely to feel that the second language can simply be added to the first rather than having to replace it. Regrettably, there is a common attitude among educators, sometimes pursued with almost religious fervor, that socially "inferior" or "uneducated" varieties of a language are a moral threat and should be completely eradicated.

The nature of language learning

Much of your own L1 acquisition was completed before you ever came to school, and this development normally takes place without any conscious effort. By the age of six months an infant has produced all of the vowel sounds and most of the consonant sounds of any language in the world, including some that do not occur in the language(s) their parents speak. If children hear English spoken around them, they will learn to discriminate among those sounds that make a difference in the meaning of English words (the **phonemes**), and they will learn to disregard those that do not. If the children hear Spanish spoken around them, they will learn to discriminate among some sounds the English speaker learns to ignore, as between the flapped *r* in *pero* 'but' and the trilled *rr* in *perro* 'dog,' and to disregard some differences that are not distinctive in Spanish, but vital to English word-meaning, as the *sh* and *ch* of *share* and *chair*.

On average children have mastered most of the distinctive sounds of their first language before they are three years old, and an awareness of basic discourse patterns such as conversational turn-taking appear at an even earlier age. Children control most of the basic L1 grammatical patterns before they are five or six, although complex grammatical patterns continue to develop through the school years.

The same natural and generally effortless learning processes take place when there is significant exposure to more than one language in early childhood. If young children hear and respond to two (or more) languages in their environment, the result will be **simultaneous multilingualism** (multiple L1s acquired by about three years of age). As noted in the first chapter, simultaneous multilingualism is not within the usual scope of study in SLA, which focuses on **sequential multilingualism** (L2s acquired after L1).

Our understanding of (and speculation about) how children accomplish the early mastery of L1(s) has changed radically in the past fifty years or so, primarily owing to developments in linguistics and psychology. It was once suggested that first language acquisition is in large part the result of children's natural desire to please their doting parents, who wait impatiently for them to utter a recognizable word. Yet the offspring of even relatively indifferent parents successfully acquire language at about the same rate. Others argued that children's language acquisition is purposive, that they develop language because of their urge to communicate their wants and needs to the people who take care of them. This has not proven to be an adequate explanation, however, since within children's limited sphere of activity, communicative needs seem to be largely satisfied by gesture and such non-speech sounds as squeals, whines, grunts, and cries.

Perhaps the most widely held view by the middle of the twentieth century was that children learn language by imitation (the **stimulus-response theory**). While it is true that much of children's initial language learning can be attributed to their imitation of sounds and words around them, many of their utterances are quite original and cannot be explained as imitations at all, since they can never have heard them before.

The role of natural ability

Humans are born with a natural ability or **innate capacity** to learn language. Such a predisposition must be assumed in order to explain several facts:

- Children begin to learn their L1 at the same age, and in much the same way, whether it is English, Bengali, Korean, Swahili, or any other language in the world.
- Children master the basic phonological and grammatical operations in their L1 by the age of about five or six, as noted above, regardless of what the language is.
- Children can understand and create novel utterances; they are not limited to repeating what they have heard, and indeed the utterances

that children produce are often systematically different from those of the adults around them.

- There is a cut-off age for L1 acquisition, beyond which it can never be complete.
- Acquisition of L1 is not simply a facet of general intelligence.

In viewing the natural ability to acquire language in terms of **innate capacity**, we are saying that part of language structure is genetically "given" to every human child. All languages are incredibly complex systems which no children could possibly master in their early years to the degree they succeed in doing so if they had to "learn" them in the usual sense of that word. Children's ability to create new utterances is remarkable, and their ability to recognize when a string of common words does *not* constitute a grammatical sentence in the language is even more so. For example, children acquiring English L1 can recognize early on that *Cookies me give* is ungrammatical. They have never been told, surely, that the particular group of words is not an English sentence, but they somehow know, nevertheless. If a child had to consciously learn the set of abstract principles that indicate which sequences of words are possible sentences in their language as opposed to those that are not, only the smartest would learn to talk, and it would take them many more years than it actually does. This is part of "the logical problem of language acquisition," which is discussed further below.

A hypothesis which many linguists and psychologists support is that a great many of these abstract principles are common to all language, as opposed to the principles that are language-specific (i.e. specific to particular languages). According to this view, those principles that are universal are "programmed" into all human children just by virtue of their being human, and this accounts for children's ability to process the smorgasbord of sounds and words that they hear, and their ability to come up with essentially the same structures as other children.

To explain why all L1 development follows essentially the same sequence, we may view children's language development as a gradual process of acquiring a more and more complex set of structures and rules for combining them. Because the stages and levels of language development can be delineated and studied, it is possible to talk about **child grammar**: that is, it is possible to systematically describe the kinds of utterances a child can produce or understand at a given maturational level. The differences between their grammar and that used by adults are not viewed as failures on the part of the children, but are considered the normal output of children at that level of development. As children mature, so do their language abilities. Since certain grammatical processes are more complex than others, they require a higher maturational level than simpler ones. As Jean Piaget observed several decades ago (e.g. 1926), in order to master complexities in their L1 which are beyond their present linguistic grasp, what normal children need is additional time, not additional stimuli.

The *rate* of progression through stages of language development can vary radically among individual children, even as the *order* of development is relatively invariant both for different children and for different languages. This is because the rate may be influenced by individual factors, while the order is "primarily determined by the relative semantic and grammatical complexity of constructions" (Brown 1973:59).

Saying that there is a "cut-off point" for L1 acquisition means that normal development does not occur if the process does not begin in childhood. Even when acquisition starts at an early age, there is evidence that progress in language development usually begins to slow sharply at about the age of puberty – no matter what level has been reached. Severely retarded children, who have a slower rate of development (but in the same relative sequence), are likely never to develop a complete adult grammar for this reason. The effects of age on both L1 and L2 acquisition are discussed in Chapter 4 as the **Critical Period Hypothesis**.

Given the complexity of language, it is no wonder that even adults with their mature intellects seldom attain native fluency in a new language. But almost all children, with their limited memories, restricted reasoning powers, and as yet almost nonexistent analytical abilities, acquire perfect fluency in any language to which they are adequately exposed, and in which they interact with others. The ability to acquire language could not be dependent upon intellectual powers alone, since children with clearly superior intelligence do not necessarily begin to speak earlier, or with better results, than children of ordinary intellect.

The role of social experience

Not all of L1 acquisition can be attributed to innate ability, for language-specific learning also plays a crucial role. Even if the universal properties of language are preprogrammed in children, they must learn all of those features which distinguish their L1 from all other possible human languages. Children will never acquire such language-specific knowledge unless that language is used with them and around them, and they will learn to use only the language(s) used around them, no matter what their linguistic heritage. American-born children of Korean or Greek ancestry will never learn the language of their grandparents if only English surrounds them, for instance, and they will find their ancestral language just as hard to learn as any other English speakers do if they attempt to learn it as an adult. Appropriate social experience, including L1 input and interaction, is thus a necessary condition for acquisition.

Intentional L1 teaching to young children is not necessary and indeed may have little effect. Some parents "correct" their children's immature pronunciation and grammar but most do not, and there is no noticeable change in rate of acquisition among children who receive such instruction. Some adults simplify both grammar and word choice, adding more complex structures as the child does, but adults' notion of "simplicity" does not correspond to the actual sequence in language acquisition. Some adults imitate children's language production, and in this imitation, they sometimes provide expansions of children's structures (such as saying *Yes, that's a big, brown dog* in response to the child saying *That dog*). The expansion may play a role in developing children's ability to understand new forms, but it cannot be considered necessary since many children do not receive this type of input and still develop language at essentially the same rate.

Sources of L1 input and interaction vary depending on cultural and social factors. Mothers' talk is often assumed to be the most important source of early language input to children, but fathers or older siblings have major childrearing responsibilities in many societies and may be the dominant source of input, and wealthier social classes in many cultures delegate most of the childrearing responsibilities to nannies or servants. The relative importance of input from other young children also varies in different cultures, as does the importance of social institutions such as nursery schools.

As long as children are experiencing adequate L1 input and interaction from people around them, the rate and sequence of their phonological and grammatical development does not appear to vary systematically according to its source, although children's pronunciation is naturally influenced by the regional and social varieties or styles of the L1 which they hear. There is considerable variance in vocabulary knowledge depending on social context, however, because vocabulary is typically learned in conjunction with social experiences. There is also variation to some extent in what functions of speaking children learn to use at an early age depending on social experience. For example, I have found that children who attend nursery school are often more advanced in development of verbal skills that are needed for controlling and manipulating other children than are children who are raised at home without the experience of interacting and competing with peers.

When young children's social experience includes people around them using two or more languages, they have the same innate capacity to learn both or all of them, along with the same ability to learn the language-specific features of each without instruction. Acquiring other languages after early childhood presents some significant differences, which we will explore in the following section.

L1 versus L2 learning

This brief comparison of L1 and L2 learning is divided into three phases. The first is the initial state, which many linguists and psychologists believe includes the underlying knowledge about language structures and principles that is in learners' heads at the very start of L1 or L2 acquisition. The second phase, the intermediate states, covers all stages of basic language development. This includes the maturational changes which take place in what I have called "child grammar," and the L2 developmental sequence which is known as learner language (also interlanguage or IL). For this phase, we will compare processes of L1 and L2 development, and then compare the conditions which are necessary or which facilitate language learning. The third phase is the final state, which is the outcome of L1 and L2 learning.

A simplified representation of these three phases is included in 2.2, along with a listing of some major points of contrast between L1 and L2 learning which we will consider here.

2.2 First vs. second language development	
L1	L2
INITIAL STATE	
Innate capacity	Innate capacity? L1 knowledge World knowledge Interaction skills
INTERMEDIATE STATES	
Child grammar	**Learner language**
Basic processes	
Maturation	Transfer
Necessary conditions	
Input Reciprocal interaction	Input
Facilitating conditions	
	Feedback Aptitude Motivation Instruction . . . .
FINAL STATE	
Native competence	Multilingual competence

Initial state

While the initial state in children's minds for L1 almost surely is an innate capacity to learn language, it is not at all certain whether or not such natural ability is part of the initial state in older learners for L2 acquisition (hence the "?" in 2.2). Some linguists and psychologists believe that the genetic predisposition which children have from birth to learn language remains with them throughout life, and that differences in the final outcomes of L1 and L2 learning are attributable to other factors. Others believe that some aspects of the innate capacity which children have for L1 remain in force for acquisition of subsequent languages, but that some aspects of this natural ability are lost with advancing age. Still others believe that no innate capacity for language acquisition remains beyond childhood, and that subsequent languages are learned by means which are more akin to how older learners acquire other domains of knowledge, such as mathematics or history.

Because it is impossible for us to observe mental capacity for language learning directly, the different beliefs are based largely on theoretical assumptions and are tested by indirect methods which individuals who come from different disciplinary perspectives may not agree on. For example, many linguists rely on learners' ability to judge which L2 utterances are not possible (such as the *Cookies me give* example mentioned above), an aspect of children's L1 competence which is attributed to innate capacity. Many who take a social perspective tend to reject such judgments of (un)grammaticality as convincing evidence because they result from artificial tasks which do not include actual circumstances of L2 interpretation and use. Many who take a psychological perspective in turn reject socially constituted evidence (such as natural language production) because the many variables which go along with actual social usage cannot be controlled for experimental investigation. So, although the question of the extent to which innate capacity for language acquisition remains available in SLA is a very interesting and important one, it is likely to remain unresolved for some years to come.

There is complete agreement, however, that since L2 acquisition follows L1 acquisition, a major component of the initial state for L2 learning must be prior knowledge of L1. This entails knowledge of how language (in general) works, as well as a myriad of language-specific features which are only partially relevant for production of the new L2. This prior knowledge of L1 is responsible for the **transfer** from L1 to L2 during second language development, which we will consider as part of the second phase of L1 versus L2 learning.

L2 learners also already possess real-world knowledge in their initial state for language acquisition which young children lack at the point they begin learning their L1. This has come with cognitive development and with experience by virtue of being older. The initial state for L2 learning also includes knowledge of means for accomplishing such interactional functions as requesting, commanding, promising, and apologizing, which have developed in conjunction with L1 acquisition but are not present in the L1 initial state.

The initial state of L1 learning thus is composed solely of an innate capacity for language acquisition which may or may not continue to be available for L2, or may be available only in some limited ways. The initial state for L2 learning, on the other hand, has resources of L1 competence, world knowledge, and established skills for interaction, which can be both an asset and an impediment.

Intermediate states

Both L1 and L2 learners go through intermediate states as they progress from their initial to their final state linguistic systems. There is similarity in that the development of both L1 and L2 is largely systematic, including predictable sequencing of many phenomena within each and some similarity of sequencing across languages, and in the fact that L1 and L2 learners both play a creative role in their own language development and do not merely mimic what they have heard or been taught.

Processes

Development, as we have seen, is a spontaneous and largely unconscious process in L1 child grammar, where it is closely correlated with cognitive maturation. As noted above, as children mature, so do their language abilities. In contrast, the development of **learner language** (or **interlanguage**) for L2 learners occurs at an age when cognitive maturity cannot be considered a significant factor; L2 learners have already reached a level of maturity where they can understand and produce complex utterances in their L1, and level of maturity is not language-specific. Processes other than maturation must be involved to explain development in SLA.

Just as we cannot directly observe mental capacity, we cannot directly observe developmental processes, but we can infer from the utterances which learners understand and produce at different stages what processes are possibly taking place. This addresses the fundamental *how* question of SLA, which we will explore from different perspectives in the chapters which follow. While answers to this question vary, there is general agreement that cross-linguistic influence, or **transfer** of prior knowledge from L1 to L2, is one of the processes that is involved in interlanguage development. Two major types of transfer which occur are:

- **positive transfer**, when an L1 structure or rule is used in an L2 utterance and that use is appropriate or "correct" in the L2; and
- **negative transfer** (or **interference**), when an L1 structure or rule is used in an L2 utterance and that use is inappropriate and considered an "error."

Cross-linguistic influence occurs in all levels of IL: vocabulary, pronunciation, grammar, and all other aspects of language structure and use. Positive transfer facilitates L2 learning because an L1 structure or rule that also works for L2 means that a new one doesn't have to be learned. For example, a word that has essentially the same form and meaning in both languages can transfer appropriately from L1 to L2: e.g. *exterior* 'outside' is a word in both Spanish and English (pronounced differently, but with the same spelling and meaning). Negative transfer of L1 features can often be inferred from forms in the second language which are unlike any that are likely to be produced by a native speaker of the L2, or are an integration of elements which would not occur in monolingual speech. Inappropriate transfer of L1 pronunciation to L2 is detectable as a "foreign accent" in a nonnative speaker's production, and is probably the most common and most easily recognized aspect of L1 influence. Interference at the grammatical level is illustrated in the following utterances made by learners of English L2, which a native English speaker would be unlikely to produce:

Can I assist to your class?
I have been always to class on time.

We have noted that, in addition to L1 competence, older children and adults have access to world knowledge that has come with cognitive development and with experience, and this is also available for L2 use during the intermediate states. The concepts associated with advanced world knowledge are often much too complex for adequate expression with limited L2 ability, but they may be at least partially conveyed in context, and they are likely to stimulate L2 vocabulary learning. For example, older children in immigrant families may enroll in US schools with prior knowledge of academic subject areas (such as science and mathematics) which are at least equal to or more advanced than US curriculum expectations, but they may lack the English L2 competence to express what they know. These students do not need to learn those concepts again, since the concepts themselves are not dependent on any specific language; they merely require new language-specific forms to represent them in L2. Even advanced international students in such fields as engineering and computer science find it much easier to learn English L2 terms for concepts they have already acquired than native English speakers do for acquiring those terms and concepts to begin with.

Adults in immigrant families to the USA often know how to drive a car, and they are likely to have vocational knowledge and skills which transfer to the new social setting. Some English must be learned before they can pass a test for a driver's license in the USA along with a few new rules and regulations, but they don't need to learn how to drive all over again. Similarly, job-related English can generally be added with relative ease to prior vocational knowledge and skills. Transfer of knowledge and skills to an L2 setting is clearly made easier when L1 support is available as part of L2 learning, and when key terminology is shared across languages, but conceptual transfer occurs in any case.

Many skills for social interaction which have been developed in L1 also transfer to L2, as I suggested above. These often also involve positive transfer and facilitate IL development, but some are inappropriate for L2 contexts. Examples of how communication can be achieved with limited shared linguistic means are presented in Chapter 5.

Necessary conditions

Language input to the learner is absolutely necessary for either L1 or L2 learning to take place. Children additionally require interaction with other people for L1 learning to occur. In contrast, while reciprocal social interaction generally facilitates SLA, it is not a necessary condition. It is possible for some individuals to reach a fairly high level of proficiency in L2 even if they have input only from such generally non-reciprocal sources as radio, television, or written text. The role of input and interaction in SLA is also discussed in Chapter 5.

Facilitating conditions

While L1 learning by children occurs without instruction, and while the rate of L1 development is not significantly influenced by correction of immature forms or by degree of motivation to speak, both rate and ultimate level of development in L2 can be facilitated or inhibited by many social and individual factors. Identifying and explaining facilitating conditions essentially addresses the fundamental *why* question of SLA: *why* are some L2 learners more successful than others?

Some of the conditions which will be explored in chapters that follow are:

- **feedback**, including correction of L2 learners' errors;
- **aptitude**, including memory capacity and analytic ability;
- **motivation**, or need and desire to learn;
- **instruction**, or explicit teaching in school settings.

Final state

The final state is the outcome of L1 or L2 learning. The final state of L1 development – by definition – is native linguistic competence. While vocabulary learning and cultivation of specialized registers (such as formal academic written style) may continue into adulthood, the basic phonological and grammatical systems of whatever language(s) children hear around them are essentially established by the age of about five or six years (as we have already noted), along with vocabulary knowledge and interaction skills that are adequate for fulfilling communicative functions. This is a universal human achievement, requiring no extraordinary aptitude or effort.

On the other hand, the final state of L2 development – again by definition – can never be totally native linguistic competence, and the level of proficiency which learners reach is highly variable. Some learners reach "near-native" or "native-like" competence in L2 along with native competence in L1, but many cease at some point to make further progress toward the learning target in response to L2 input, resulting in a final state which still includes instances of L1 interference or creative structures different from any that would be produced by a native speaker of the L2 (a "frozen" state of progress known as fossilization in SLA). The complex of factors which contribute to differential levels of ultimate multilingual development is of major interest for both SLA theory and second language teaching methods.

The logical problem of language learning

How is it possible for children to achieve the final state of L1 development with general ease and complete success, given the complexity of the linguistic system which they acquire and their immature cognitive capacity at the age they do so? This question forms the logical problem of language learning. The "problem" as it has been formulated by linguists relates most importantly to syntactic phenomena. As noted in the preceding section, most linguists and psychologists assume this achievement must be attributed to innate and spontaneous language-learning constructs and/or processes. The notion that innate linguistic knowledge must underlie language acquisition was prominently espoused by Noam Chomsky (1957, 1965), who subsequently formulated a theory of Universal Grammar which has been very influential in SLA theory and research (to be discussed in Chapter 3). This view has been supported by arguments such as the following:

1. Children's knowledge of language goes beyond what could be learned from the input they receive

This is essentially the poverty-of-the-stimulus argument. According to this argument, children often hear incomplete or ungrammatical utterances along with grammatical input, and yet they are somehow able to filter the language they hear so that the ungrammatical input is not incorporated into their L1 system. Further, children are commonly recipients of simplified input from adults, which does not include data for all of the complexities which are within their linguistic competence. In addition, children hear only a finite subset of possible grammatical sentences, and yet they are able to abstract general principles and constraints which allow them to interpret and produce an infinite number of sentences which they have never heard before. Even more remarkable, children's linguistic competence includes knowledge of which sentences are *not* possible, although input does not provide them with this information: i.e. input "underdetermines" the grammar that develops. Almost all L1 linguistic input to children is **positive evidence**, or actual utterances by other speakers which the children are able to at least partially comprehend. Unlike many L2 learners, children almost never receive any explicit instruction in L1 during the early years when acquisition takes place, and they seldom receive any **negative evidence**, or correction (and often fail to recognize it when they do).

2. Constraints and principles cannot be learned

Children's access to general constraints and principles which govern language could account for the relatively short time it takes for the L1 grammar to emerge, and for the fact that it does so systematically and without any "wild" divergences. This could be so because innate principles lead children to organize the input they receive only in certain ways and not others. In addition to the lack of negative evidence mentioned above, constraints and principles cannot be learned in part because children acquire a first language at an age when such abstractions are beyond their comprehension; constraints and principles are thus outside the realm of learning processes which are related to general intelligence. Jackendoff (1997) approaches this capacity in children as a "paradox of language acquisition":

If general-purpose intelligence were sufficient to extract the principles of mental grammar, linguists (or psychologists or computer scientists), at least some of whom have more than adequate general intelligence, would have discovered the principles long ago. The fact that we are all still searching and arguing, while every normal child manages to extract the principles unaided, suggests that the normal child is using something other than general-purpose intelligence.   (p. 5)

3. Universal patterns of development cannot be explained by language-specific input

Linguistic input always consists of the sounds, words, phrases, sentences, and other surface-level units of a specific human language. However, in spite of the surface differences in input (to the point that people who are speaking different languages can't understand one another), there are similar patterns in child acquisition of any language in the world. The extent of this similarity suggests that language universals are not only constructs derived from sophisticated theories and analyses by linguists, but also innate representations in every young child's mind.

The logical problem of language learning

For a long time, people thought that children learned language by imitating those around them. More recent points of view claim that children have an innate language ability. There are three major arguments supporting this notion.

First of all, children often say things that adults do not. This is especially true of children's tendency to use regular patterns to form plurals or past tenses on words that would have irregular formation. Children frequently say things like *goed*, *mans*, *mouses*, and *sheeps*, even though it is highly unlikely that any adult around them ever produced such forms in front of them.

We also know that children do not learn language simply by imitation because they do not imitate adult language well when asked to do so. For example (adapted from Crystal 1997b:236):

CHILD: He taked my toy!
MOTHER: No, say "he took my toy."
CHILD: He taked my toy!
(*Dialogue repeated seven times.*)
MOTHER: No, now listen carefully: say *"He took my toy."*
CHILD: Oh! He taked my toy!

Next, children use language in accordance with general universal rules of language even though they have not yet developed the cognitive ability necessary to understand these rules. Therefore, we know that these rules are not learned from deduction or imitation.

Finally, patterns of children's language development are not directly determined by the input they receive. The age at which children begin to produce particular language elements does not correspond to their frequency in input. Thus, we must assume that something besides input triggers the developmental order in children's language.

If we extend the logical problem from L1 acquisition to SLA, we need to explain how it is possible for individuals to achieve multilingual competence when that also involves knowledge which transcends what could be learned from the input they receive. In other words, L2 learners also develop an underlying system of knowledge about that language which they are not taught, and which they could not infer directly from anything they hear (see White 1996). As we have already seen, however, in several important respects L1 and L2 acquisition are fundamentally different; the arguments put forth for the existence of an innate, language-specific faculty in young children do not all apply to L2 learners since they are not uniformly successful, they are typically more cognitively advanced than young children, they may receive and profit from instruction and negative evidence, and they are influenced by many factors which seem irrelevant to acquisition of L1.

It is widely accepted that there is an innate capacity involved in L1 acquisition by young children (although many do not agree with Chomsky's particular formulation of its nature), but there is less certainty about the continued availability of that capacity for acquiring an L2. Still, we do need to explain how multilingual competence transcends input, and why there are such widely differential outcomes of SLA – ranging from L2 performance which may be perceived as native to far more limited L2 proficiency. This will be an important question to keep in mind as we review theories and findings on SLA from different perspectives, since it has provided a topic of inquiry for much of the history of this field.

Frameworks for SLA

Interest in second language learning and use dates back many centuries (e.g. see McCarthy 2001), but it is only since the 1960s that scholars have formulated systematic theories and models to address the basic questions in the field of SLA which were listed in Chapter 1: (1) *What* exactly does the L2 learner know? (2) *How* does the learner acquire this knowledge? (3) *Why* are some learners more successful than others? As I noted earlier, different approaches to the study of SLA can be categorized as primarily based on *linguistic*, *psychological*, and *social* frameworks. Each of these perspectives will be the subject of a separate chapter, although we should keep in mind that there are extensive interrelationships among them.

Important theoretical frameworks that have influenced the SLA approaches which we will consider are listed in 2.3, arranged by the discipline with which they are primarily associated, and sequenced according to the decade(s) in which they achieved relevant academic prominence:

Prior to the 1960s, interest in L2 learning was tied almost exclusively to foreign language teaching concerns. The dominant linguistic model through the 1950s was Structuralism (e.g. Bloomfield 1933), which emphasized the

2.3 Frameworks for study of SLA			
Timeline	Linguistic (Chapter 3)	Psychological (Chapter 4)	Social (Chapter 5)
1950s and before	Structuralism	Behaviorism	Sociocultural Theory
1960s	Transformational-Generative Grammar	Neurolinguistics Information Processing	Ethnography of Communication Variation Theory
1970s	Functionalism	Humanistic models	Acculturation Theory Accommodation Theory
1980s	Principles and Parameters Model	Connectionism	Social Psychology
1990s	Minimalist Program	Processability	

description of different levels of production in speech: phonology (sound systems), morphology (composition of words), syntax (grammatical relationships of words within sentences, such as ordering and agreement), semantics (meaning), and lexicon (vocabulary). The most influential cognitive model of learning that was applied to language acquisition at that time was Behaviorism (Skinner 1957), which stressed the notion of habit formation resulting from S-R-R: stimuli from the environment (such as linguistic input), responses to those stimuli, and reinforcement if the responses resulted in some desired outcome. Repeated S-R-R sequences are "learned" (i.e. strong stimulus-response pairings become "habits"). The intersection of these two models formed the disciplinary framework for the Audiolingual Method, an approach to language teaching which emphasized repetition and habit formation that was widely practiced in much of the world at least until the 1980s. Although it had not yet been applied to second language concerns, Vygotsky's Sociocultural Theory (1962 in English translation) was also widely accepted as a learning theory by mid-century, emphasizing interaction with other people as critical to the learning process. This view is still influential in SLA approaches which are concerned with the role of input and interaction.

Linguistic

There have been two foci for the study of SLA from a linguistic perspective since 1960: internal and external. The internal focus has been based primarily on the work of Noam Chomsky and his followers. It sets the goal of study as accounting for speakers' internalized, underlying knowledge of language (linguistic competence), rather than the description of surface forms as in earlier Structuralism. The external focus for the study of SLA has emphasized language use, including the functions of language which are realized in learners' production at different stages of development.

Internal focus

The first linguistic framework with an internal focus is Transformational-Generative Grammar (Chomsky 1957, 1965). The appearance of this work revolutionized linguistic theory and had a profound effect on the study of both first and second languages. Chomsky argued convincingly that the behaviorist theory of language acquisition is wrong because it cannot explain the creative aspects of our linguistic ability. He called attention to the "logical problem of language acquisition" which we discussed earlier in this chapter, and claimed the necessity of assuming that children begin with an innate capacity which is biologically endowed. These views have dominated most linguistic perspectives on SLA to the present day.

This framework was followed by the Principles and Parameters Model and the Minimalist Program, also formulated by Chomsky. Specification of what constitutes "innate capacity" in language acquisition has been revised to include more abstract notions of general principles and constraints that are common to all human languages as part of Universal Grammar. The Minimalist Program adds distinctions between lexical and functional category development, as well as more emphasis on the acquisition of feature specification as a part of lexical knowledge.

External focus

The most important linguistic frameworks contributing to an external focus on SLA are categorized within **Functionalism**, which dates back to the early twentieth century and has its roots in the Prague School of Eastern Europe. They differ from the Chomskyan frameworks in emphasizing the information content of utterances, and in considering language primarily as a system of communication. Some of them emphasize similarities and differences among the world's languages and relate these to sequence and relative difficulty of learning; some emphasize acquisition as largely a process of mapping relations between linguistic functions and forms, motivated by communicative need; and some emphasize the means learners have of structuring information in L2 production and how this relates to acquisition. Approaches based on functional frameworks have dominated European study of SLA and are widely followed elsewhere in the world.

Psychological

There have been three foci in the study of SLA from a psychological perspective: languages and the brain, learning processes, and learner differences.

Languages and the brain

The location and representation of language in the brain has been of interest to biologists and psychologists since the nineteenth century, and the expanding field of **Neurolinguistics** was one of the first to influence cognitive perspectives on SLA when systematic study began in the 1960s. Lenneberg (1967) generated great interest when he argued that there is a **critical period** for language acquisition which has a neurological basis, and much age-related research on SLA is essentially grounded in this framework. As we will see in Chapter 4, exploratory procedures associated with brain surgery on multilingual patients, as well as the development of modern noninvasive imaging techniques, are dramatically increasing knowledge in this area.

Learning processes

The focus on learning processes has been heavily influenced by computer-based **Information Processing (IP)** models of learning, which were established in cognitive psychology by the 1960s. Explanations of SLA phenomena based on this framework involve assumptions that L2 is a highly complex skill, and that learning L2 is not essentially unlike learning other highly complex skills. Processing itself (of language or any other domain) is believed to cause learning. A number of approaches to SLA have been based on IP, including several that will be discussed in Chapter 4. They have been especially productive in addressing the question of *how* learners acquire knowledge of L2, and in providing explanations for sequencing in language development. **Processability** is a more recently developed framework which extends IP concepts of learning and applies them to teaching second languages.

Connectionism is another cognitive framework for the focus on learning processes, beginning in the 1980s and becoming increasingly influential. It differs from most other current frameworks for the study of SLA in not considering language learning to involve either innate knowledge or abstraction of rules and principles, but rather to result from increasing strength of associations (connections) between stimuli and responses. Because this framework considers frequency of input an important causative factor in learning, it is also providing a theoretical base for research on language teaching.

Learner differences

The focus on learner differences in SLA has been most concerned with the question of *why* some learners are more successful than others. It arises in part from the humanistic framework within psychology, which has a long history in that discipline, but has significantly influenced second language teaching and SLA research only since the 1970s (see Williams and Burden 1997). This framework calls for consideration of emotional involvement in learning, such as affective factors of attitude, motivation, and anxiety level. This focus also considers biological differences associated with age and sex, as well as some differences associated with aspects of processing.

Social

Some of the frameworks that I categorize within a social perspective can also be considered linguistic, since they relate to language form and function; some can also be considered cognitive, since they explore learning processes or attitude and motivation. We will review them in this section because (in addition to linguistic and cognitive factors) they all emphasize the importance of social context for language acquisition and use.

There are two foci for the study of SLA from this perspective: microsocial and macrosocial.

Microsocial focus

The concerns within the microsocial focus relate to language acquisition and use in immediate social contexts of production, interpretation, and interaction. The frameworks provided by Variation Theory and Accommodation Theory include exploration of systematic differences in learner production which depend on contexts of use, and they consider why the targets of SLA may be different even within groups who are ostensibly learning the "same" language. Vygotsky's Sociocultural Theory also contributes to this focus, viewing interaction as the essential genesis of language.

Macrosocial focus

The concerns of the macrosocial focus relate language acquisition and use to broader ecological contexts, including cultural, political, and educational settings. The Ethnography of Communication framework extends the notion of what is being acquired in SLA beyond linguistic and cultural factors to include social and cultural knowledge that is required for appropriate use, and leads us to consider second language learners as members of groups or communities with sociopolitical as well as linguistic bounds. The frameworks provided by Acculturation Theory and Social Psychology offer broader understandings of how such factors as identity, status, and values affect the outcomes of SLA.

2.4 Perspectives, foci, and frameworks		
Perspective	Focus	Framework
Linguistic	Internal	Transformational-Generative Grammar Principles and Parameters Model Minimalist Program
	External	Functionalism
	Languages and the brain	Neurolinguistics
Psychological	Learning processes	Information Processing Processability Connectionism
	Individual differences	Humanistic models
Social	Microsocial	Variation Theory Accommodation Theory Sociocultural Theory
	Macrosocial	Ethnography of Communication Acculturation Theory Social Psychology

We will consider the foci and frameworks since 1960 in the next three chapters (see 2.4). As we now start to explore each of these in more depth, we should remind ourselves that no one perspective or framework among those surveyed in this book has the "final answer" or is more privileged, and that all are needed to provide an adequate understanding of SLA.

Chapter summary

For a variety of reasons, the majority of people in the world know more than one language. The first language is almost always learned effortlessly, and with nearly invariant success; second language learning involves many different conditions and processes, and success is far from certain. This may be at least partly because older learners no longer have the same natural ability to acquire languages as do young children, and because second language learning is influenced by prior knowledge of the first and by many individual and contextual factors.

This chapter has identified a number of theoretical frameworks which provide the bases for different approaches to the study of SLA that we will consider. All of these approaches address the basic *what*, *how*, and *why* questions that we posed, but they have different foci of interest and attention. Linguistic frameworks differ in taking an internal or external focus on language; psychological frameworks differ in whether they focus on languages and the brain, on learning processes, or on individual differences; and social frameworks differ in placing their emphasis on micro or macro factors in learning. Like the lenses with different color filters used in photographing Mars, these complement one another and all are needed to gain a full spectrum picture of the multidimensional processes involved in SLA. Even so, much remains a mystery, stimulating continued research.

Activities

Questions for self-study

1. List at least five possible motivations for learning a second language at an older age.
2. Sounds that make a difference in the identity of words are called_____.
3. Match the following terms to their definitions:

1. innate capacity	a. when a second language is introduced after the native language has been acquired
2. sequential bilingualism	b. when young children acquire more than one language at the same time
3. simultaneous bilingualism	c. natural ability

4. What is the initial state of language development for L1 and L2 respectively?
5. What is a necessary condition for language learning (L1 or L2)?
6. Give at least two reasons that many scientists believe in some innate capacity for language.
7. Linguists have taken an internal and/or external focus to the study of language acquisition. What is the difference between the two?

Active learning

1. If you can use two or more languages, why is this so? What has been your reason for learning second language(s)? If you can use only one, why haven't you learned other languages? Compare your response to this question with those of other individuals and make a list of reasons for multilingualism or monolingualism. Categorize these reasons as primarily based on individual preference and need or on social and political circumstances.

2. Think about the facilitating conditions to language learning discussed in this chapter. Have you had any of these experiences facilitate your own learning? If so, which ones? Have there been other factors as well that influenced your learning? In your answer to question 2 in Chapter 1, did you consider any of these conditions?

3. Based on your personal and educational experience, do you expect to prefer or feel more comfortable with one of the perspectives on SLA (linguistic, psychological, social)? Why or why not? If so, what are some strategies you can use to keep an open mind to the perspectives you might not privilege?

4. It is a matter of debate what level of proficiency is needed before one claims to have multilingual competence, or to 'know' a second language. How did you decide what to count as L2(s) in question 1 of Chapter 1? Do you have exposure to other languages that you did not list? If so, explain why you did not list those languages. Now that you have read Chapter 2, have your ideas changed about how proficient one must be to be considered to have an L2?

Further reading

Lightbown, P. M. & Spada, N. (1999). *How Languages are Learned* (Second Edition). Oxford: Oxford University Press.

Lightbown and Spada present a highly accessible overview of second language learning, with discussion of theories of learning and factors that affect second language learning. Additionally, second language learning and teaching in the school setting are treated, as are popular myths about language learning.

Bialystok, E. & Hakuta, K. (1994). *In Other Words: The Science and Psychology of Second-Language Acquisition*. New York: Basic Books.

Chapter 1, "First word," is a clear introduction to the important questions of second language acquisition from psychological and social perspectives, such as why there are learning differences among individuals who are different ages, are acquiring related versus unrelated languages, or have different educational experiences.

3 The linguistics of Second Language Acquisition

CHAPTER PREVIEW

KEY TERMS

Interference

*Interlanguage
(IL)*

Natural order

*Universal
Grammar (UG)*

Language faculty

Principles

Parameters

Initial state

Final state

Markedness

*Grammaticali-
zation*

In this chapter we survey several approaches to the study of SLA that have been heavily influenced by the field of linguistics since the middle of the twentieth century. We begin with a characterization of the nature of language, and with a consideration of the knowledge and skills which people must have in order to use any language fluently. We follow this with a survey of early linguistic approaches to SLA, beginning with **Contrastive Analysis** and then several which take an **internal focus** on learners' **creative construction** of language: **Error Analysis, Interlanguage, Morpheme Order Studies,** and the **Monitor Model.** We bring the internal focus up to date with discussion of **Universal Grammar (UG),** and what constitutes the **language faculty** of the mind. Finally, to complete the chapter, we switch to approaches which involve an **external focus** on the functions of language that emerge in the course of second language acquisition: **Systemic Linguistics, Functional Typology, Function-to-Form Mapping, and Information Organization.**

The Nature of language

What is it that we learn when we learn a language? If we look up a definition of "language" in a dictionary, we will probably see reference to its verbal features (oral and written), to its function in communication, and to its uniquely human character. Most linguists would agree that all naturally occurring languages also share the following characteristics:

- **Languages are systematic.** They consist of recurrent elements which occur in regular patterns of relationships. All languages have an infinite number of possible sentences, and the vast majority of all sentences which are used have not been memorized. They are created according to rules or principles which speakers are usually unconscious of using – or even of knowing – if they acquired the language(s) as a young child. Although we use the same stock of words over and over, it is safe to assume that, for instance, most of the particular combinations of words making up the sentences in a daily newspaper have never been used before. How, then, do we understand them? We can do so because we understand the principles by which the words are combined to express meaning. Even the sounds we produce in speaking, and the orders in which they occur, are systematically organized in ways that we are totally unaware of.

- **Languages are symbolic.** Sequences of sounds or letters do not inherently possess meaning. The meanings of symbols in a language come through the tacit agreement of a group of speakers. For example, there is no resemblance between the four-legged animal that eats hay and the spoken symbol [*hors*] or the written symbol *horse* which we use to represent it in English. English speakers agree that the hay-eating animal will be called a *horse*, Spanish speakers *caballo*, German *Pferd*, Chinese *ma*, and Turkish *at*.

- **Languages are social.** Each language reflects the social requirements of the society that uses it, and there is no standard for judging whether one language is more effective for communication than another, other than to estimate the success its users may have in achieving the social tasks that are demanded of them. Although the capacity for first language acquisition is inherent in the neurological makeup of every individual, no one can develop that potential without interaction with others in the society he or she grows up in. We use language to communicate, to categorize and catalogue the objects, events, and processes of human experience. We might well define language at least in part as "the expressive dimension of culture." It follows that people who function in more than one cultural context will communicate more effectively if they know more than one language.

Linguists traditionally divide a language into different levels for description and analysis, even though in actual use all levels must interact and function simultaneously. The human accomplishment of learning language(s) seems all the more remarkable when we consider even a simplified list of the areas of knowledge which every L1 or L2 learner must acquire at these different levels:

- lexicon (vocabulary)
  - word meaning
  - pronunciation (and spelling for written languages)
  - grammatical category (part of speech)
  - possible occurrence in combination with other words and in idioms
- phonology (sound system)
  - speech sounds that make a difference in meaning (phonemes)
  - possible sequences of consonants and vowels (syllable structure)
  - intonation patterns (stress, pitch, and duration), and perhaps tone in words
  - rhythmic patterns (pauses and stops)
- morphology (word structure)
  - parts of words that have meaning (morphemes)
  - inflections that carry grammatical information (like number or tense)
  - prefixes and suffixes that may be added to change the meaning of words or their grammatical category
- syntax (grammar)
  - word order
  - agreement between sentence elements (as number agreement between subject and verb)
  - ways to form questions, to negate assertions, and to focus or structure information within sentences
- discourse
  - ways to connect sentences, and to organize information across sentence boundaries
  - structures for telling stories, engaging in conversations, etc.
  - scripts for interacting and for events

All of this knowledge about language is automatically available to children for their L1 and is somehow usually acquired with no conscious effort. Completely comparable knowledge of L2 is seldom achieved, even though much time and effort may be expended on learning. Still, the widespread occurrence in the world of high levels of multilingual competence attests to the potential power and effectiveness of mechanisms for SLA. Explaining what these mechanisms are has been a major objective in the study of SLA from a variety of linguistic perspectives.

Early approaches to SLA

We begin our survey of early approaches with Contrastive Analysis (CA), which predates the establishment in the 1960s of SLA as a field of systematic study. This is an important starting point because aspects of CA procedures are still incorporated in more recent approaches, and because CA introduced a continuing major theme of SLA research: the influence of L1 on L2. The revolution in linguistic theory introduced by Noam Chomsky (1957) redirected much of SLA study to an internal focus, which is manifested in the other early (i.e. predating 1980) approaches included in this section.

Contrastive Analysis

Contrastive Analysis (CA) is an approach to the study of SLA which involves predicting and explaining learner problems based on a comparison of L1 and L2 to determine similarities and differences. It was heavily influenced by theories which were dominant in linguistics and psychology within the USA through the 1940s and 1950s, Structuralism and Behaviorism. The goal of CA (as that of still earlier theories of L2 learning) was primarily pedagogical in nature: to increase efficiency in L2 teaching and testing. Robert Lado states this clearly in his introduction to *Linguistics Across Cultures* (1957), a book which became a classic guide to this approach:

The plan of the book rests on the assumption that we can predict and describe the patterns that will cause difficulty in learning, and those that will not cause difficulty, by comparing systematically the language and culture to be learned with the native language and culture of the student. In our view, the preparation of up-to-date pedagogical and experimental materials must be based on this kind of comparison.   (vii)

Following notions in structuralist linguistics, the focus of CA is on the surface forms of both L1 and L2 systems, and on describing and comparing

Robert Lado (b. Tampa, Florida) 1915–1995

Linguistics

Robert Lado's pioneering work on contrastive analysis, *Linguistics Across Cultures*, was published in 1957. Lado was an exemplary applied linguist, seeking to discover the problems that foreign language students would encounter in the learning process. On the faculty of Georgetown University from 1960–80, he was the first dean of the School of Languages and Linguistics there from 1961 to 1973. Altogether, he wrote more than 100 articles and 60 books on language and linguistics.

Interesting note: Though born in the United States, Robert Lado was the son of Spanish immigrants and grew up in Spain. He returned to the United States as an adult to attend college, and studied with Charles Fries at the University of Michigan.

the languages one level at a time – generally contrasting the phonology of L1 and L2 first, then morphology, then syntax, with the lexicon receiving relatively little attention, and discourse still less. A "bottom-up" priority for analysis (generally from smaller to larger units) is also expressed as a priority for language learning, of structures before meaning. Charles Fries, who was a leading figure in applying structural linguistics to L2 teaching, makes this priority very clear: "In learning a new language, . . . the chief problem is not at first that of learning vocabulary items. It is, first, the mastery of the sound system. . . . It is, second, the mastery of the features of arrangement that constitute the structure of the language" (Fries 1945:3).

Following notions in behaviorist psychology, early proponents of CA assumed that language acquisition essentially involves habit formation in a process of Stimulus – Response – Reinforcement (S-R-R). Learners respond to the stimulus (linguistic input), and reinforcement strengthens (i.e. habituates) the response; they imitate and repeat the language that they hear, and when they are reinforced for that response, learning occurs. The implication is that "practice makes perfect."

Another assumption of this theory is that there will be transfer in learning: in the case of SLA, this means the transfer of elements acquired (or habituated) in L1 to the target L2. The transfer is called positive (or facilitating) when the same structure is appropriate in both languages, as in the transfer of a Spanish plural morpheme -*s* on nouns to English (e.g. *lenguajes* to *languages*). The transfer is called negative (or interference) when the L1 structure is used inappropriately in the L2, as in the additional transfer of Spanish plural -*s* to a modifier in number agreement with the noun: e.g. *lenguajes modernas* to *Moderns Languages* (a translation which was printed at the top of a letter that I received from South America), or *greens beans* (for 'green beans,' which I saw posted as a vegetable option in a US cafeteria near the Mexican border).

The process of CA involves describing L1 and L2 at each level, analyzing roughly comparable segments of the languages for elements which are likely to cause problems for learners. This information provides a rationale for constructing language lessons that focus on structures which are predicted to most need attention and practice, and for sequencing the L2 structures in order of difficulty.

To summarize Lado's (1957) position: the easiest L2 structures (and presumably first acquired) are those which exist in L1 with the same form, meaning, and distribution and are thus available for positive transfer; any structure in L2 which has a form not occurring in L1 needs to be learned, but this is not likely to be very difficult if it has the same meaning and distribution as an "equivalent" in L1; among the most difficult are structures where there is partial overlap but not equivalence in form, meaning, and/or distribution, and these are most likely to cause interference. Lado gives examples in Spanish and English for some of the types of contrasts he describes, which I include in the accompanying box. I have ordered them from least to most probable difficulty for speakers of one of these languages learning the other.

Types of Interference

Same form and meaning, different distribution

Spanish: *la paloma blanca* 'the dove white'; *las palomas blancas* 'the (pl) doves whites'

English: *the white dove; the white doves*

> The form -*s* and the meaning "plural" are the same in both languages, but the distribution of occurrence is different. Spanish attaches the -*s* to articles, modifiers, and nouns, but English attaches it only to nouns. This is the same contrast which was illustrated in the earlier examples of *Moderns Languages* and *greens beans*. (The difference in word order is a contrast in form at another level of analysis.)

Same meaning, different form

Spanish: *iré* '(I) will go'

English: I *will go*

> The meaning "future" is expressed by different grammatical elements in the two languages. In Spanish it is conveyed by the future tense suffix -*é* added to the infinitive form of the verb *ir* 'to go,' while it is conveyed by the auxiliary verb *will* in English. (The first person subject is another contrast in form, also conveyed by the Spanish suffix -*é* while the overt pronoun *I* is required in English.)

Same meaning, different form and distribution

Spanish: *agua* 'water'

English: *water*

> The English word *water* may occur as a noun in *a glass of water*, as a verb in w*ater the garden*, and as a modifier noun in the compound *water meter*. The Spanish word *agua* may occur only as a noun unless its form is changed: i.e. its distribution is more limited than that of the equivalent in English.

Different form, partial overlap in meaning

Spanish: *pierna* 'leg of humans'; *pata* 'leg of animals or furniture'; *etapa* 'leg of a race or trip'

English: *leg*

> The scope of meaning for the English word *leg* covers the scope of three different words in Spanish; no single equivalent term can be used in both languages.

Similar form, different meaning

Spanish: *asistir* 'to attend'

English: *assist*

> Similar words like these are sometimes called "false friends," and are predicted to cause great difficulty for speakers of one language learning the other. Since the words look and sound so much alike, L2 learners are likely to assume that they also share meaning.

While CA highlighted potential learning problems, behaviorist learning theory attributed variable success by L2 learners in part to the nature of the relationship between L1 and L2 (and thus to the potential for negative versus positive transfer), but most importantly to circumstances of learning which promote poor versus good habit formation. Fries related L2 accuracy in English to the priorities he set for learning: "one can achieve mere fluency in a foreign language too soon . . . Such students, with fluency in vocabulary but with no basic control of either the sound system or the structure, are almost without exception hopeless so far as ever achieving a satisfactory control of English is concerned" (1945:3).

The CA approach of the 1940s to 1960s was not adequate for the study of SLA in part because the behaviorist learning theory to which it is tied cannot explain the logical problem of language learning that was addressed in Chapter 2 (how learners know more than they have heard or have been taught). Another problem was that CA analyses were not always validated by evidence from actual learner errors. Many of the L2 problems which CA predicts do not emerge; CA does not account for many learner errors; and much predicted positive transfer does not materialize. A major limitation in application to teaching has been that instructional materials produced according to this approach are language-specific and unsuitable for use with speakers of different native languages. Still, CA stimulated the preparation of hundreds of comparative grammars (including many unpublished masters theses and doctoral dissertations at universities around the world), and its analytic procedures have been usefully applied to descriptive studies and to translation, including computer translation. Further, there has been a more recent revival and revision of CA procedures, including contrasts of languages at more abstract levels, and extension of the scope of analysis to domains of cross-cultural communication and rhetoric.

Error Analysis

Error Analysis (EA) is the first approach to the study of SLA which includes an internal focus on learners' creative ability to construct language. It is based on the description and analysis of actual learner errors in L2, rather than on idealized linguistic structures attributed to native speakers of L1 and L2 (as in CA). EA largely augmented or replaced CA by the early 1970s because of the following developments:

- Predictions made by CA did not always materialize in actual learner errors, as noted above. More importantly, perhaps, many real learner errors could not be attributed to transfer from L1 to L2.
- As linguistic theory changed, the exclusive focus on surface-level forms and patterns by structural linguists shifted to concern for underlying rules.
- The behaviorist assumption that habit formation accounts for language acquisition was seriously questioned by many linguists and psychologists. There was a shift to Mentalism in explanations of

language acquisition, with emphasis on the innate capacity of the language learner rather than on external influences.

- The study of SLA was no longer motivated as strongly by teaching concerns as it had been for CA. L2 learning came to be thought of as independent of L2 teaching to some extent, and researchers began to separate issues in SLA from pedagogical concerns. Learning processes became an important focus for study in their own right.

The shift in primary focus from surface forms and patterns to underlying rules, and the parallel shift in efforts to explain acquisition from Behaviorism to Mentalism, are attributable in large part to the revolution in linguistics which resulted from Noam Chomsky's introduction of Transformational-Generative (TG) Grammar (1957, 1965). Chomsky claimed that languages have only a relatively small number of essential rules which account for their basic sentence structures, plus a limited set of transformational rules which allow these basic sentences to be modified (by deletions, additions, substitutions, and changes in word order). The finite number of basic rules and transformations in any language accounts for an infinite number of possible grammatical utterances. (Note that these "rules" merely describe what native speakers say, not what someone thinks they *should* say.) "Knowing" a language was seen as a matter of knowing these rules rather than memorizing surface structures. Since speakers of a language can understand and produce millions of sentences they have never heard before, they cannot merely be imitating what they have heard others say, but must be applying these underlying rules to create novel constructions. Language thus came to be understood as rule-governed behavior.

Under this influence from linguistics and related developments in psychology, the study of first language acquisition adopted notions that inner forces (interacting with the environment) drive learning, and that the child is an active and *creative* participant in the process rather than a passive recipient of language "stimuli." Structures of child language production began to be described and analyzed as grammatical systems in their own right rather than in terms of how they are "deficient" in comparison to adult norms (Miller 1964; McNeil 1966). Similar notions began to be applied to the study of second language learning at about the same time, in part to address the issue of how L1 and L2 acquisition processes might be the same or different.

The most influential publication launching Error Analysis as an approach in SLA was S. Pit Corder's (1967) article on "The significance of learners' errors," which calls on applied linguists to focus on L2 learners' errors not as "bad habits" to be eradicated, but as sources of insight into the learning processes. Corder claimed that errors provide evidence of the system of language which a learner is using at any particular point in the course of L2 development, and of the strategies or procedures the learner is using in his "discovery of the language." In a sense, errors are windows into the language learner's mind. In this approach, learner language is viewed as a target of analysis which is potentially independent of L1 or L2, and the state of learner knowledge is seen as **transitional competence** on the path of SLA. Further, Corder claimed that the making of errors is significant because it is part of the learning process itself: "a way the learner has of testing his hypothesis about the nature of the language he is learning." This includes testing whether aspects of existing L1 knowledge can be used in the L2. Errors are thus a sign that the learner is (perhaps unconsciously) exploring the new system rather than just experiencing "interference" from old habits.

The procedure for analyzing learner errors includes the following steps (Ellis 1994):

- **Collection of a sample of learner language.** Most samples of learner language which have been used in EA include data collected from many speakers who are responding to the same kind of task or test (as in **Morpheme Order Studies,** which are discussed below). Some studies use samples from a few learners that are collected over a period of weeks, months, or even years in order to determine patterns of change in error occurrence with increasing L2 exposure and proficiency.

- **Identification of errors**. This first step in the analysis requires determination of elements in the sample of learner language which deviate from the **target** L2 in some way. Corder (1967) distinguishes between systematic **errors** (which result from learners' lack of L2 knowledge) and **mistakes** (the results from some kind of processing failure such as a lapse in memory), which he excludes from the analysis.

- **Description of errors.** For purposes of analysis, errors are usually classified according to language level (whether an error is phonological, morphological, syntactic, etc.), general linguistic category (e.g. auxiliary system, passive sentences, negative constructions), or more specific linguistic elements (e.g. articles, prepositions, verb forms).

- **Explanation of errors.** Accounting for why an error was made is the most important step in trying to understand the processes of SLA. Two of the most likely causes of L2 errors are **interlingual** ("between languages") factors, resulting from negative transfer or **interference** from L1 and **intralingual** ("within language") factors, not attributable to cross-linguistic influence. Intralingual errors are also considered **developmental** errors and often represent incomplete learning of L2 rules or overgeneralization of them. Distinguishing between interlingual and intralingual errors implicitly builds upon CA procedures, since the distinction requires comparative knowledge of L1 and L2. For example, the following passage was in a letter written to me by a native Korean speaker. I have underlined and numbered the errors.

The weather is been[1] very hot in the[2] Washington D.C. There climate[3] last week warm[4].

(1) Use of *is* instead of *has* with *been* (**intralingual/developmental error**). This is evidence that the speaker/writer is learning the English auxiliary verb system, but hasn't yet mastered the distinction between forms of *be* and *have*, which doesn't exist in Korean.

(2) Use of *the* with a place name (**intralingual/developmental** error). This is evidence that the speaker/writer is learning to use articles in front of nouns (no articles are used in Korean) but hasn't yet learned that they don't occur before most place names.

(3) *There climate* is a direct translation of the Korean phrase which would be used in this context (**interlingual/interference** error).

(4) In Korean the word for 'warm' is a verb itself, so no additional verb corresponding to English *was* would be used (**interlingual/interference** error).

- **Evaluation of errors.** This step involves analysis of what effect the error has on whoever is being addressed: e.g. how "serious" it is, or to what extent it affects intelligibility, or social acceptability (such as qualifying for a job). In the example I gave of the Korean L1 speaker making errors in a letter to me, the errors are not serious at all. We are friends, and the ungrammaticality of many of her sentences has no bearing on the social relationship; furthermore, there is no resulting misinterpretation of meaning.

EA continues as a useful procedure for the study of SLA, but a number of shortcomings have been noted and should be kept in mind. These include:

- **Ambiguity in classification.** It is difficult to say, for instance, if a Chinese L1 speaker who omits number and tense inflections in English L2 is doing so because of L1 influence (Chinese is not an inflectional language) or because of a universal developmental process (also present in L1 acquisition) which results in simplified or "telegraphic" utterances.
- **Lack of positive data.** Focus on errors alone does not necessarily provide information on what the L2 learner *has* acquired (although I have inferred from the examples I gave above what the Korean L1 speaker/writer has learned about English auxiliary verbs and articles); further, correct uses may be overlooked.
- **Potential for avoidance.** Absence of errors may result from learners' avoidance of difficult structures, and this will not be revealed by EA (e.g. Shachter [1974] makes the point that Chinese and Japanese L1 speakers make few errors in English L2 relative clauses because they avoid using them).

Interlanguage

Under the same influences from linguistics and psychology as Corder, and building on his concepts and procedures for EA, Larry Selinker (1972) introduced the term Interlanguage (IL) to refer to the intermediate states (or interim grammars) of a learner's language as it moves toward the target L2. As in EA and first language studies of the 1960s and 1970s, Selinker and others taking this approach considered the development of the IL to be a creative process, driven by inner forces in interaction with environmental factors, and influenced both by L1 and by input from the target language. While influence from L1 and L2 language systems in a learner's IL is clearly recognized, emphasis is on the IL itself as a third language system in its own right which differs from both L1 and L2 during the course of its development.

An interlanguage has the following characteristics:

- **Systematic.** At any particular point or stage of development, the IL is governed by rules which constitute the learner's internal grammar. These rules are discoverable by analyzing the language that is used by the learner at that time – what he or she can produce and interpret correctly as well as errors that are made.
- **Dynamic.** The system of rules which learners have in their minds changes frequently, or is in a state of flux, resulting in a succession of interim grammars. Selinker views this change not as a steady progression along a continuum, but discontinuous progression "from stable plateau to stable plateau" (1992:226).
- **Variable.** Although the IL is systematic, differences in context result in different patterns of language use (discussed in Chapter 5).
- **Reduced system, both in form and function.** The characteristic of **reduced form** refers to the less complex grammatical structures that typically occur in an IL compared to the target language (e.g. omission of inflections, such as the past tense suffix in English). The characteristic of **reduced function** refers to the smaller range of communicative needs typically served by an IL (especially if the learner is still in contact with members of the L1 speech community).

Selinker (1972) stresses that there are differences between IL development in SLA and L1 acquisition by children, including different cognitive processes involved (from McLaughlin 1987:61):

- **Language transfer** from L1 to L2.
- **Transfer of training,** or how the L2 is taught.
- **Strategies of second language learning,** or how learners approach the L2 materials and the task of L2 learning.
- **Strategies of second language communication,** or ways that learners try to communicate with others in the L2.
- **Overgeneralization of the target language linguistic material,** in which L2 rules that are learned are applied too broadly. (Overgeneralizations include some of the **intralingual or developmental errors** which were illustrated in the previous section.)

Also unlike L1 acquisition is the strong likelihood of **fossilization** for L2 learners – the probability that they will cease their IL development in some respects before they reach target language norms, in spite of continuing L2 input and passage of time. This phenomenon relates to age of learning, with older L2 learners more likely to fossilize than younger ones, but also to factors of social identity and communicative need (e.g. see Selinker 1992). Such factors are at the core of discussions concerning the basic question of *why* some learners are more successful than others. "Relative success" can be defined in this approach as the level of IL development reached before learning stops.

L1 ___ | .... | ___ L2

Interlanguage

The beginning and end of IL are defined respectively as whenever a learner first attempts to convey meaning in the L2 and whenever development "permanently" stops, but the boundaries are not entirely clear. A schematization of the construct is presented in 3.1. The initial state and very early stages of L2 development in naturalistic (i.e. unschooled or untutored) settings often involve only isolated L2 words or memorized routines inserted in an L1 structural frame for some period of time. For example, we recorded the following utterances from children who were just beginning to acquire English (Saville-Troike, Pan, and Dutkova 1995):

Chinese L1: *Zheige delicious*. 'This is delicious.'

Navajo L1: *Birthday cake deedąą'*. 'We ate a birthday cake.'

Czech L1: *Yili sme bowling*. 'We went bowling.'

IL probably cannot properly be said to begin until there is some evidence of systematic change in grammar. The endpoint of IL is difficult to identify with complete certainty since additional time and different circumstances might always trigger some resumption in learning.

Identification of **fossilization,** or cessation of IL development before reaching target language norms, is even more controversial (though primarily for social and political rather than linguistic reasons). Should individuals be considered "fossilized" in L2 development because they retain a foreign accent, for instance, in spite of productive fluency in other aspects of the target language? (One thinks of Arnold Schwarzenegger, US motion picture actor and politician, who retains a strong Austrian-German accent, or of many faculty members and students who are identifiably nonnative speakers of English although they speak and write fluently in this language – often even more fluently than many native speakers. There may even be an advantage in retaining a nonnative accent, since "sounding native" may be misinterpreted by native speakers as implying corresponding native social and cultural knowledge.)

There is also the issue of what the concept of "target language" entails as the goal of SLA, especially as it applies to English usage in parts of the world where English has been adopted as an auxiliary or official language but differs from any native variety in Great Britain or the USA (see Kachru and Nelson 1996). "Native-like" production is neither intended nor desired by many speakers, and assuming that it is or should be the ultimate goal for all L2 learners may be considered somewhat imperialistic.

The concept of an IL as a system of learner language which is at least partially independent of L1 and L2 has been highly productive in the study of SLA. It is generally taken for granted now, although controversies remain concerning its specific nature and whether "progress" should be measured against native-speaker norms (e.g. Eubank, Selinker, and Sharwood Smith 1995; Johnson and Johnson 1998:174–76).

Morpheme Order Studies

One important question in the study of SLA which the concept of IL highlighted during the 1970s is whether there is a natural order (or universal sequence) in the grammatical development of L2 learners. This is interesting because if we find that the same elements of an L2 are learned first no matter what the learner's L1 is, we might assume that transfer from L1 is less important than if we were to find that the order of acquisition is different for speakers of different native languages. If the same order of acquisition is found in L2 as in children's L1 learning, there is the additional implication that the acquisition processes may be very much the same for all of language development.

What is inflection?

Inflection adds one or more units of meaning to the base form of a word, to give it a more specific meaning. This is how we code for plural nouns, past tense and progressive aspect in English.

	Basic form	Unit of meaning	Function of the unit of meaning	Example
Noun	Cat	s	Plural	Three cats
Verbs	walk	ed	Past	I walked yesterday.
	walk	ing	Progressive	We were walking.

Roger Brown (1973) provided the first baseline information on an L1 acquisition sequence by tracking the order in which three children mastered the production of a set of grammatical morphemes in English, including inflections which mark tense on verbs and plural number on nouns. His work was soon validated by studies of larger numbers of English L1 children. The claim that this sequence constituted a natural order for English L2 as well as English L1 was first made by Heidi Dulay and Marina Burt, based on studies of children learning English who were native speakers of Spanish and Chinese. A list of morphemes that were included in the Brown (1973) and Dulay and Burt (1974) findings is given in 3.2. These results indicate, for example, that the progressive suffix -*ing* and plural -*s*

3.2 English L1 and L2 Morpheme Acquisition Order			
English L1	Morpheme	Example	English L2
1	Progressive -*ing*	He is tal*king*.	3
2	Plural -*s*	There are two cat*s*.	4
3	Past irregular	We *ate*.	7
4	Possessive -*s*	The child*'s* toy	8
5	Articles *a/the*	*The* cat/*A* sunny day	1
6	Past regular -*ed*	They talk*ed*.	6
7	Third person -*s*	He sing*s*.	9
8	Copula *be*	He*'s* tall.	2
9	Auxiliary *be*	She*'s* singing.	5

are the first of this set of morphemes to be mastered by both L1 and L2 learners of English; the irregular past tense form of verbs and possessive -*s* are acquired next in sequence for L1, but relatively later for learners of L2 (after forms of *be* and *a/the*).

Although not identical, the order of morpheme acquisition reported was similar in L1 and L2. Further, the order was virtually the same in English L2 whether children were L1 speakers of Spanish or Chinese. The existence of such a "natural order" strengthened claims for internally driven acquisition processes, which Dulay and Burt (1973) labeled creative construction. They concluded that L2 learners are neither merely imitating what they hear nor necessarily transferring L1 structures to the new code, but (subconsciously) creating a mental grammar which allows them to interpret and produce utterances they have not heard before.

A claim was originally made that this evidence of similar morpheme order supports an Identity Hypothesis (or L1 = L2): that processes involved in L1 and L2 acquisition are the same. The strong form of this hypothesis was rejected largely because the basic question of *what* is being acquired in SLA was limited here to a list of isolated English morphemes, with no principled relation to other aspects of English or to other languages, and also because of weaknesses in the research methodology.

The concept of natural order remains very important for understanding SLA, however, both from linguistic and from cognitive approaches. The morpheme acquisition studies were followed by research which indicated that there are also regular sequences in acquisition of some syntactic constructions by both children and adults (e.g. negation, questions, and relative clauses). These findings form part of the basis for continuing speculation that innate mechanisms for language acquisition may not be limited to early childhood.

Monitor Model

One of the last of the early approaches to SLA which has an internal focus is the Monitor Model, proposed by Stephen Krashen (1978). It explicitly and essentially adopts the notion of a language acquisition device (or LAD), which is a metaphor Chomsky used for children's innate knowledge of language.

Krashen's approach is a collection of five hypotheses which constitute major claims and assumptions about how the L2 code is acquired. Caution is required, however, that Krashen's model has frequently been criticized by researchers because many of its constructs (e.g. what constitutes comprehensible input) and the claimed distinction between learning and acquisition are vague and imprecise, and because several of its claims are impossible to verify (see McLaughlin 1987). The hypotheses forming the model are the following:

- *Acquisition-Learning Hypothesis.* There is a distinction to be made between acquisition and learning. Acquisition is subconscious, and involves the innate language acquisition device which accounts for children's L1. Learning is conscious and is exemplified by the L2 learning which takes place in many classroom contexts.
- *Monitor Hypothesis.* What is "learned" is available only as a monitor, for purposes of editing or making changes in what has already been produced.
- *Natural Order Hypothesis.* We acquire the rules of language in a predictable order.
- *Input Hypothesis.* Language acquisition takes place because there is comprehensible input. If input is understood, and if there is enough of it, the necessary grammar is automatically provided.
- *Affective Filter Hypothesis.* Input may not be processed if the affective filter is "up" (e.g. if conscious learning is taking place and/or individuals are inhibited).

In spite of being severely criticized by researchers, Krashen's model had a major influence on language teaching in the USA in the 1980s and 1990s, including avoidance of the explicit teaching of grammar in many hundreds of classrooms. The pendulum has since begun to swing back in the opposite direction, with formal grammar teaching increasingly being introduced, especially with adults, who are able to benefit from (and may even need) an explicit explanation of grammatical structure.

The early period for linguistic study of SLA which we have just reviewed ended with some issues in rather spirited debate among proponents of different approaches, but there was widespread consensus on some important points. These include:

- *What* is being acquired in SLA is a "rule-governed" language system. Development of L2 involves progression through a dynamic interlanguage system which differs from both L1 and L2 in significant respects. The final state of L2 typically differs (more or less) from the native speakers' system.

- *How* SLA takes place involves creative mental processes. Development of both L1 and L2 follows generally predictable sequences, which suggests that L1 and L2 acquisition processes are similar in significant ways.
- *Why* some learners are more (or less) successful in SLA than others relates primarily to the age of the learner.

As we reach the 1980s in this survey, new proposals in Chomskyan theoretical linguistics were about to have a major impact on the study of SLA, and Universal Grammar was to become (and continues to be) the dominant approach with an internal focus.

Universal Grammar

Universal Grammar (UG) continues the tradition which Chomsky introduced in his earlier work. Two concepts in particular are still of central importance:

(1) What needs to be accounted for in language acquisition is linguistic competence, or speaker-hearers' underlying knowledge of language. This is distinguished from linguistic performance, or speaker-hearers' actual use of language in specific instances.
(2) Such knowledge of language goes beyond what could be learned from the input people receive. This is the logical problem of language learning, or the poverty-of-the stimulus argument.

Noam Chomsky (b. Philadelphia), 1928–present

Linguistics

A professor at the Massachusetts Institute of Technology since 1961, Noam Chomsky has had a revolutionary impact on the field of linguistics. His Transformational-Generative Grammar was the first linguistic framework with an internal focus. His theories have evolved from there to the Principles and Parameters Model and to the Minimalist Program.

Interesting note: The sentence *Colorless green ideas sleep furiously* was constructed by Chomsky to show that a grammatically correct sentence can still be void of meaning. This sentence was later used in one 1985 literary competition where the goal was to make it meaningful in 100 words or less!

Chomsky and his followers have claimed since the 1950s that the nature of speaker-hearers' competence in their native language can be accounted for only by innate knowledge that the human species is genetically endowed with. They argue that children (at least) come to the task of acquiring a specific language already possessing general knowledge of what all languages have in common, including constraints on how any natural language can be structured. This innate knowledge is in what Chomsky calls the **language faculty,** which is "a component of the human mind, physically represented in the brain and part of the biological endowment of the species" (Chomsky 2002:1). What all languages have in common is Universal Grammar.

If a language faculty indeed exists, it is a potential solution to the "logical problem" because its existence would mean that children already have a rich system of linguistic knowledge which they bring to the task of L1 learning. They wouldn't need to learn this underlying system, but only build upon it "on the basis of other inner resources activated by a limited and fragmentary linguistic experience" (Chomsky 2002:8). In other words, while children's acquisition of the specific language that is spoken by their parents and others in their social setting requires input in that language, the acquisition task is possible (and almost invariably successful) because of children's built-in capacity. One of the most important issues in a UG approach to the study of SLA has been whether this innate resource is still available to individuals who are acquiring additional languages beyond the age of early childhood.

Until the late 1970s, followers of this approach assumed that the language acquisition task involves children's induction of a system of rules for particular languages from the input they receive, guided by UG. How this could happen remained quite mysterious. (Linguistic input goes into a "black box" in the mind, something happens, and the grammatical system of a particular language comes out.) A major change in thinking about the acquisition process occurred with Chomsky's (1981) reconceptualization of UG in a **Principles and Parameters** framework (often called the **Government and Binding [GB]** model), and with his subsequent introduction of the **Minimalist Program** (1995).

Principles and Parameters

Since around 1980, the construct called **Universal Grammar** has been conceptualized as a set of **principles** which are properties of all languages in the world. Some of these principles contain **parameters,** or points where there is a limited choice of settings depending on which specific language is involved. Because knowledge of principles and parameters is postulated to be innate, children are assumed to be able to interpret and unconsciously analyze the input they receive and construct the appropriate L1 grammar. This analysis and construction is considered to be strictly constrained and channeled by UG, which explains why L1 acquisition for children is relatively rapid and always successful; children never violate core principles nor do they select parametric values outside of the channel imposed by UG, even though there might be other logical possibilities.

An example of an early principle which Chomsky posited stipulates that every phrase in every language has the same elements including a Head: e.g. a noun phrase (NP) must always have a noun head (N), a verb phrase (VP) must always have a verb head (V), a prepositional or postpositional phrase (PP) must always have a preposition or postposition head (P), and so forth. The only choice, or parameter setting, that speakers have in different languages is Head Direction, or the position of the head in relation to other elements in the phrase. There are only two possible choices: **head-initial** or **head-final**.

Children who are learning English L1 receive input that lets them know that English generally has a head-initial parameter setting. This is because they hear sentences with the following word order:

a. *John [kicked the ball]*$_{VP}$
   I have put brackets around the VP in this example, and underlined the head of that phrase, which is the verb *kicked*. The word order of this VP provides evidence that the English parameter setting is head-initial, because the verb *kicked* comes in front of the ball.
b. *John rode [in the car]*$_{PP}$
   Brackets are around the PP in this example, and its head is the preposition *in*. This provides additional evidence that the parameter setting for English is head-initial, because the preposition comes in front of *the car* in the phrase.

In contrast, children who are learning Japanese L1 receive input that lets them know that Japanese has a head-final parameter setting. They hear sentences with the following word order:

a. *John-wa [booru-wo ketta]*$_{VP}$ (Literally: 'John ball kicked')
   This provides evidence that the Japanese parameter setting is head-final, because the verb *ketta* 'kicked' comes after *booru-wo* 'ball' in the VP.
b. *John-wa [kuruma-ni]*$_{PP}$ *notta* (Literally: 'John car-in rode')
   This provides additional evidence that Japanese is head-final because the postposition *-ni* 'in' comes after *kuruma* 'car' in the PP.

Japanese and English word orders are largely, though not entirely, a "mirror image" of one another. Children acquiring English or Japanese as their L1 need to hear only a limited amount of input to set the parameter for this principle correctly. That parameter setting then presumably guides them in producing the correct word order in an unlimited number of utterances which they have not heard before, since the general principle stipulates that all phrases in a language tend to have essentially the same structure. (Not all languages are completely consistent, however. In English and Chinese, for example, since modifiers precede the noun head, the NP is head-final, but the object NP follows the Verb.)

Other principles and parameter settings that account for variations between languages include those that determine whether or not agreement between subject and verb must be overtly expressed, and whether or not a subject must be overtly present (the "null subject" parameter). For example, English speakers must say <u>It</u> *is raining*, with a meaningless overt subject *it*, whereas subjects are omitted in Chinese *Xia yu* 'Down rain' and

Spanish *Está lloviendo* 'Is raining.' There is no complete listing of invariant principles and principles with parametric choices in UG, and there perhaps will never be one, since proposals concerning their identity change as the theory evolves. In any case, the specification of universal principles and parameters is relevant to theoretical developments and understandings, and may have practical value in L2 teaching. But children have no use for such a list, of course, and could not understand it if one were available. Principles and parameters per se are not, cannot, and need not be learned in L1 acquisition, as they are assumed to be built into the Language Acquisition Device (LAD) we are born with. This may also partially hold true for older second language learners, though an awareness of parameter settings in an L2 may help focus perception on input and thus facilitate learning.

What is acquired in L1 acquisition is not UG itself; UG is already present at birth as part of the innate language faculty in every human being, although maturation and experience are required for the manifestation of this capacity. Child acquisition of a specific language involves a process of selecting from among the limited parametric options in UG those that match the settings which are encountered in linguistic input.

In a radical change from his earlier Transformational-Generative (TG) theory, Chomsky no longer believes that acquisition involves induction of a language-specific system of rules, based on input and guided by UG. Rather, he argues that there are just extremely general principles of UG and options to be selected. The acquisition of vocabulary has become much more important in his recent theory, because lexical items are thought to include rich specification of properties that are needed for parameter setting and other features of grammar, as well as for interpretation of semantic meaning. "Knowing" the noun *foot* in English, for instance, means knowing how it is pronounced and what it refers to, that it is a noun and can function as the head of an NP, and that it takes an irregular plural form; "knowing" the verb *chi* 'eat' in Chinese means knowing its pronunciation and meaning, that it is a verb and the head of a VP, and that it normally requires a direct object, often the "dummy object" *fan* (literally 'rice').

The starting point (or initial state) for child L1 acquisition is thus UG, along with innate learning principles that are also "wired in" in the language faculty of the brain. *What* is acquired in the process of developing a specific language is information from input (especially vocabulary) that the learner matches with UG options. The eventual product is the final state, or adult grammar (also called "stable state"). Intermediate states in development are "state L" (L_1, L_2, L_3, . . .). As summarized by Chomsky:

> The initial state changes under the triggering and shaping effect of experience, and internally determined processes of maturation, yielding later states that seem to stabilize at several stages, finally at about puberty. We can think of the initial state of [the language faculty] as a device that maps experience into state L attained: a "language acquisition device" (LAD).   (2002:85)

From this perspective, *how* acquisition occurs for children is "natural", "instinctive," and "internal to the cognitive system." Unlike SLA, attitudes, motivation, and social context (beyond provision of the minimal input that is required) play no role. The question of *why* some learners are more successful than others is not considered relevant for L1 acquisition, since all native speakers in this view attain essentially the same "final state." (This conceptualization does not take into account further development of different registers, such as hip-hop, sports reporting, or formal written English.)

UG and SLA

Three questions are of particular importance in the study of SLA from a UG perspective:

- What is the initial state in SLA?
- What is the nature of interlanguage, and how does it change over time?
- What is the final state in SLA?

Initial state

As discussed in the section on L1 versus L2 acquisition in the previous chapter, learners already have knowledge of L1 at the point where L2 acquisition begins; they already have made all of the parametric choices that are appropriate for that L1, guided by UG. Some L1 knowledge is clearly transferred to L2, although exactly which features may transfer and to what degree appears to be dependent on the relationship of L1 and L2 (perhaps involving markedness of features similar to those discussed under Functional Typology below), the circumstances of L2 learning, and other factors. When L1 and L2 parameter settings for the same principle are the same, positive transfer from L1 to L2 is likely; when L1 and L2 parameter settings are different, negative transfer or interference might occur.

For example, I once heard one Navajo girl (who was at an early stage of English L2 acquisition) describe the location of a doll to her teacher:

Dollie is wagon in.

The child's phrase *wagon in* is a postpositional phrase with the head P *in* placed after *wagon*. This does not match the English head-first parameter setting, which requires the head *in* at the beginning of the phrase. The Navajo language (like Japanese) has a head-final setting, and *wagon in* is a direct translation of Navajo word order for *tsinaabąąs bi-í*? 'wagon it-in.' The child who produced this English sentence was inappropriately transferring a parameter setting from Navajo L1 to English L2.

L2 learners may still have access to UG in the initial state of SLA as well as knowledge of L1, but there is no agreement on this. Four possibilities have been suggested (e.g. see Cook 1988):

(1) Learners retain *full access* to UG as an innate guide to language acquisition, even when they are learning languages subsequent to their L1.

(2) Learners retain *partial access* to UG, keeping some of its components but not others.

(3) Learners retain *indirect access* to UG through knowledge that is already realized in their L1 but have no remaining direct access.

(4) Learners retain *no access* to UG and must learn L2 via entirely different means than they did L1.

Nature and development of interlanguage

Interlanguage (IL) is defined in the Principles and Parameters perspective as intermediate states of L2 development (IL_1, IL_2, IL_3, etc.), which is compatible with the notion of IL as "interim grammars" that was introduced in the 1960s and 1970s. If at least some access to UG is retained by L2 learners, then the process of IL development is in large part one of resetting parameters on the basis of input in the new language. For example, the L1 speaker of Japanese or Navajo who is learning English L2 needs to reset the Head Direction parameter from head-final to head-initial; the L1 speaker of English who is learning Japanese or Navajo needs to reset it from head-initial to head-final.

Learners change the parameter setting (usually unconsciously) because the L2 input they receive does not match the L1 settings they have. If access to UG is still available, then that will limit their choices (as it does in L1) and their IL grammars will never deviate from structures that are allowed by UG. If learning principles that are part of the **language faculty** are also still available, then sufficient information to make these changes is available from the **positive evidence** they receive, i.e. the input that is provided from experiencing L2 in natural use or formal instruction. **Negative evidence,** including explicit correction, is often also provided to L2 learners (especially if they receive formal language instruction), and this probably plays a role in parameter resetting for older learners. (Evidence for different positions on why and how parameter resetting occurs is discussed in Gregg 1996 and White 2003.)

Constructionism, an approach to SLA which has been formulated within Chomsky's Minimalist Program (e.g. Herschensohn 2000), considers IL development as the progressive mastery of L2 vocabulary along with the morphological features (which specify word form) that are part of lexical knowledge. While the general principles and parameters that constitute UG do not need to be learned, "morphological paradigms must gradually be added to the lexicon, just like words" (White 2003:194). The stages and variability which characterize IL development are accounted for because of initially incomplete specification of these features in learners' competence. While parameter setting and mastery of morphological features are linked in L1 acquisition, this approach claims that they are not necessarily linked for older learners in SLA. Failure to reach a state of full feature specification in the lexicon is seen as the primary reason that many L2 learners **fossilize** at an intermediate level of development without attaining near-native competence.

Of particular relevance for L2 learners and teachers is the critical role of lexical acquisition in providing information for parameter (re)setting and other aspects of grammar in a UG approach. This is in sharp contrast to the structuralist and behaviorist position which was reviewed near the beginning of this chapter, that all of the basic grammatical structures of L2 could (indeed should) be learned in conjunction with minimal vocabulary.

If access to UG or the learning principles of the language faculty are no longer available for SLA, then IL development would need to be explained as a fundamentally different learning process than that which takes place for L1. Evidence that IL does not violate the constraints of UG, and that it cannot be accounted for completely by either L1 transfer or L2 input, are used to argue against the *no access* position.

Final state

While the question of *why* some learners are more successful than others is not relevant for basic L1 acquisition (since all children achieve a native "final state"), the question is highly relevant for SLA. All approaches to this topic need to account for the great variability which is found in the ultimate level of attainment by L2 learners. There are several possibilities within the UG framework. These include:

- All learners may not have the same degree of access to UG.
- Different relationships between various L1s and L2s may result in differential transfer or interference.
- Some learners may receive qualitatively different L2 input from others.
- Some learners may be more perceptive than others of mismatches between L2 input and existing L1 parameter settings.
- Different degrees of specification for lexical features may be achieved by different learners.

However, there are other issues in SLA that are not addressed, or are not addressed satisfactorily, by a narrow UG approach, with its strictly **internal** focus on the mental organization of the learner. We now turn to consider some major alternative views.

Functional approaches

While UG has been the dominant linguistic approach to SLA for many years, many researchers have rather chosen to take an external focus on language learning. The more influential of these approaches are based on the framework of Functionalism.

Functional models of analysis date back to the early twentieth century, and have their roots in the Prague School of linguistics that originated in Eastern Europe. They differ from structuralist and early generative models by emphasizing the information content of utterances, and in considering language primarily as a system of communication rather than as a set of rules.

The term function has several meanings in linguistics, including both structural function (such as the role which elements of language structure play as a subject or object, or as an actor or goal) and pragmatic function (what the use of language can accomplish, such as convey information, control others' behavior, or express emotion). Approaches to SLA which are characterized as functional differ in emphasis and definition but share the following characteristics in general opposition to those in the Chomskyan tradition:

- Focus is on the use of language in real situations (performance) as well as underlying knowledge (competence). No sharp distinction is made between the two.
- Study of SLA begins with the assumption that the purpose of language is communication, and that development of linguistic knowledge (in L1 or L2) requires communicative use.
- Scope of concern goes beyond the sentence to include discourse structure and how language is used in interaction, and to include aspects of communication beyond language (Tomlin 1990).

Four of the functional approaches which have been influential in SLA are Systemic Linguistics, Functional Typology, function-to-form mapping, and information organization.

Systemic Linguistics

Systemic Linguistics has been developed by M. A. K. Halliday, beginning in the late 1950s. This is a model for analyzing language in terms of the interrelated systems of choices that are available for expressing meaning. Basic to the approach is the notion, ultimately derived from the anthropologist Malinowski, that language structures cannot be idealized and studied without taking into account the circumstances of their use, including the extralinguistic social context.

From this functional view,

> language acquisition . . . needs to be seen as the mastery of linguistic functions. Learning one's mother tongue is learning the uses of language, and the meanings, or rather the meaning potential, associated with them. The structures, the words and the sounds are the realization of this meaning potential. Learning language is learning how to mean.
>
> (Halliday 1973:345)

To relate this notion to the question about *what* language learners essentially acquire, in Halliday's view it is not a system of rules which govern language structure, but rather "meaning potential": "what the speaker/hearer *can* (what he can mean, if you like), not what he knows" (1973:346). The process of acquisition consists of "mastering certain basic functions of language and developing a meaning potential for each" (1975:33).

Halliday (1975) describes the evolution of the following pragmatic functions in early L1 acquisition (he calls them "functions of language as a whole"), which are universal for children:

- *Instrumental* – language used as a means of getting things done (one of the first to be evolved): the "I want" function.
- *Regulatory* – language used to regulate the behavior of others: the "do as I tell you" function.
- *Interactional* – use of language in interaction between self and others: the "me and you" function.
- *Personal* – awareness of language as a form of one's own identity: the "here I come" function.
- *Heuristic* – language as a way of learning about things: the "tell me why" function.
- *Imagination* – creation through language of a world of one's own making: the "let's pretend" function.
- *Representational* – means of expressing propositions, or communicating about something (one of the last to appear): the "I've got something to tell you" function.

Linguistic structures which are mastered in the developmental process are "direct reflections" of the functions that language serves; their development is closely related to the social and personal needs they are used to convey.

One application of Halliday's model to the study of SLA comes with seeing L2 learning as a process of adding multilingual meaning potential to what has already been achieved in L1. This is an approach that some of my colleagues and I have taken in our research. We have concluded that "Second language acquisition is largely a matter of learning new linguistic forms to fulfill the same functions [as already acquired and used in L1] within a different social milieu" (Saville-Troike, McClure, and Fritz 1984:60). In studying children who had just arrived in the USA from several different countries, for instance, we found that all of them could accomplish a wide range of communicative functions even while they still had very limited English means at their disposal. What we observed and recorded over a period of several months for every child in our study was not the emergence of new functions (as we would expect in early L1 development), but emergence of new language structures to augment existing choices for expressing them. This structural emergence follows the same general sequence for each function (not unlike early stages of L1). For example:

1. **Nonlinguistic**
   Regulatory: (Hitting another child who is annoying.)
   Interactional: Unh? *(Uttered as a greeting.)*
   Heuristic: (Pointing at an object [with a questioning look] to request the English term for it.)
2. **L2 formula or memorized routine**
   Regulatory: Don't do that!
   Interactional: Hi!
   Heuristic: What's it?

3. **Single L2 word**
   Regulatory: He! *(Pointing out another child's offending behavior to a teacher.)*
   Interactional: Me? *(An invitation to play.)*
   Heuristic: What? *(Asking for the English term for an object.)*

4. **L2 phrase or clause**
   Regulatory: That bad!
   Interactional: You me play?
   Heuristic: What name this?

5. **Complex L2 construction**
   Regulatory: The teacher say that wrong!
   Interactional: I no like to play now.
   Heuristic: What is name we call this?

Other applications of Halliday's model can be found in the study of SLA in relation to social contexts of learning and use. That perspective is discussed in Chapter 5.

Functional Typology

Another approach within the functional framework is Functional Typology, which is based on the comparative study of a wide range of the world's languages. This study involves the classification of languages and their features into categories (or "types"; hence "typology"), with a major goal being to describe patterns of similarities and differences among them, and to determine which types and patterns occur more/less frequently or are universal in distribution. The approach is called "functional" because analysis integrates considerations of language structure, meaning, and use.

Functional Typology has been applied to the study of SLA most fruitfully in accounting for developmental stages of L2 acquisition, for why some L2 constructions are more or less difficult than others for learners to acquire, and for the selectivity of crosslinguistic influence or transfer (i.e. for why some elements of L1 transfer to L2 and some do not). A particularly important concept which is tied to these accounts is markedness – the notion of markedness deals with whether any specific feature of a language is "marked" or "unmarked." A feature is "unmarked" if it occurs more frequently than a contrasting element in the same category, if it is less complex structurally or conceptually, or if it is more "normal" or "expected" along some other dimension. The concept applies to all levels of linguistic analysis. For example:

- In phonology, the most common syllable structure which occurs in languages of the world is CV (consonant + vowel, as in *me* and *ba-na-na*), so this structure is "unmarked". It is much less common to have a sequence of consonants at the beginning or end of syllables; English sequences like *street* [stri:t] and *fence* [fɛnts] are "marked" in this respect.
- In vocabulary, the preposition *in* denotes location while the preposition *into* is more complex, denoting both location and

3.3 Markedness Differential Predictions for SLA

Feature in L1	Feature in L2	Prediction
Marked	Unmarked	L2 feature will be easy to learn;
		L1 feature will not transfer to L2
Unmarked	Marked	L1 feature will transfer to L2

directionality. *Into* is thus "marked" in contrast with *in* because it is both structurally and conceptually more complex.

- In syntax, the basic word order in sentences of SVO (subject–verb–object) is more common in languages of the world than is SOV. SVO is thus relatively "unmarked" and SOV relatively "marked."
- In discourse, the expected "unmarked" response to the English formulaic greeting *How are you?* is *Fine. How are you?* (no matter how the respondent is actually feeling). A response which reports information about one's health or other personal conditions is not expected in this routine exchange, and is "marked." Similarly, the "unmarked" response to a question requesting information is an answer about the same topic. Silence or a comment on a different topic is a "marked" response because it is not in accord with "normal" conversational practice.

In accounting for order and relative difficulty for acquisition, unmarked elements are likely to be acquired before marked ones in children's L1 (Jakobson 1941), and to be easier for a learner to master in L2. In phonology, for instance, the babbling and first words of a child in L1 are likely to have an unmarked CV syllabic structure (no matter what the native language), and marked CC sequences appear only at a later stage of development. It is also likely that L2 learners will find marked CC sequences more difficult to produce, especially if they do not occur at all in the speakers' L1. A markedness account of selective transfer from L1 to L2 (proposed as the Markedness Differential Hypothesis by Eckman 1977) predicts that unmarked features in L1 are more likely to transfer, as well as that marked features in L2 will be harder to learn. A simplified summary of this hypothesis is shown in 3.3.

For example, the pronunciation of the marked consonant sequence [sk] in *school* should be difficult for Spanish L1 speakers, whose native phonological system is "simpler" than English in this respect because it does not allow two voiceless consonants to occur together. It is indeed common for beginning Spanish L1 learners of English L2 to break this [sk] combination apart into two syllables and pronounce the word as [ɛs-kul], thus avoiding the marked structure. In reverse, learners of Spanish L2 should have no comparable problem pronouncing *escuela* [ɛs-kwe-la] 'school,' since it contains no consonant cluster in any syllable.

Functional Typology resembles Contrastive Analysis in comparing elements of different languages in order to predict or explain transfer from

L1 to L2, but it goes beyond the surface-level structural contrasts of CA to more abstract patterns, principles, and constraints. The Markedness Differential Hypothesis is also an advance over the traditional CA approach in that:

Eckman's work suggests that transfer is not always a bidirectional process, as might be inferred from a strict contrastive analysis approach. Instead, this work on linguistic universals indicates that the reason why some first-language structures are transferred and others are not relates to the degree of markedness of the structures in the various languages.

(McLaughlin 1987:90)

One implication that we might draw from this approach is that some aspects of some languages are more difficult to learn than others, in spite of the traditional claim within linguistics that all languages are equally complex. Another issue that we might speculate about is why some types and patterns of features are more or less frequent than others in both native and second languages. Functional explanations tend to refer to extralinguistic factors, or elements outside of language. Certain factors that have been suggested are: perceptual salience, ease of cognitive processing, physical constraints (e.g. the shape of the human vocal tract), and communicative needs (see Ramat 2003).

Function-to-form mapping

Another functional approach which has been applied to the description and analysis of interlanguage emphasizes function-to-form mapping in the acquisitional sequence. A basic concept from this perspective is that acquisition of both L1 and L2 involves a process of grammaticalization in which a grammatical function (such as the expression of past time) is first conveyed by shared extralinguistic knowledge and inferencing based on the context of discourse, then by a lexical word (such as *yesterday*), and only later by a grammatical marker (such as the suffix *-ed*). For example, if you ask a beginning learner of English what he did the day before he might say *I play soccer*, relying on context to convey the meaning of past time; a somewhat more advanced learner might say *Yesterday I play soccer*, using an adverb to convey the meaning of past; and a still more advanced learner might say *I played soccer*, using the grammatical inflection *-ed*.

The general principle of increasing reliance on grammatical forms and reducing reliance on context and lexical words to express functions such as time is followed in all languages. In Chinese L2, for example, learners tend to use the lexical adverb *jiu* 'then' to express temporal sequencing of events before they use the grammatical marker *le* 'finished' in expressing this notion. The following utterances were produced by a beginning learner (a) and a more advanced learner (b) who were retelling the same event in a film (*The Pear Story*) that they had viewed (Yang 2002):

a. *Ta kan neige ne haizi de shihou, ta jiu shuai xia, ta shuiguo jiu diao xiagu.*

   'When he looked at that girl, he then fall off (the bike), his fruit then fall down (on the ground).'

b. *Suoyi tade zixingche shui dao le, suoyi suoyou de neige shuiguo dou diao xialai le.*

'So his bike fell down, so all the fruit fell off.'

Talmy Givón (1979) proposed the distinction between a style of expressing meaning which relies heavily on context (which he calls a **pragmatic mode**) and a style which relies more on formal grammatical elements (a **syntactic mode**), and the notion that change from one to the other is evolutionary in nature. He lists a number of contrasts in addition to the evolution from no use of grammatical morphology to elaborate use of grammatical morphology, which I illustrated above. Additional developmental contrasts include:

- From **topic-comment** to **subject-predicate** structure. A subject-predicate structure involves more grammatical marking because of the agreement it requires between sentence elements, while a topic-comment structure requires no such marking in stating what the topic is and then giving some information about it.
- From loose conjunction (with elements merely juxtaposed or connected with *and*) to tight subordination (with elements connected by words like *since* or *because*).
- From slow rate of delivery (under several intonation contours) to fast rate of delivery (under a single intonational contour).
- From word order governed mostly by the pragmatic principle of old information first, followed by new information (as in topic-comment structures) to word order used to signal semantic case functions (such as subject or object).
- From roughly one-to-one ratio of verbs to nouns in discourse to a larger ratio of nouns over verbs. The increase in the ratio of nouns to verbs indicates that more semantic case functions are being expressed: e.g. not just subject (only one noun with one verb), but also object and indirect object (a total of three nouns).

According to this approach, language acquisition importantly involves developing linguistic forms to fulfill semantic or pragmatic functions. **Grammaticalization** is driven by communicative need and use and is related to the development of more efficient cognitive processing (e.g. via **automatization**) as part of language learning. This aspect of language acquisition will be considered in Chapter 4.

Information organization

Information organization refers to a functional approach which focuses on **utterance structure**, or "the way in which learners put their words together" (Klein and Perdue 1993:3). The task of studying SLA from this perspective includes describing the structures of **interlanguage** (called **learner varieties** by Klein and Perdue), discovering what organizational principles guide learners' production at various stages of development, and analyzing how these principles interact with one another.

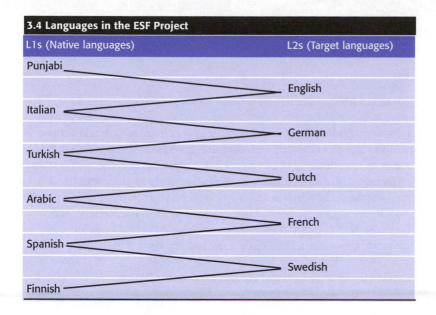

3.4 Languages in the ESF Project

L1s (Native languages)	L2s (Target languages)
Punjabi	
	English
Italian	
	German
Turkish	
	Dutch
Arabic	
	French
Spanish	
	Swedish
Finnish	

The evidence for this description and analysis comes primarily from the European Science Foundation (ESF) project (e.g. Klein and Perdue 1992; Perdue 1993). Over a period of almost three years, Klein, Perdue, and other linguists regularly recorded the L2 production of speakers of six L1s who were learning five different L2s. All of the learners were adult immigrants in Europe who needed to use the L2 to communicate but did not receive a significant amount of formal instruction in that language.

The number of L1s and L2s in this study is important because it allows the researchers to make generalizations about the nature of interlanguage (or learner varieties) which would not be possible if all of the participants were speakers of the same L1, or if all were learning the same L2. The combinations of native and target languages are shown in 3.4 (adapted from Klein and Perdue 1992:5).

This list indicates that the participants are native speakers of both Punjabi and Italian learning English, of Italian and Turkish learning German, of Turkish and Arabic learning Dutch, of Arabic and Spanish learning French, and of Spanish and Finnish learning Swedish. Most of the L2s are related Germanic languages, but the L1s represent several very different language families: Turkic (Turkish), Semitic (Arabic), Indo-Iranian (Punjabi), Romance (Italian and Spanish), and Finno-Ugric (Finnish).

Developmental levels

All of the learners in this study, no matter what their L1 and L2, go through a remarkably similar sequence of development in their interlanguage. The examples are from narratives about a Charlie Chaplin film that were told by learners in English L2 (as reported in Huebner, Carroll, and Perdue 1992).

- *Nominal Utterance Organization (NUO).* Learners generally begin with the seemingly unconnected naming of subjects and objects (i.e. with nouns and pronouns, or "nominals"). They may also use adverbs and adjectives or other elements but seldom use a verb to help organize an utterance.

PUNJABI L1: *charlie and girl accident*
ITALIAN L1: *this man one idea from the window*

- *Infinite Utterance Organization (IUO).* Learners increasingly add verbs to their utterances, but they seldom use grammatical morphemes to convey the meaning of tense, person, or number (i.e. the verb is uninflected, or "infinite"). There is also increasing use of grammatical relators such as prepositions. At this stage, learners have constructed an interlanguage grammar which is called the **Basic Variety**. They may be able to express themselves adequately at this stage in some contexts, and not all continue development beyond this level.

PUNJABI L1: *charlie and girl and policeman put on the floor*
ITALIAN L1: *the blonde friend tell other woman about the son*

- *Finite Utterance Organization (FUO).* Learners who continue interlanguage development beyond the IUO level next add grammatical morphemes to the verb (i.e. the verb becomes inflected, or "finite"). This is the process of progressive **grammaticalization,** which was described in the previous section on **function-to-form mapping.**

PUNJABI L1: *after she said to charlie "you eat dinner"*
ITALIAN L1: *he has finished the work*

The sequence of structural development shows minimal crosslinguistic influence for the NUO and IUO levels; speakers of all languages follow the same pattern. More L1 transfer occurs as learners increase their L2 resources and produce more complicated utterances (Perdue 2000).

Organizing principles

There is a limited set of principles which learners make use of for organizing information. These interact, and the balance or weight of use among them shifts during the process of interlanguage development. These principles may be classified as:

- *Phrasal constraints*, or restrictions on the phrasal patterns which may be used. Once the verb has emerged, for example, a basic pattern is noun phrase plus verb (NP + V), with a second NP after the verb possible. There are also restrictions on the composition and complexity of each phrasal category. For example, at one stage of development a noun phrase (NP) may consist only of a noun (N) or a pronoun. At the next stage of development it may consist of a determiner (e.g. *the*) plus noun (D + N) or an adjective plus noun (Adj + N), but not D + Adj + N.

Possible phrasal composition increases in complexity with developmental level.

- *Semantic constraints*, or features of categories like NP which determine their position in a sentence and what case role they are assigned (e.g. agent or "doer" of the action, or patient or recipient of the action). When an utterance has more than one NP, learners use such semantic factors to decide which one should come first. The principle that learners follow is to put the agent first, or the NP that refers to the thing that is most likely to be in control of other referents.
- *Pragmatic constraints*, including restrictions that relate to what has been said previously, or to what the speaker assumes that the hearer already knows. The general pragmatic principle is to put what is known (the topic) first, and new information or what the speaker is focusing on last.

While all learners follow essentially the same principles in organizing their utterances, there is individual variation, in part attributable to how the principles apply in their L1 and influence interlanguage use. These constraints are therefore not seen as deterministic, but as "something like 'guiding forces' whose interplay shapes the utterance" (Perdue 1993:25).

In summarizing results, Klein and Perdue (1993:261–66) offer four "bundles of explanations" for the sequence of acquisition they find, and for why some L2 learners are more successful than others:

- *Communicative needs.* Discourse tasks push the organization of utterances, in part to overcome communicative inadequacies. Linguistic means are acquired to overcome limitations of earlier levels or stages of expression.
- *Cross-linguistic influence.* Influence from L1 affects rate of interlanguage development and ultimate level of success, although not order of acquisition. L1 influence is a factor in rate and achievement because it more or less facilitates learners' analysis of L2 input and plays a role in their selection from among possible L2 organizational devices.
- *Extrinsic factors.* Progress beyond the basic variety is dependent both on "propensity" factors such as attitudes and motivation, and on "environmental" factors such as extent and nature of learners' exposure to L2. The everyday environment has more influence on progress at this level than does classroom learning.
- *Limits on processing.* Learners' current internalized interlanguage system must be ready to integrate new linguistic features or they cannot be put to immediate use in communication. Learners cannot attend to all communicative needs at the same time.

Klein and Perdue conclude:

The emerging picture is one of a *creative learner* who does not try, item by item and as closely as possible, to replicate the various structural features of the input offered by the social environment, but rather draws on some of the material from the input and uses it to construct his or her own language. This construction is permanently challenged – by the permanent influx of new input, on the one hand, and by various structural inadequacies, on the other. The extent to which the learner tackles these challenges, and the way in which it is done, depends on the particular learner and on the particular languages involved.

(1993:38–39)

All of the functional approaches discussed here basically agree on the following:

- *what* is being acquired in SLA is a system for conveying meaning,
- *how* language is acquired importantly involves creative learner involvement in communication, and
- understanding of SLA processes is impossible if they are isolated from circumstances of use.

However, for many who take a functional approach, concern with communicative meaning and context does not preclude belief in the existence of an innate (and possibly language-specific) faculty as an explanatory mechanism, nor does it rule out concern with addressing the "logical problem," that learners somehow know much more about language than can be accounted for by the input they receive.

Chapter summary

Ability to use a language requires a complex of knowledge and skills that is automatically available to everyone when they acquire L1 as a child. However, a comparable level is seldom achieved in L2, even if learners expend a great deal of time and effort on the learning task. Different linguistic approaches have explored the basic questions about SLA with either an internal or an external focus of attention. Views on *what* is being acquired range from underlying knowledge of highly abstract linguistic principles and constraints, to ability to structure and convey information in a second language; views on *how* SLA takes place differ in their emphasis on continued innate UG capacity for language learning or on requirements of communicative processing; views on *why* some learners are more or less successful range from factors which are largely internal to language and mind, to explanations which involve communicative need and opportunity. Purely linguistic approaches, though, have largely excluded psychological and social factors. To gain an in-depth, "stereoscopic" understanding of L2 acquisition, we unquestionably need to view the process through more than one lens. The still-fuzzy nature of the present picture reflects the need for more refined theoretical models and additional research.

Activities

Questions for self-study

1. Briefly explain how language is (a) systematic (b) symbolic, and (c) social.
2. Match the following linguistic terms to their corresponding synonyms/definitions:

1. lexicon	a. word structure
2. phonology	b. grammar
3. morphology	c. vocabulary
4. syntax	d. sound system

3. Match the following theories with their central figures:

1. Contrastive Analysis	a. Krashen
2. Error Analysis	b. Dulay and Burt
3. Interlanguage	c. Corder
4. Morpheme Order Studies	d. Chomsky
5. Monitor Model	e. Lado
6. Universal Grammar	f. Selinker

4. When interlanguage development stops before a learner reaches target language norms, it is called _____ .
5. As they can be understood in Chomsky's theory of Universal Grammar, what is the difference between linguistic performance and linguistic competence?
6. According to a Functionalist perspective, what is the primary purpose of language?
7. Choose which developmental levels from the framework of Information Organization the following sentences represent: (choose from Nominal Utterance Organization, Infinite Utterance Organization, Finite Utterance Organization)
   a. my manager say I get raise
   b. they have eaten
   c. girl nice but she not pretty
   d. later we talked
   e. he call his mother, say "come over"
   f. man wife restaurant

Active learning

1. Read the following scenarios and decide which aspect of language is mentioned in each instance. (Choose from lexicon, morphology, phonology, and syntax.)
   a. If we see the word "talks" alone, outside of any context, we could consider it to be composed of the root "talk" and a plural -s to make a noun (more than one talk/discussion/address), or we could consider it to be made up of the root "talk" and a third person -s to make a conjugated verb (like "he talks," "she talks," or "it talks").
   b. The English word "talk" has near synonyms like "speak," "say," "express," "shout," "yell," and "whisper."
   c. The English word "talk" can be pronounced differently depending on the geographical locations of the speakers.

d. In English, appropriate word order is Subject–Verb–Object, like saying "The man was talking to the child." In Japanese, word order is subject–object–verb, so one would say "The man the child to was talking."

2. Reread the section on the poverty-of-the-stimulus argument and make a definition of this theory in your own words. Do you think this theory holds true for SLA as well as for first language acquisition? Why or why not?

3. Make a timeline to indicate when the following theories or schools of thought were flourishing as they are discussed in this text. Think about the progression of theories. When they change, are they building upon old theories or rejecting them? Select one theory and explain how it builds upon or rejects those that came before it.

a. Contrastive Analysis	h. Mentalism
b. Behaviorism	i. Interlanguage
c. Structuralism	j. Morpheme Order Studies
d. Error Analysis	k. Monitor Model
e. Universal Grammar	l. Constructionism
f. Systemic Linguistics	m. Functional Typology
g. Function-to-form mapping	n. Information organization

4. Listen to someone who speaks your language non-natively and write down some ungrammatical sentences they have spoken. Using principles of Contrastive Analysis and the procedures of Error Analysis on pages 37–40 of this chapter, try to classify each error. Remember that there may not be a specific "right" answer available; these are just your predictions.

5. If you have studied a second language, what are some of the linguistic elements that have been most difficult for you to master (morphology, phonology, syntax, etc.)? Why do you think they have been harder?

6. Proponents of Universal Grammar believe that language ability is innate, whereas Functionalists believe that we develop language primarily because of a need to communicate. Which theory do you believe in? Why?

Further reading

Pinker, S. (1994). *The Language Instinct*. New York: William Morrow and Company.

A highly readable explanation of modern linguistics, wherein chapters 4, 5, and 6 include discussion of syntax, morphology, phonology, and the arbitrariness of language.

Yaguello, M. (1981/1998). *Language through the Looking Glass: Exploring Language and Linguistics*. Oxford: Oxford University Press.

Language through the Looking Glass provides explanation of the classical categories of linguistic study (phonology, morphology, semantics, syntax) in addition to treating the questions of arbitrariness and universality of language largely based upon literary examples from Lewis Carroll's *Alice in Wonderland*.

Selinker, L. (1992). *Rediscovering Interlanguage*. New York: Longman.

Selinker treats contrastive analysis and error analysis as the beginnings that eventually led to the concept of interlanguage. In addition, he presents work on fossilization and how the concept of interlanguage is used

today, as opposed to when it was coined in 1972. This is done with the overall goal
in the history of its field.

Baker, M. (2001). *The Atoms of Language*. New York: Basic Books.
 Baker explains the concepts of Chomsky's Principles and Parameters theory in term
general audience.

Bialystok, E. & Hakuta, K. (1994). *In Other Words: The Science and Psychology of Se*
Acquisition. New York: Basic Books.
 In Chapter 2, "Language," Bialystok and Hakuta clearly present much of the linguistic background
(discussing Chomskyan and Functionalist perspectives) needed to understand the basic tenets of Second
Language Acquisition as a field today.

Mitchell, R. & Myles, F. (2004). Functional/pragmatic perspectives on second language learning. *Second*
Language Learning Theories (Second Edition) (pp. 100–20). London: Arnold.
 This chapter offers an overview of several functionalist perspectives as they relate to L1 development and
L2 learning. It also includes a brief section outlining the contributions of functionalism to the body of
knowledge in the SLA field.

The psychology of Second Language Acquisition

CHAPTER PREVIEW

In this chapter we survey several approaches to SLA that have been heavily influenced by the field of psychology. They are ordered according to their primary focus of attention: first those that focus on *languages and the brain*, then those that focus on the *learning processes* that are involved in SLA, and finally those that focus on *differences among learners*.

Study of languages and the brain is based largely on the framework provided by **neurolinguistics**, which seeks to answer questions about how the location and organization of language might differ in the heads of monolingual versus multilingual speakers, and of multilinguals who acquire second languages at different ages or under differing circumstances. It primarily addresses *what* is being acquired in a physical sense: what is added or changed in the neurological "wiring" of people's brains when they add another language?

The study of learning processes draws especially on the frameworks of **Information Processing (IP)** and **Connectionism**, and includes questions about stages and sequences of acquisition. This focus primarily addresses *how* acquisition takes place. Is there a specialized **language faculty** in the brain (as we read in the last chapter), or does all learning involve the same mechanisms?

Approaches to the study of learner differences derive largely from **humanistic** traditions that take affective factors into account, but some consider factors associated with age and sex, and some consider possible individual differences in aptitude for language learning. This third focus primarily addresses the question of *why* some second language learners are more successful than others. Does it make a difference if learners are ten or twenty years old when they begin a new language, or whether they are male or female, or whether they are gregarious or introverted?

Finally, we will explore how being multilingual might affect the ways people think, and how multilinguals perform on tests of intelligence.

Languages and the brain

Notions that particular locations in the brain may be specialized for language functions date back at least into the nineteenth century. Paul Pierre Broca (1861, 1865) observed that an area in the left frontal lobe (Broca's area) appeared to be responsible for the ability to speak and noted that an injury to the left side of the brain was much more likely to result in language loss than was an injury to the right side. Wernicke (1874) further identified a nearby area which is adjacent to the part of the cortex that processes audio input (Wernicke's area) as also being central to language processing. Some exceptions have been found, but for the vast majority of individuals, language is represented primarily in the left half (or hemisphere) of the brain within an area (including both Broca's area and Wernicke's area) around the Sylvian fissure (a cleavage that separates lobes in the brain). Subsequent research has shown that many more areas of the brain are involved in language activity than was thought earlier: language activity is not localized, but core linguistic processes are typically housed in the left hemisphere.

Such specialization of the two halves of the brain is known as lateralization, and is present to some extent even in infancy (e.g. Mills, Coffey-Corina, and Neville 1993). There is increased specialization as the brain matures and has less plasticity: i.e. one area of the brain becomes less able to assume the functions of another in the event it is damaged. Lenneberg (1967) proposed that children had only a limited number of years during which they could acquire their L1 flawlessly if they suffered brain damage to the language areas; brain plasticity in childhood would allow other areas of the brain to take over the language functions of the damaged

Paul Pierre Broca (b. Sainte-Foy-la-Grande, France) 1824–1880

Neuroscience

After becoming a professor and researcher at the University of Paris, Paul Pierre Broca made a most important discovery about the anatomy of the brain: he found its speech center, now called *Broca's Area*. Broca arrived at his discovery by studying the brains of patients with aphasia (the inability to talk).

Interesting note: Broca was considered a child prodigy and earned baccalaureates in literature, mathematics, and physics. He began medical school at age seventeen, and finished at age twenty, when most medical students were just beginning their studies.

areas, but beyond a certain age, normal language would not be possible. This is the Critical period hypothesis, mentioned in Chapter 2 and to be discussed below in relation to the influence of age on SLA.

Communicative functions for which each hemisphere of the brain is primarily specialized are listed in 4.1, as suggested by L1 research reviewed in Obler and Gjerlow (1999).

4.1 Principal communicative specializations of L and R hemispheres	
Principal hemispheric specializations	
Left hemisphere	Right hemisphere
Phonology	Nonverbal (as babies' cries)
Morphology	Visuospatial information
Syntax	Intonation
Function words and inflections	Nonliteral meaning and ambiguity
Tone systems	Many pragmatic abilities
Much lexical knowledge	Some lexical knowledge

In discussing hemispheric specialization, Obler and Gjerlow emphasize that, "while localizing language phenomena in the brain is the eventual goal of neurolinguistics, we no longer expect that there are language areas that are entirely "responsible" for language, or even "dominant" for language, to be contrasted with areas that have nothing to do with it" (1999:11–12).

Hemispheric specialization for language is the same regardless of whether the language is spoken or not; core linguistic functions for sign languages used in deaf communities are also located in the left hemisphere. The visuospatial information listed for the right hemisphere in 4.1 refers to movement which may be meaningful but is nonlinguistic in nature. When movement incorporates linguistic units of phonology, morphology, and syntax (as in sign language), it is left-hemisphere based (Emmorey 2002). The typical distribution of primary functions is probably due to the left hemisphere's being computationally more powerful than the right and therefore better suited for processing the highly complex elements of language.

Interest in how the brain might be organized for multiple languages also dates back to the nineteenth century (e.g. Freud 1891). The initial questions arose from observing differing patterns for the interruption and recovery of languages following brain damage in multilinguals. Most individuals lose or recover multiple languages equally (Paradis 1987), but some recover one before the other, and some never recover use of one (either L1 or L2). These findings suggest that two or more languages may be represented in somewhat different locations in the brain and/or have different networks of activation. This possibility has stimulated observation and research on the topic for the past century, although research procedures have changed radically with changing technology. Methods for gathering data have included the following:

- Correlations of location of brain damage with patterns of loss/ recovery in cases where languages are affected differentially.
- Presentation of stimuli from different languages to the right versus the left visual or auditory fields to investigate which side of the brain is most involved in processing each language. What is presented to the right fields will be processed faster and more accurately by the left hemisphere and vice versa.
- Mapping the brain surface during surgery by using electrical stimulation at precise points and recording which areas are involved in which aspects of speech, and in which language. (This mapping procedure is often used prior to or even during removal of brain tissue because of a tumor or other abnormality, allowing the neurosurgeon to avoid disrupting language functions as much as possible.)
- Positron Emission Tomography (PET-scans) and other non-invasive imaging techniques that allow direct observation of areas of the brain that are activated by different language stimuli and tasks.

In spite of many years of research, some questions remain unanswered or answers remain controversial. In part this is because study has generally involved limited numbers of subjects and there is considerable individual variation in how the brain is "wired"; in part it is because research efforts have not used the same procedures for data collection and analysis and therefore do not yield entirely comparable results. Still, there are a number of findings which shed increasing light on the representation and organization of multiple languages in the brain. Specific questions which have been explored are listed below, along with a brief summary of results from some of the research conducted on them.

1. How independent are the languages of multilingual speakers?

There is no single answer to this question, both because there appears to be considerable individual variation among speakers, and because there are very complex factors which must be taken into account. It seems reasonable to conclude, however, that multiple language systems are neither completely separate nor completely fused.

Ervin and Osgood (1954; following Weinreich 1953) suggested a three-way possibility for how languages relate in an individual's mind, which are called **coordinate, compound,** and **subordinate bilingualism**. **Coordinate** refers to parallel linguistic systems, independent of one another; **compound** to a fused or unified system; and **subordinate** to one linguistic system accessed through another. Ervin and Osgood claim that these different relationships result in part because of different contexts for language learning. An extreme case of coordinate bilingualism would be the rare individual who has learned two or more languages in different contexts and is not able (even with conscious effort) to translate between them. More common would be compound bilingualism, believed by many to characterize simultaneous bilingualism in early childhood (before the age of three years), and subordinate bilingualism, believed to result from learning L2 through the medium of L1 (as in grammar-translation approaches to foreign language instruction). There is evidence that suggests the relationship may depend on L2 proficiency, changing from compound or subordinate to coordinate at higher knowledge and skill levels (Kroll and Steward 1994).

Other researchers stress the interdependence of languages, although separation can be maintained for many purposes. Obler and Gjerlow conclude that multiple linguistic systems ". . . are only as independent as necessary, and reliance on a single system is the rule whenever possible" (1999:140).

2. How are multiple language structures organized in relation to one another in the brain? Are both languages stored in the same areas?

Again, there is considerable variation among speakers. For at least some multilinguals, it appears that L1 and L2 are stored in somewhat different areas of the brain, but both are predominantly in (probably overlapping) areas of the left hemisphere. However, the right hemisphere might be more involved in L2 than in L1.

Researchers have stimulated certain segments of the brain during surgery (Ojemann and Whitaker 1978) and found that disturbing some points in the brain blocks people from being able to name things in both languages, while disturbing other points does not have this effect. The area common to both L1 and L2 storage is near the Sylvian fissure in the left hemisphere (already established as the primary language area for monolinguals, including Broca's and Wernike's areas), but only L1 or L2 (more likely L2) is disrupted by stimulation of points further away from the Sylvian fissure. Using PET-scan imaging on one Spanish–English subject in repetition tasks, Fedio et al. (1992) also found more diffuse brain activation for L2 than for L1, and different areas involved, which the authors interpreted as indicating that greater memorization of words and phrases is involved in L2 (as opposed to direct processing of words for meaning in L1).

3. Does the organization of the brain for L2 in relation to L1 differ with age of acquisition, how it is learned, or level of proficiency?

The answer is probably "yes" to all three, with the strongest body of evidence showing that age of acquisition influences brain organization for many second language learners.

After reviewing research on lateralization in bilinguals, Vaid (1983) concludes that individuals who acquire L2 later in life show more right-hemisphere involvement. Supporting this conclusion, Wuillemin and Richards (1994) report more right-hemisphere involvement for individuals who acquire L2 between ages nine and twelve than for those who acquire

L2 before age 4. Cook suggests that how people learn languages might be a factor: "The variation in right hemisphere involvement may be due to the lack of a single route to L2 knowledge: second languages may be learnt by many means rather than the single means found in L1 acquisition and, consequently, may have a greater apparent hemispheric spread" (1992:572).

We know very little so far about how organization of knowledge in the brain might be related to level of proficiency in a second language, but it appears probable that the organization of L2 knowledge is more diffuse for lower levels of proficiency and more compact for highly fluent L2 users. As we have just seen (Fedio et al. 1992), a PET-scan of the brain shows that a multilingual person may use more memorization for L2 and more direct processing of meaning for L1. Other types of research (e.g. analysis of errors in reading) show L2 learners' increasing reliance on meaning over memory as their proficiency in L2 increases. With the availability of non-invasive imaging techniques, we can hope that researchers might gather data from the same individuals over time as they progress in L2 learning, so we can actually see whether there are changes in the brain's organization of knowledge in relation to interlanguage development.

4. Do two or more languages show the same sort of loss or disruption after brain damage? When there is differential impairment or recovery, which language recovers first?

As noted in the first part of this section, brain damage results in the same or very similar patterns of loss and recovery for both/all of most multilingual persons' languages, but many exceptions have been reported. One early hypothesis was that in cases of such brain damage, the last-learned language would be the first lost, the next-to-the-last learned the second to be lost, and so forth, with L1 the last to remain; recovery was speculated to be L1 first. This in fact does not appear to occur at a level greater than chance, at least with respect to order of recovery. Obler and Gjerlow (1999) conclude rather that a significant factor in initial recovery is which language was most used in the years prior to the incident which caused the damage, whether this is L1 or L2.

Research on this question also shows that not only can different languages be affected differentially by brain damage, but different abilities in the same language may be differentially impaired: e.g. syntax versus vocabulary, production versus comprehension, or oral versus written modality. These observations have possible implications for claims that different elements of language are located in separate parts of the brain.

We may conclude that *what* is being added in the brain when a second language is acquired is not very different from, nor usually entirely separate from, what is already there for the first. But there are intriguing differences: some differences may be due to level of L2 proficiency, some to circumstances of L2 learning, and some to the fact that our brains are not "wired" in exactly the same way. Research on this focus is expanding rapidly with the help of brain-imaging technology, and it promises also to contribute more neurological answers to questions of *how* second languages are learned and *why* some people are more successful than others.

Learning processes

Psychology provides us with two major frameworks for the focus on learning processes: Information Processing (IP) and Connectionism. IP has had more influence on the study of SLA than any other psychological perspective, following an approach developed by John Anderson (e.g. 1976, 1983). It makes the claim that learning language is essentially like learning other domains of knowledge: that whether people are learning mathematics, or learning to drive a car, or learning Japanese, they are not engaging in any essentially different kind of mental activity. *Learning is learning.* We take a general look at the information processing framework and then discuss three approaches based on it, the Multidimensional Model, Processability, and the Competition Model, respectively. The Connectionism framework also claims that "learning is learning," but considers learning processes as a matter of increasing strength of associations rather than as the abstraction of rules or principles.

Information Processing (IP)

Approaches based on IP are concerned with the mental processes involved in language learning and use. These include perception and the input of new information; the formation, organization, and regulation of internal (mental) representations; and retrieval and output strategies.

   The information processing approach makes a number of assumptions (McLaughlin 1987):

(1) Second language learning is the acquisition of a complex cognitive skill. In this respect language learning is like the acquisition of other complex skills.
(2) Complex skills can be reduced to sets of simpler component skills, which are hierarchically organized. Lower-order component skills are prerequisite to learning of higher-order skills.
(3) Learning of a skill initially demands learners' attention, and thus involves controlled processing.
(4) Controlled processing requires considerable mental "space," or attentional effort.
(5) Humans are limited-capacity processors. They can attend to a limited number of controlled processing demands at one time.
(6) Learners go from controlled to automatic processing with practice. Automatic processing requires less mental "space" and attentional effort.
(7) Learning essentially involves development from controlled to automatic processing of component skills, freeing learners' controlled processing capacity for new information and higher-order skills.

(8) Along with development from controlled to automatic processing, learning also essentially involves **restructuring** or reorganization of mental representations.

(9) Reorganizing mental representations as part of learning makes structures more coordinated, integrated, and efficient, including a faster response time when they are activated.

(10) In SLA, restructuring of internal L2 representations, along with larger stores in memory, accounts for increasing levels of L2 proficiency.

Our mental capacity requirements for controlled processing are obvious when we are beginning to learn a second language, as we need to concentrate our attention to comprehend or produce basic vocabulary and syntactic structures. It is only after these have been automatized that we can attend to more complex, higher-order features and content. We encounter similar capacity limitations (we easily experience "information overload") in learning a new "language" for computerized word processing: we must initially use controlled processing to select appropriate symbols and apply the right rules, and it is difficult or impossible to simultaneously pay attention to higher-order content or creative processing. It is only after we have automatized the lower-level skills that our processing capacity is freed for higher-order thought. Writers usually cannot compose "online" effectively until lower-level word-processing skills such as typing, saving documents, and changing fonts have become automatized. Further examples can readily be drawn from learning other complex nonverbal skills, such as driving or skiing, where tasks that initially require attentional control become automatized with practice; they then generally remain out of conscious awareness unless some unusual occurrence returns them to controlled processing. Behaviors under attentional control are permeable, i.e. they are changeable; but once automatized, they are both more efficient and more difficult to change. In fact, one explanation for L2 **fossilization** (or apparent cessation of learning) from an IP perspective is that aspects of L2 may become automatized before they have developed to target levels, and positive input no longer suffices to lead to their improvement.

Information Processing has three stages, as shown in 4.2 (adapted from Skehan 1998).

4.2 Stages of Information Processing		
Input	Central processing	Output
Perception	Controlled–automatic processing	Production
	Declarative–procedural knowledge	
	Restructuring	

Input for SLA is whatever sample of L2 that learners are exposed to, but it is not available for processing unless learners actually notice it: i.e. pay attention to it. Then it can become **intake**. It is at this point of perception of input where priorities are largely determined, and where attentional resources are channeled. Richard Schmidt (1990) lists the following features as likely contributors to the degree of noticing or awareness which will occur:

- Frequency of encounter with items
- Perceptual saliency of items
- Instructional strategies that can structure learner attention
- Individuals' processing ability (a component of **aptitude**)
- Readiness to notice particular items (related to hierarchies of complexity)
- Task demands, or the nature of activity the learner is engaged in

In line with this IP approach to learning, developing and testing strategies to heighten learner awareness of input and to structure attention has been a major thrust in foreign language instructional design and pedagogy, so that successful intake can occur.

Output for SLA is the language that learners produce, in speech/sign or in writing. The importance of output for successful L2 learning has been most fully expounded by Merrill Swain (e.g. Swain and Lapkin 1995). Meaningful production practice helps learners by:

- Enhancing fluency by furthering development of automaticity through practice
- Noticing gaps in their own knowledge as they are forced to move from semantic to syntactic processing, which may lead learners to give more attention to relevant information
- Testing hypotheses based on developing interlanguage, allowing for monitoring and revision
- Talking about language, including eliciting relevant input and (collaboratively) solving problems

Fluency is achieved in production both through use of automatized rule-based systems and through memory-based chunks which serve as exemplars or templates and are "retrieved and used as wholes" (Skehan 1998:60).

Central processing is the heart of this model, where learning occurs. It is here that learners go from controlled to automatic processing, and where restructuring of knowledge takes place. It is possible to test for degree of automatization because controlled processing requires more time. Research that measures the amount of time it takes multilinguals to recall words and grammatical structures shows that the L2 of even fluent speakers of both languages is generally less automatized than their L1, and less proficient L2 is less automatized than more fluent L2.

In the model of learning that was proposed by Anderson (1976), development from **declarative** to **procedural** stages of knowledge is parallel to development from controlled to automatic processing in many respects. The declarative stage involves acquisition of isolated facts and rules; processing is relatively slow and often under attentional control. Development to the procedural stage involves processing of longer associated units and increasing automatization, which frees attentional resources for higher-level skills. Proceduralization requires practice.

As noted in the assumptions about IP listed above, the restructuring that takes place during central processing makes mental representations more coordinated, integrated, and efficient. It involves qualitative changes, meaning that L2 development cannot be characterized as a seamless continuum along which new forms are added to old, but as a partially discontinuous plane along which there is regular systemic reorganization and reformulation. Two types of evidence from learners' speech and writing are often cited. One is the sequence of acquisition which learners exhibit when they produce unanalyzed chunks of L2 correctly and then make errors as they restructure the elements they have processed in accord with newly formulated patterns and rules: i.e. an onset or increase of ungrammaticality in utterances is often an indicator of "progress" in SLA. A related type of evidence is found in U-shaped development: i.e. learners' use of an initially correct form such as plural *feet* in English, followed by incorrect *foots*, eventually again appearing as *feet*. In this case, *feet* is first learned as an unanalyzed word, without recognition that it is a combination of *foot* plus plural. The later production of *foots* is evidence of systemic restructuring that takes place when the regular plural *-s* is added to the learner's grammar. *Feet* reappears when the learner begins to acquire exceptions to the plural inflection rule.

Theories regarding order of acquisition

Psychological approaches to SLA have made significant contributions to understanding why certain elements are acquired in a fixed sequence. One of the best known of these approaches is the Multidimensional Model, developed by researchers who initially studied the German L2 learning of adult L1 speakers of Italian, Spanish, and Portuguese in the ZISA project (see Clahsen, Meisel, and Pienemann 1983). This model includes the following claims:

- Learners acquire certain grammatical structures in a developmental sequence.
- Developmental sequences reflect how learners overcome processing limitations.
- Language instruction which targets developmental features will be successful only if learners have already mastered the processing operations which are associated with the previous stage of acquisition.

The processing strategies which account for developmental sequences in perception and production are explained by Clahsen (1984) in relation to the IP constraint of limited capacity: "linguistic structures which require a high degree of processing capacity will be acquired late" (p. 221). Which syntactic structures require more processing capacity (i.e. are more complex) is determined by the extent to which their underlying relations are preserved in output, and by the perceptual salience of any reordering that does occur. Clahsen infers the following hierarchy:

(1) *Canonical Order Strategy*:   There is no reordering from "basic" word order. Structures which can be processed with this strategy will be acquired first.

(2) *Initialization/Finalization Strategy*:   Reordering which moves underlying elements into the first or last position in a grammatical string are perceptually more salient, and thus easier to process than permutations to internal positions.

(3) *Subordinate Clause Strategy*:   Reordering in subordinate clauses is not allowed. This accounts for why "learners initially use certain reorderings only in main clauses and [. . .] thus the order of the elements in subordinate clauses is less varied" (1984:223).

A reorientation of the Multidimensional Model is known as **Processability Theory** (Pienemann 1998); it also has the aim of determining and explaining the sequences in which processing skills develop in relation to language learning. The following acquisitional hierarchy of processing skills is proposed (from Pienemann and Håkansson 1999):

(1) *Lemma/word access*:   Words (or **lemmas**) are processed, but they do not yet carry any grammatical information, nor are they yet associated with any ordering rules.

(2) *Category procedure*:   Lexical items are categorized, and grammatical information may be added (e.g. number and gender to nouns, tense to verbs).

(3) *Phrasal procedure*:   Operations within the phrase level occur, such as agreement for number or gender between adjective and noun within the noun phrase.

(4) *S-procedure*:   Grammatical information may be exchanged across phrase boundaries, such as number agreement between subject and verb.

(5) *Clause boundary*:   Main and subordinate clause structures may be handled differently.

This is an implicational hierarchy in the sense that processing skill at level 1 is a prerequisite for processing skill at level 2, level 2 is prerequisite for level 3, and so forth. The sequence of strategies describes the developing learner grammar in terms of processing prerequisites needed to acquire grammatical (syntactic and morphological) rules at successive stages.

The universality of this sequence in SLA is being tested by researchers, with generally supportive results. In addition to Pienemann's analysis of German L2 (1998) and reanalysis of data from prior research on Swedish L2 (Pienemann and Håkansson 1999), the most extensive studies thus far have been on Danish, Norwegian, and Swedish (Glahn et al. 2001).

Claims that language instruction will be effective only if it targets the next stage in an L2 learner's developmental sequence (rather than more advanced levels) have been tested on many languages since the 1970s (reviewed in Spada and Lightbown 1999). Results are mixed concerning the interaction of developmental order and instructional level, with indication that at least for some structures, and for some learners, instruction at a more advanced level can be more efficient. Complexities include the type of instruction (e.g. whether explicit contrastive L1-L2 information on the structure is presented), and the degree to which L1 knowledge may be applicable. However, these complexities do not appear to invalidate claims about order of acquisition; even when learners profit from more advanced levels of instruction, they progress through the same developmental sequence.

Competition Model

Another psychological approach that has addressed the general question of how languages are learned is the Competition Model (Bates and MacWhinney 1981; MacWhinney 2001). This is a functional approach which assumes that all linguistic performance involves "mapping" between external form and internal function. The form of a lexical item is represented by its auditory properties, and its function by its semantic properties; the forms of strings of lexical items are word-order patterns and morphological inflections, and their functions are grammatical. For example, for the word *horse* the form is represented by the sounds [hors]; the function is the meaning of a four-legged, hay-eating animal. In the sentence *Horses eat hay*, the word orders of *horses* before and *hay* after the verb are forms; the functions are to convey that *horses* is the subject and *hay* is the object. The inflection *-s* on *horses* is also a form; its function is to convey that more than one horse is being referred to.

This approach considers that learning the system of form–function mapping is basic for L1 acquisition. SLA involves adjusting the internalized system of mapping that exists in the learner's L1 to one that is appropriate for the target language. This is accomplished by detecting cues in language input which are associated with a particular function, and by recognizing what weight to assign each possible cue (the cue strength). The cue in English that *horses* is the subject in the sentence *Horses eat hay* is word order – *horses* comes in front of the verb. If the sentence were in

Brian MacWhinney (b. New York), 1945–present

Psychology

MacWhinney's studies of language processing across languages led to the co-development of the Competition Model with Elizabeth Bates (MacWhinney and Bates, 1989). In this research, many areas of processing were studied: normal adult sentence processing, the development of child sentence processing, and language processing of people with aphasia. MacWhinney has also developed a set of computer programs and a database called CHILDES (Child Language Data Exchange System), which is used by more than 800 researchers in forty-six different countries.

Japanese, the cue would be a **case marker,** the inflection -*ga* that is attached to the end of a word which means it is the subject (i.e. that it has nominative case).

Multiple cues are available simultaneously in input; language processing essentially involves "competition" among the various cues. For example, for the grammatical function of subject, possible cues are *word order*, *agreement*, *case marking*, and *animacy* (i.e. capacity for volitional action). All of these possible cues are illustrated in the following sentences (some are not grammatical or grammatically felicitous):

(a) *The cow kicks the horse.*
(b) *The cow kick the horses.*
(c) *Him kicks the horse.*
(d) *The fence kicks the horse.*

The relative strength of word order as a cue in English over the other possibilities can be tested by presenting native speakers with sentences such as these and asking them to identify the subject or agent in each (i.e. who/what does the "kicking").

In spite of the ungrammaticality of (b-c), or in the case of (d) its anomalous character, native English speakers are most likely to identify the first noun phrase in each of these sentences as subject, even though in (b) the verb agrees with the second noun phrase rather than the first, in (c) *him* is case-marked as object (the receiver of the action) rather than subject, and in (d) *fence* is inanimate and cannot be interpreted literally as a "doer" of the verb *kick*. If these sentences were translated into other languages, different identifications of subject would likely be made depending on whether agreement, case marking, or animacy carried more weight. In Japanese, for instance, the case marker -*ga* attached to a noun phrase (if no other -*ga* occurred) would generally carry more weight in identifying that NP as the subject, no matter where in the word order it occurred. An English L1 speaker learning Japanese as L2 might inappropriately transfer the strong word-order cue to initial form–function mapping (and identify the wrong noun phrase as subject if it occurred first), whereas native speakers of Japanese might transfer their L1 cue weights to English L2 and also provide nonnative interpretations.

Acquisition of appropriate form–function mappings is driven primarily by the probability that a particular functional interpretation should be chosen in the presence of a particular cue. If the probability is high, the cue is reliable. The following determinants of cue strength are also discussed by MacWhinney (2001:74–75; see Ellis 1994:373–77):

- *Task frequency*:   how often the form–function mapping occurs. The vast majority of English sentences have a subject before the verb, so the mapping of word-order form to subject function is very frequent.
- *Contrastive availability*:   when the cue is present, whether or not it has any contrastive effect. In example (a) above, for instance (*The cow kicks the horse*), the third person singular -*s* on the verb agrees with both noun phrases and so the agreement cue tells nothing about

which is the subject. An available cue must occur contrastively if it is to be useful.

- *Conflict reliability*:   how often the cue leads to a correct interpretation when it is used in comparison to other potential cues.

Transfer of L1 cue strengths to L2 is the most likely outcome in early stages of SLA when the systems differ, but research has shown that some learners ultimately abandon L1 cue strengths in favor of L2, while some compromise and merge the two systems, and some differentiate between the languages in this aspect of processing.

Connectionist approaches

Connectionist approaches to learning have much in common with IP perspectives, but they focus on the increasing strength of associations between stimuli and responses rather than on the inferred abstraction of "rules" or on restructuring. Indeed, from a connectionist perspective learning essentially *is* change in the strength of these connections. Some version of this idea has been present in psychology at least since the 1940s and 1950s (see McClelland, Rumelhart, and Hinton 1986 for an overview of historical developments), but Connectionism has received widespread attention as a model for first and second language acquisition only since the 1980s.

The best-known connectionist approach within SLA is Parallel Distributed Processing, or PDP. According to this viewpoint, processing takes place in a network of nodes (or "units") in the brain that are connected by pathways. As learners are exposed to repeated patterns of units in input, they extract regularities in the patterns; probabilistic associations are formed and strengthened. These associations between nodes are called connection strengths or patterns of activation. The strength of the associations changes with the frequency of input and nature of feedback. The claim that such learning is not dependent on either a store of innate knowledge (such as Universal Grammar) or rule-formation is supported by computer simulations. For example, Rumelhart and McClelland (1986) demonstrated that a computer that is programmed with a "pattern associator network" can learn to associate English verb bases with their appropriate past tense forms without any *a priori* "rules," and that it does so with much the same learning curve as that exhibited by children learning English L1. The model provides an account for both regular and irregular tense inflections, including transfer to unfamiliar verbs, and for the "U-shaped" developmental curve (discussed in the previous section on order of acquisition) which is often cited in linguistic models and in other cognitive approaches as evidence for rule-based learning.

Assumptions about processing from a connectionist/PDP viewpoint differ from traditional IP accounts in other important ways. For example (McClelland, Rumelhart, and Hinton 1986; Robinson 1995):

(1) Attention is not viewed as a central mechanism that directs information between separate memory stores, which IP claims are available for controlled processing versus automatic processing.

Rather, attention is a mechanism that is distributed throughout the processing system in local patterns.

(2) Information processing is not serial in nature: i.e. it is not a "pipeline . . . in which information is conveyed in a fixed serial order from one storage structure to the next" (Robinson 1995:288). Instead, processing is parallel: many connections are activated at the same time.

(3) Knowledge is not stored in memory or retrieved as patterns, but as "connection strengths" between units which account for the patterns being recreated.

It is obvious that parallel processing is being applied when tasks simultaneously tap entirely different resources such as talking on a cell phone while riding a bicycle, but it also less obviously occurs within integrated tasks such as simply talking or reading, when encoding/decoding of phonology, syntactic structure, meaning, and pragmatic intent occur simultaneously. Many connections in the brain must be activated all at once to account for successful production and interpretation of language, and not processed in sequence (i.e. one after the other).

Little research based on this approach has been conducted in SLA, but the assumption is that transfer from L1 to L2 occurs because strong associations already established in L1 interfere with establishment of the L2 network. Because frequency is the primary determinant of connection strength, it might be predicted that the most common patterns in L1 would be the most likely to cause interference in L2, but research on transfer from linguistic perspectives does not support this conclusion in any strong sense; L1-L2 relationships are not that simple. Proponents of connectionist approaches to language acquisition note that while frequency is "an all-pervasive causal factor" (Ellis 2002:179), it interacts with other determinants, including how noticeable the language patterns are in the input learners receive, and whether the patterns are regular or occur with many variations and exceptions.

Many linguists and psychologists would argue against a strong deterministic role for frequency of input in language learning. One counterargument is that some of the most frequent words in English (including the most frequent, *the*) are relatively late to appear, and among the last (if ever) to be mastered. Still, whatever one's theoretical perspective, the effects of frequency on SLA clearly merit more attention than they have typically received since repetition drills went out of fashion in language teaching. Researchers from several approaches to SLA which focus on learning processes are taking a renewed look at how frequency influences learning.

Differences in learners

In Chapter 3, we considered the basic question of *why* some L2 learners are more successful than others from a linguistic perspective, and in Chapter 5 we will again consider this question from the perspective of the social contexts of learning. Here we address this question from a psychological perspective, focusing on differences among learners themselves.

The differences we explore here are age, sex, aptitude, motivation, cognitive style, personality, and learning strategies. Some of the relevant research looks at neurological representation and organization (such as the research reported above in the section on languages and the brain), some is of an experimental nature (which manipulates variables and makes direct claims about cause and effect), and some relies on "good language learner" studies (which deal with correlations between specific traits and successful SLA). Some of this research remains quite speculative.

Age

It is a common belief that children are more successful L2 learners than adults, but the evidence for this is actually surprisingly equivocal. One reason for the apparent inconsistency in research findings is that some studies define relative "success" as initial rate of learning (where, contrary to popular belief, older learners have an advantage) while other studies define it as ultimate achievement (where learners who are introduced to the L2 in childhood indeed do appear to have an edge). Also, some studies define "success" in terms of how close the learner's pronunciation is to a native speaker's, others in terms of how closely a learner approximates native grammaticality judgments, and still others in terms of fluency or functional competence. It is very important to keep evaluative criteria clearly in mind while judging conflicting claims.

The question of whether, and how, age affects L2 outcomes has been a major issue in SLA for several decades, and a number of recent publications provide reviews from different points of view (e.g. Birdsong 1999; Scovel 2000; Singleton 2001). Some of the advantages which have been reported for both younger and older learners are listed in 4.3.

4.3 Age differences in SLA	
Younger advantage	**Older advantage**
• Brain plasticity	• Learning capacity
• Not analytical	• Analytic ability
• Fewer inhibitions (usually)	• Pragmatic skills
• Weaker group identity	• Greater knowledge of L1
• Simplified input more likely	• Real-world knowledge

We noted in the earlier section of this chapter on languages and the brain that there is a critical period for first language acquisition: children have only a limited number of years during which normal acquisition is possible. Beyond that, physiological changes cause the brain to lose its plasticity, or capacity to assume the new functions that learning language demands. Individuals who for some reason are deprived of the linguistic input which is needed to trigger first language acquisition during the critical period will never learn any language normally. One famous documented case which provides rare evidence for this point is that of

Genie, an abused girl who was kept isolated from all language input and interaction until she was thirteen years old. In spite of years of intensive efforts at remediation, Genie never developed linguistic knowledge and skills for her L1 (English) that were comparable to those of speakers who began acquisition in early childhood (Curtiss 1977).

Genie:

Evidence for the Critical Period Hypothesis

The tragic case of "Genie" bears directly on the critical period hypothesis. Genie was discovered in 1970, at the age of thirteen, having been brought up in conditions of inhuman neglect and extreme isolation. She was severely disturbed and underdeveloped, and had been unable to learn language. In the course of her treatment and rehabilitation, great efforts were made to teach her to speak. She had received next to no linguistic stimulation between the ages of two and puberty, so the evidence of her language-learning ability would bear directly on the Lenneberg hypothesis.

Analysis of the way Genie developed her linguistic skills showed several abnormalities, such as a marked gap between production and comprehension, variability in using rules, stereotyped speech, gaps in the acquisition of syntactic skills, and a generally retarded rate of development. After various psycholinguistic tests, it was concluded that Genie was using her right hemisphere for language (as well as for several other activities), and that this might have been the result of her beginning the task of language learning after the critical period of left-hemisphere development. The case was thus thought to support Lenneberg's hypothesis, but only in a weak form. Genie was evidently able to acquire some language from exposure after puberty (she made great progress in vocabulary, for example, and continued to make gains in morphology and syntax), but she did not do so in a normal way. (After S. Curtiss 1977, in Crystal 1997b.)

Lenneberg (1967) speculated that the critical period applies to SLA as well as to first language acquisition, and that this accounts for why almost all L2 speakers have a "foreign accent" if they do not begin learning the language before the cut-off age. Seliger (1978) and Long (1990) argue instead that there are multiple periods which place constraints on different aspects of language: e.g. different periods relate to the acquisition of phonology versus the acquisition of syntax. They also suggest that these periods do not impose absolute cut-off points; it is just that L2 acquisition will more *likely* be complete if begun in childhood than if it does not start until a later age. This weaker claim seems warranted since some older learners can achieve native-like proficiency, although they definitely constitute a minority of second language learners.

While most would agree that younger learners achieve ultimately higher levels of L2 proficiency, evidence is just as convincing that adolescents and adults learn faster in initial stages. While "brain plasticity" is listed as a younger learner advantage in 4.3, older learners are advantaged by greater learning capacity, including better memory for vocabulary. Greater analytic ability might also be an advantage for older learners, at least in the short run, since they are able to understand and apply explicit grammatical rules. On the other hand, Newport (1990) suggests that "less is more" in this respect: one reason younger learners develop more native-like grammatical intuitions is that they are in a non-analytic processing mode. This calls for another qualification: younger learners are probably more successful in informal and naturalistic L2 learning contexts, and older learners in formal instructional settings.

Other advantages that younger learners may have are being less inhibited than older learners, and having weaker feelings of identity with people (other than close family or caregivers) who speak the same native language. Children are also more likely to receive simplified language input from others, which might facilitate their learning (a factor that will be discussed in Chapter 5). Other advantages that older learners may have include higher levels of pragmatic skills and knowledge of L1, which may transfer positively to L2 use; more real-world knowledge enables older learners to perform tasks of much greater complexity, even when their linguistic resources are still limited.

Sex

Most research on the relation of learner sex and SLA has been concerned with cognitive style or learning strategies, or to issues of what variety of L2 is being acquired or opportunities for input and interaction (social factors to be discussed in Chapter 5). There is widespread belief in many western cultures that females tend to be better L2 learners than males, but this belief is probably primarily a social construct, based on outcomes which reflect cultural and sociopsychological constraints and influences.

There do appear to be some sex differences in language acquisition and processing, but the research evidence is mixed. For example, women outperform men in some tests of verbal fluency (such as finding words that begin with a certain letter), and women's brains may be less asymmetrically organized than men's for speech (Kimura 1992). Of particular potential relevance to SLA are findings in relation to mental representations in the lexicon versus the grammar: females seem to be better at memorizing complex forms, while males appear to be better at computing compositional rules (e.g. Halpern 2000). Other differences may be related to hormonal variables: higher androgen level correlates with better automatized skills, and high estrogen with better semantic/interpretive skills (Mack 1992). Kimura (1992) reports that higher levels of articulatory and motor ability have been associated in women with higher levels of estrogen during the menstrual cycle.

Aptitude

The assumption that there is a talent which is specific to language learning has been widely held for many years. The following four components were proposed by Carroll (1965) as underlying this talent, and they constitute the bases for most aptitude tests:

- Phonemic coding ability
- Inductive language learning ability
- Grammatical sensitivity
- Associative memory capacity

Phonemic coding ability is the capacity to process auditory input into segments which can be stored and retrieved. It is particularly important at very early stages of learning when this ability "is concerned with the extent to which the input which impinges on the learner can become input that is worth processing, as opposed to input which may simply be an auditory blur or alternatively only partially processed" (Skehan 1998:203). In other words, if the hearer cannot analyze the incoming stream of speech into phonemes in order to recognize morphemes, input may not result in intake.

Inductive language learning ability and grammatical sensitivity are both concerned with central processing. They account for further processing of the segmented auditory input by the brain to infer structure, identify patterns, make generalizations, recognize the grammatical function of elements, and formulate rules. It is in central processing that restructuring occurs.

Associative memory capacity is importantly concerned with how linguistic items are stored, and with how they are recalled and used in output. Associative memory capacity determines appropriate selection from among the L2 elements that are stored, and ultimately determines speaker fluency.

The concept of language-learning aptitude is essentially a hypothesis that possessing various degrees of these abilities predicts correlated degrees of success in L2 acquisition. Skehan (1998) reviews research in this area which largely supports this assumption, although he concludes that individual ability may vary by factor: e.g. a learner who has a high level of grammatical sensitivity may have a poor associative memory or vice versa. Talent in all factors is not a requirement for success in L2 learning. Some good learners achieve success because of their linguistic-analytic abilities, and some because of their memory aptitude. Skehan further concludes that language-learning aptitude "is not completely distinct from general cognitive abilities, as represented by intelligence tests, but it is far from the same thing" (1998:209).

The findings that aptitude is an important predictor of differential success in L2 learning holds both for naturalistic contexts and for formal classroom instruction. It is not completely deterministic, however, and is but one of several factors which may influence ultimate L2 proficiency.

Motivation

Another factor which is frequently cited to explain why some L2 learners are more successful than others is individual motivation. Motivation largely determines the level of effort which learners expend at various stages in their L2 development, often a key to ultimate level of proficiency.

Motivation is variously defined, but it is usually conceived as a construct which includes at least the following components (see Oxford and Ehrman 1993; Dörnyei 2001):

- Significant goal or need
- Desire to attain the goal
- Perception that learning L2 is relevant to fulfilling the goal or meeting the need
- Belief in the likely success or failure of learning L2
- Value of potential outcomes/rewards

The most widely recognized types of motivation are integrative and instrumental. Integrative motivation is based on interest in learning L2 because of a desire to learn about or associate with the people who use it (e.g. for romantic reasons), or because of an intention to participate or integrate in the L2-using speech community; in any case, emotional or affective factors are dominant. Instrumental motivation involves perception of purely practical value in learning the L2, such as increasing occupational or business opportunities, enhancing prestige and power, accessing scientific and technical information, or just passing a course in school. Neither of these orientations has an inherent advantage over the other in terms of L2 achievement. The relative effect of one or the other is dependent on complex personal and social factors: e.g. L2 learning by a member of the dominant group in a society may benefit more from integrative motivation, and L2 learning by a subordinate group member may be more influenced by instrumental motivation. Other reported motivations include altruistic reasons, general communicative needs, desire to travel, and intellectual curiosity (Skehan 1989; Oxford and Ehrman 1993).

Most of the research on this topic has been conducted using data collected with questionnaires that ask individuals to report on their reasons for learning another language. The reliability of such information has been questioned, but the consistently high correlation between reported strength of motivation and level of L2 achievement make it seem quite likely that the connection is indeed significant. Whether any cause–effect relationship is a "chicken-and-egg" matter is more uncertain. Does high motivation cause high L2 achievement, or is the satisfaction which results from successful L2 learning responsible for increasing motivation? In the process of language learning (which usually requires several years), there is probably a reciprocal effect.

More recent developments in SLA theory (Schumann 1997, 2001) suggest that motivation for second language learning, along with L2 representation and processing, is controlled by neurological mechanisms. Specific areas within our brain conduct a "stimulus appraisal," which assesses the motivational relevance of events and other stimuli and determines how we respond, including what our attitudes and ultimately degree of effort will be.

   The potential power of motivation can be seen in rare cases where even
older learners may overcome the "odds" of not acquiring native-like pronunciation – if sounding "native" is perceived to be important enough.

Cognitive style

Cognitive style refers to individuals' preferred way of processing: i.e. of
perceiving, conceptualizing, organizing, and recalling information.
Unlike factors of age, aptitude, and motivation, its role in explaining why
some L2 learners are more successful than others has not been well established, but extravagant claims have sometimes been made which need to
be viewed with skepticism and caution. We do know that, whatever the
relation of cognitive style to success, it involves a complex (and as yet poorly understood) interaction with specific L2 social and learning contexts.
Cognitive style is also closely related to and interacts with personality factors and learning strategies, which will be discussed below.
   Categories of cognitive style are commonly identified as pairs of traits on
opposite ends of a continuum; individual learners are rarely thought to be
at one extreme or the other, but are located somewhere along the continuum between the poles. Researchers typically correlate individuals' ratings
on different dimensions of cognitive style with various measures of L2 proficiency. Some of the traits which have been explored are listed in 4.4.

4.4 Cognitive styles		
Field-dependent	–	Field-independent
Global	–	Particular
Holistic	–	Analytic
Deductive	–	Inductive
Focus on meaning	–	Focus on form

   The field-dependent/field-independent (FD/FI) dimension is the one
most frequently referred to in SLA-related research (reviewed in Chapelle
and Green 1992). This distinction was originally introduced by Witkin et al.
(1954) in a study of how individual perceptual differences relate to general
cognitive processes, and was only later applied to language learning. A commonly used criterion for FD/FI is performance on an embedded figures test,
which requires subjects to find a simple shape within a more complex
design. Individuals who have difficulty discerning a figure apart from the
ground (or field) within which it is embedded are judged to be relatively FD;
individuals who have no difficulty with this test are judged relatively FI.
The cognitive tasks are to disassemble or restructure visual stimuli and to
rely on internal versus external referents. As this dimension has been
applied to learning, individuals who are FD are also considered more global and holistic in processing new information; individuals who are FI are
considered more particularistic and analytic. FD learners are thought to
achieve more success in L2 acquisition via highly contextualized interactive

communicative experiences because that fits better with their holistic "cognitive style," and FI learners to profit more from decontextualized analytic approaches and formal instruction. In terms of an Information Processing model of learning, FI learners may have better attentional capacities (Skehan 1998). This distinction has been metaphorically extended by some investigators to cultural differences between whole national or ethnic populations, with highly questionable results.

Another partially related dimension is preference for deductive or inductive processing. Deductive (or "top-down") processing begins with a prediction or rule and then applies it to interpret particular instances of input. Inductive (or "bottom-up") processing begins with examining input to discover some pattern and then formulates a generalization or rule that accounts for it and that may then in turn be applied deductively. An inductive cognitive style is related to the linguistic-analytic ability discussed above as one component of language aptitude, which does appear to contribute to success in L2 learning in either naturalistic or instructed circumstances.

Some evidence can also be found for differential success in relation to relative focus on meaning versus focus on form. In a study of exceptionally talented L2 learners, for instance, Novoa, Fein, and Obler (1988) found that they possess "a cognitive style whereby subjects are able to focus on form perhaps better than meaning (but certainly in conjunction with meaning)" (Obler and Hannigan 1996:512-13).

Another difference in cognitive style may be related to age. Ellen Bialystok (1997) suggests that L2 learners have two options when adapting their existing categories of linguistic structure to adequately represent the structure of the new language. One option is extending the existing categories to include new instances from L2: in phonological structure, an L2 sound which is actually slightly different from a similar sound in L1 may be identified as the same as the L1 sound and pronounced with that value, resulting in a foreign accent. The second option is creating new categories: in phonological structure, this would mean recognizing the slightly different L2 sound as phonetically different, and learning to keep it distinct from the similar (and often functionally equivalent) L1 sound. For example, both English and Spanish have a sound that we can broadly represent as [t], but the English [t] is usually pronounced with the tongue touching the bony ridge that is behind the teeth (the alveolar ridge), while the Spanish [t] is usually pronounced with the tongue further forward, touching the back of the teeth. If English L1 learners of Spanish L2 fail to perceive the difference and produce these sounds as "the same," this will contribute to an English accent in their Spanish. If they recognize the difference and learn to develop motor control of the tongue to produce the Spanish [t] differently, they will sound more like a native speaker of that language. (The reverse, of course, contributes to a Spanish accent in L2 learners' English.)

Bialystok claims that adults tend to extend existing categories (i.e. not notice small differences), while children notice differences and tend to create new categories accordingly. She suggests that this difference in cognitive style, rather than a critical or sensitive period, may account for why many people consider children to be superior in L2 learning. Since the age–style relationship is a tendency rather than absolute, children might pronounce L2 with a foreign accent (but be less likely to) and adults might achieve native-like pronunciation (but are less likely to do so). However, as we will see in the next chapter, children might intentionally choose to adopt nonnative pronunciation in their L2 because of social factors.

Another dimension sometimes considered as a matter of cognitive style is sensory preference for processing input: visual, auditory, kinesthetic (movement-oriented), or tactile (touch-oriented). Apparently no one means of processing has an inherent advantage over others, but L2 learners reportedly feel more comfortable when teachers' instructional strategies are congruent with their sensory preference. This dimension may also be age-related, with younger learners showing more preference for kinesthetic and tactile modalities (cited in Reid 1987).

Criticisms of research on cognitive style and the implications which are drawn for L2 instruction have been primarily directed at the field-dependent/field-independent (FD/FI) distinction and related continua. One criticism is that the embedded figure test used to assess traits is not applicable to language acquisition and therefore is not relevant. Another concerns analytic procedures which often correlate a single cognitive trait and a single language proficiency measure without taking other influencing factors and complexities of performance into account. Still other criticisms concern lack of consideration given to differences in cultural background, prior educational experiences, possibilities of change over time, and stages of language learning. While cognitive style is interesting, and is ultimately likely to prove significant in some way in explaining differential L2 learning outcomes, we must be cautious in drawing conclusions at the present time.

Personality

Personality factors are sometimes added to cognitive style in characterizing more general learning style. Speculation and research in SLA has included the following factors, also often characterized as endpoints on continua, as shown in 4.5. As with cognitive styles, most of us are

4.5 Personality traits		
Anxious	—	**Self-confident**
Risk-avoiding	—	**Risk-taking**
Shy	—	**Adventuresome**
Introverted	—	Extroverted
Inner-directed	—	Other-directed
Reflective	—	Impulsive
Imaginative	—	Uninquisitive
Creative	—	Uncreative
Empathetic	—	Insensitive to others
Tolerant of ambiguity	—	Closure-oriented

somewhere in between the extremes. Boldface print in this figure indicates positive correlation with success in L2 learning.

Research in this area is almost always correlational: individuals are assessed for some personality trait (usually using questionnaires and scales), and the strength of the relationship between that score and the result of an L2 language proficiency measure is calculated. Evidence in some cases is very limited or contradictory.

Anxiety has received the most attention in SLA research, along with lack of anxiety as an important component of self-confidence (see Horwitz 2001 for a review). Anxiety correlates negatively with measures of L2 proficiency including grades awarded in foreign language classes, meaning that higher anxiety tends to go with lower levels of success in L2 learning. In addition to self-confidence, lower anxiety may be manifested by more risk-taking or more adventuresome behaviors.

We need to keep some complex issues in mind when we read about or interpret research on anxiety:

(1) The direction of cause and effect is uncertain. Lower anxiety levels might very well facilitate language learning; conversely, however, more successful language learners might feel less anxious in situations of L2 learning and use, and thus be more self-confident.
(2) Instructional context or task influences anxiety level and reporting. For example, foreign language classes or tests which require oral performance normally generate more anxiety than do those in which production is in writing. Small-group performance generates less anxiety than whole-class activity.
(3) Although personality factors are defined as individual traits, systematic cultural differences are found between groups of learners. For example, oral performance in English classes generates relatively more anxiety for Korean students (Truitt 1995) than for Turkish students (Kunt 1997). This may be because of cultural differences in concepts of "face" (i.e. projecting a positive self-image; see Liu 2001), or because of cultural differences in classroom practices and experiences.
(4) Low anxiety and high self-confidence increase student motivation to learn, and make it more likely that they will use the L2 outside of the classroom setting. It is therefore not clear whether more successful learning is directly due to lower anxiety, or to a higher level of motivation and more social interaction.

On a partially related personality dimension, introverts generally do better in school and extroverts talk more. Some SLA researchers have hypothesized that extroverts would be more successful language learners, but there is no clear support for the advantage of either trait. Nearly synonymous pairs of terms found in the research literature are "inner-directed/other-directed" and "reflective/impulsive." Most personality studies have involved adult subjects, but when I explored this dimension with children from several countries, I found no significant correlation between either trait and academic achievement measures of

English (Saville-Troike 1984). I did find that among the Japanese L1 girls in my study, higher achievers on the academic language measures tended to be less passive, less compliant, and less dependent in coping with the challenges of learning English. However, these trends did not hold true for other L1 groups (Arabic, Hebrew, Icelandic, Korean, Polish, and Spanish), nor for Japanese boys.

Little study has been carried out on other personality factors in relation to differences in L2 outcomes, but there is some evidence that being imaginative or creative, empathetic, and tolerant of ambiguity is advantageous.

Learning strategies

Differential L2 outcomes may also be affected by individuals' learning strategies: i.e. the behaviors and techniques they adopt in their efforts to learn a second language. Selection from among possible strategies is often a conscious choice on the part of learners, but it is strongly influenced by the nature of their motivation, cognitive style, and personality, as well as by specific contexts of use and opportunities for learning. The other variables we considered earlier in this section – age, sex, and aptitude – also play a role in strategy selection. Many learning strategies are culturally based: individuals learn how to learn as part of their socialization experiences, and strategies they acquire in relation to other domains are commonly transferred to language learning, which may take place under very different circumstances, sometimes within a foreign educational system.

Not all strategies are equal: some are inherently more effective than others, and some more appropriate in particular contexts of learning or for individuals with differing aptitudes and learning styles. One goal in SLA research has been to identify which strategies are used by relatively good language learners, with the hope that such strategies can be taught or otherwise applied to enhance learning.

A typology of language-learning strategies which is widely used in SLA was formulated by O'Malley and Chamot (Chamot 1987):

- *Metacognitive*: e.g. previewing a concept or principle in anticipation of a learning activity; deciding in advance to attend to specific aspects of input; rehearsing linguistic components which will be required for an upcoming language task; self-monitoring of progress and knowledge states.
- *Cognitive*: e.g. repeating after a language model; translating from L1; remembering a new word in L2 by relating it to one that sounds the same in L1, or by creating vivid images; guessing meanings of new material through inferencing.
- *Social/affective*: e.g. seeking opportunities to interact with native speakers; working cooperatively with peers to obtain feedback or pool information; asking questions to obtain clarification; requesting repetition, explanation, or examples.

Metacognitive strategies are those which attempt to regulate language learning by planning and monitoring; cognitive strategies make use of direct analysis or synthesis of linguistic material; social/affective strategies involve interaction with others.

Self-reporting is a common means for collecting information on what strategies learners select, usually with interviews and questionnaires about what they have done or usually do (retrospective reports), or with think-aloud activities which have learners talk about what they are doing while engaged in an L2 learning task (concurrent reports). Self-reports are also collected by asking learners to keep journals or diaries and to record what they are conscious of doing in their effort to learn. Because the strategies used by adults are usually not visible, observation has limited value, but it is often used to collect information on children. Some researchers (e.g. Kleifgen 1986) have also used play-back techniques with children, where they videotape learners working at L2 tasks and then interview them in their L1 about what strategies they were using along with replaying the videotape for them. Recording private speech with unobtrusive wireless microphones is also a profitable data-collection procedure with children who naturally talk to themselves while working at cognitively demanding tasks (e.g. Saville-Troike 1988). Some of my subjects as young as three years in age softly repeated the new language forms after others, drilled themselves with self-created pattern practices, translated L2 forms to L1, rehearsed what they were going to say before speaking, and played games that were based on sounds of the new language. (Examples from this research are included in the next chapter.)

Age can have an influence on learning strategies; for example, children tend to use more repetition whereas adults use more synthesis. Similarly the sex of learners can be significant, as females tend to use relatively more social/affective strategies than males, as well as more metacognitive strategies in listening tasks. A range of findings show "good learners" to have the following major traits (Ellis 1994:546):

- Concern for language form (but also attention to meaning)
- Concern for communication
- Active task approach
- Awareness of the learning process
- Capacity to use strategies flexibly in accordance with task requirements

As with other correlational research, it is difficult to establish causality, or even directionality: for example, "good learners" may approach language tasks more actively because they are more proficient (not more proficient because they are more active), or because they are more self-confident.

In spite of the extensive research documenting "good learner" traits, the extent to which strategic behavior can be initiated or changed with training is still not known. One problem in determining this, as noted above, is whether strategies are the cause or the result of L2 learning success. Another problem is the complex of other variables which must be taken into account. Inclusion of strategy training for SLA is generally viewed positively in any case, with the reasonable expectation that heightened awareness of strategic possibilities will beneficially inform L2 learners and may empower them to take control of their own learning (e.g. Jones 1998; Oxford 1992). A danger is that a researcher or instructor may have preconceived ideas as to "what works," and disrupt a student's successful strategy by imposing or encouraging a different one.

The effects of multilingualism

The possible gains/costs of multilingualism in relation to other cognitive faculties or processes has been a matter of speculation and study for many years. The strength of positive versus negative perceptions of the relationship has shifted over time, and this shift has been attributable as much to philosophical and political factors as to scientific findings.

Philosophically, the notion that multilingualism has positive effects on cognitive development was traditionally related to the belief that foreign language study (especially Greek and Latin) is good for "training the mind"; there is still an assumption in many parts of the world that multilingualism is an essential characteristic of "educated" and "cultured" members of society.

The opposite notion, that multilingualism has a negative impact on general intelligence, perhaps reached its zenith in US-based research on immigrants during the 1930s, motivated by increasingly xenophobic isolationist political sentiments at that time, and based on the low scores of immigrants who spoke languages other than English natively on the standardized tests of intelligence which then were coming into widespread use. (The point was not made until some years later that these tests were being administered in a language which the subjects did not speak fluently or understand well, and that the individuals were not being tested in their native languages.)

Research since the 1960s has largely supported claims that multilingualism has positive effects on intellectual functions, based on "measures of conceptual development, creativity, metalinguistic awareness, semantic development, and analytic skills" (Diaz 1985:18). The following list is a summary of positive findings (Diaz and Klingler 1991:184):

- Bilingual children show consistent advantages in tasks of both verbal and nonverbal abilities.
- Bilingual children show advanced metalinguistic abilities, especially manifested in their control of language processing.
- Cognitive and metalinguistic advantages appear in bilingual situations that involve systematic uses of the two languages, such as simultaneous acquisition settings or bilingual education.
- The cognitive effects of bilingualism appear relatively early in the process of becoming bilingual and do not require high levels of bilingual proficiency nor the achievement of balanced bilingualism.
- Bilingual children have advantages in the use of language for verbal mediation, as shown by their higher frequency of private-speech utterances and their larger number of private-speech functions.

Relatively recent negative claims regarding multilingualism have pri-marily addressed capacity limitations for language acquisition and main-tenance, with evidence that simultaneous bilingualism in childhood may result in a narrower range of lexical development in either language, and that intensive and continued use of L2 may reduce accessibility of L1. Common and stable multilingualism among populations in many parts of the world, however, suggests that whatever limitations there may be are not biological in nature. Some of the social factors influencing interac-tion between multilingualism and other aspects of cognitive development and academic performance are discussed in Chapter 5.

Most interesting here is that, whether evidence is positive or negative (and it is generally positive), there are *differences* in the way multilinguals perform cognitive tasks. A person who knows more than one language can perceive and experience the world through more than one lens: "Both negative and positive effects are signs that L2 users think differently from monolinguals . . . Multicompetence is a different state of mind" (Cook 1992:565). Accounting for the differences remains one of the most intrigu-ing challenges for psychological approaches to SLA.

Chapter summary

Psychological perspectives on *what* is acquired in SLA concentrate on additions or changes that occur in neurological makeup, and on how the multilingual brain is organized. We have seen that the physical representation of the second language in the brain is not very different from the first, but there are differences in brain organization which relate to how proficient people are in L2, and to how they learned it. In contrast to Chomsky's proposal that there is a species-specific Language Acquisition Device (LAD), the psychologists surveyed in this chapter generally view *how* second languages are learned as involving the same processes as the acquisition of other areas of complex knowledge and skills: i.e. "learning is learning." Some consider the processes to be largely a matter of abstracting rules or principles, and some to be more a physical neurological development of associative networks and connections. The question of *why* some learners are more successful than others leads to the examination of differences in the learners themselves. We find that language-learning outcomes are influenced by age, aptitude, and motivation. Other factors in individuals' learning styles and strategies correlate with degree of success in SLA, but we can be much less sure of claims for cause–effect relationships.

Humans are inherently social creatures, and it is difficult to assess individual cognitive factors in language learning apart from the influence of the learner's total social context, to which we turn next.

Activities

Questions for self-study

1. Match the following areas of SLA theory and research to their descriptions:

1.	learning processes	a.	considers aptitude in learning, how learning is linked to age and sex, and addresses why some second language learners are more successful than others
2.	neurolinguistics	b.	studies the stages and sequences of language acquisition, addressing how acquisition happens
3.	learner differences	c.	studies how the location and organization of language might differ in the heads of monolingual versus multilingual speakers, addressing what is added and changed in people's brains when they learn another language

2. Broca's area is responsible for the ability to _____, whereas Wernicke's area is responsible for processing _____.

3. Match the following terms to the situation that illustrates each:

1.	coordinate bilingualism	a.	Maria speaks French and English fluently, and often speaks "Frenglish," a mixture of French and English, with her other bilingual friends. She produces and understands this mixture of languages easily.
2.	subordinate bilingualism	b.	Ursula speaks French and German fluently, but cannot switch readily between the two. She must speak all German with you, or all French, even if you both know both languages.
3.	compound bilingualism	c.	Shane speaks English natively and German as an L2. Each time he learns something new in German, he translates it into English to memorize the literal translation and compare it to the English meaning and structure.

4. Input is considered whatever sample of L2 that learners are exposed to. However, according to the Information Processing framework, what must learners do to make this input available for processing? What is the term for this kind of input?

5. Swain contends that _____ is necessary for successful L2 learning because it helps develop automaticity through practice and because it helps learners notice gaps in their own knowledge.

6. The _____ approach to learning focuses on the increasing strength of associations between stimuli and response, considering learning a change in the strength of these associations.

7. _____ motivation involves emotional or affective reasons for learning an L2, such as an intention to participate or integrate in the L2 speech community. _____ motivation involves a purely practical reason for learning, such as better job opportunities or passing required courses in school.

Active learning

1. If you have learned any second languages, at what age did you begin learning them? Are you more successful now in languages that you were exposed to earlier? Based on your personal experience, what do you think of the Critical Period Hypothesis? Do you know others whose experiences would support or refute it?

2. Which models relating to L2 learning processes do you feel you can use to explain your own learning process in your L2(s)? Does one seem more plausible than the others? Explain why or why not.

3. Integrative and instrumental motivation can both play a role in the desire to learn an L2. How have these two kinds of motivation influenced your L2 learning? If you have learned more than one L2, is it different depending on the L2 in question? If you know other L2 learners, ask them about what kinds of factors motivated them to learn, and compare them to your own.

4. Some studies define "success" in L2 acquisition per the initial rate of learning, some define it per the ultimate achievement, whereas others define it based upon how closely a learner comes to native-like pronunciation, or grammaticality judgments similar to a native speaker's. How do you define "success" in L2 acquisition in general as compared to how you define it for yourself? Is your definition of success in L2 learning the same as the standards by which you are judged, or do the members of your L2 speech community (teachers, classmates, colleagues, friends, etc.) have different definitions of success in L2 learning than you do?

5. It is postulated that younger learners are probably more successful in informal and naturalistic learning contexts, and older learners are more successful in formal instructional settings. Do you agree or disagree? Use your own experience combined with theoretical support from this chapter to make your argument.

Further reading

Bialystok, E. & Hakuta, K. (1994). *In Other Words: The Science and Psychology of Second-Language Acquisition*. New York: Basic Books.

   Bialystok and Hakuta treat the Critical Period Hypothesis and different models of how language is processed by the brain in Chapters 3 and 4.

Birdsong, D. (ed.) (1999). *Second Language Acquisition and the Critical Period Hypothesis*. Mahwah, NJ: Lawrence Erlbaum.

   A compilation of articles from various scholars, this book offers competing views on the Critical Period Hypothesis, allowing readers to hear many sides of the argument before judging for themselves.

Obler, L. K. & Gjerlow, K. (1999). *Language and the Brain*. Cambridge: Cambridge University Press.

   As foundational knowledge, Chapter 1 offers a useful overview of the history and present-day state of neurolinguistics and Chapter 2 is an introduction to the brain and its language-specific areas. More related to SLA, Chapter 10 focuses on bilingualism, whereas Chapter 11 explores the relationship between linguistic theory and neurolinguistics.

Pinker, S. (1994). *The Language Instinct*. New York: William Morrow and Company.

   For clear discussion of various aspects of language acquisition, learning and processing, see Chapters 1–3, 7, 10, and 13.

Skehan, P. (1998). *A Cognitive Approach to Language Learning*. Oxford: Oxford University Press.

   This volume contains discussion of psycholinguistics and learner differences with respect to language learning, with emphasis on cognition rather than on linguistics or sociolinguistics.

CHAPTER

5 Social contexts of Second Language Acquisition

CHAPTER PREVIEW

KEY TERMS

Communicative competence
Language community
Foreigner talk
Direct correction
Indirect correction
Interaction Hypothesis
Symbolic mediation
Interpersonal interaction
Zone of Proximal Development (ZPD)
Scaffolding
Intrapersonal interaction
Acculturation
Additive bilingualism
Subtractive bilingualism

When we talk about *what* is being acquired in SLA, it is not enough just to talk about the language itself. We must also include the social and cultural knowledge embedded in the language being learned, that is required for appropriate language use. What must L2 learners know and be able to do in order to communicate effectively? Part of this knowledge involves different ways of categorizing objects and events and expressing experiences. But an important part involves learners understanding their own and others' roles as members of groups or communities with sociopolitical as well as linguistic bounds. What difference does group membership and identity make in regard to *what* is learned, *how* it is acquired, and *why* some learners are more successful than others? In this chapter, we focus attention on two levels of context that affect language learning: the **microsocial** and the **macrosocial**: The microsocial focus deals with the potential effects of different immediately surrounding circumstances, while the macrosocial focus relates SLA to broader cultural, political, and educational environments.

Communicative competence

From a social perspective, the notion of linguistic competence which was introduced in Chapter 1 is inadequate to account for what is being acquired in any language that is going to be used for communicative purposes. Dell Hymes (1966), in establishing the framework for a field he called the Ethnography of Communication, made a critical observation that speakers who can produce any and all of the grammatical sentences of a language (which satisfies Chomsky's 1965 definition of "competence") would be institutionalized if they indiscriminately went about trying to do so. The concept of communicative competence became a basic tenet in the then-emerging field of sociolinguistics, and was soon adopted as well by many specialists in the field of SLA and language teaching. This term can be defined simply as "what a speaker needs to know to communicate appropriately within a particular language community" (Saville-Troike 2003). It involves knowing not only the vocabulary, phonology, grammar, and other aspects of linguistic structure (although that is a critical component of knowledge) but also when to speak (or not), what to say to whom, and how to say it appropriately in any given situation. Further, it involves the social and cultural knowledge speakers are presumed to have which enables them to use and interpret linguistic forms.

The term language community refers to a group of people who share knowledge of a common language to at least some extent. Multilingual individuals are often members of more than one language community – generally to different degrees, and the one or ones they orient themselves to at any given moment is reflected not only in which segment of their linguistic knowledge they select, but which interaction skills they use, and which features of their cultural knowledge they activate. As we have already seen, the competence of nonnative speakers of a language may differ significantly from the competence of native speakers, even as they may participate in the same or overlapping language communities. This may include structural differences in the linguistic system, different rules for usage in writing or conversation, and even somewhat divergent meanings for the "same" lexical forms. Further, a multilingual speaker's total communicative competence differs from that of a monolingual in including knowledge of rules for the appropriate choice of language and for switching between languages, given a particular social context and communicative purpose.

Differences between monolingual and multilingual communicative competence are due in part to the different social functions of first and second language learning, and to the differences between learning language and learning culture. L1 learning for children is an integral part of their socialization into their native language community: a child's native language is normally part of his or her native culture, and thus part of the body of knowledge, attitudes, and skills which are transmitted from one generation to the next as well as a primary medium through which other aspects of culture are transmitted and through which social relations are maintained. L2 learning may be part of second culture learning and adaptation, but the relationship of SLA to social and cultural learning differs greatly with circumstances.

In discussing linguistic and psychological perspectives on SLA, I have for the most part used "second language learning" in the inclusive sense of adding another language to one's first (or native) language, but it is important at this point to return to the distinction among second language (SL) learning, foreign language (FL) learning, and auxiliary language (AL) learning which was mentioned in Chapter 2. This is relevant to differential considerations not only of *what* is being learned in the process of SLA from social perspectives, but of *how* it is being learned, and of *why* some learners are more successful than others.

What we are here distinguishing as an SL is generally learned and used within the context of a language community which dominantly includes members who speak it natively; it is needed to participate in that community socially, academically, politically, and economically. Examples of SL learners would include Spanish speakers in the USA learning English, Turkish speakers in Germany learning German, or Koreans in China learning Chinese. Communicative competence in an SL thus often requires considerable knowledge of the larger community's culture and social structure, although learners may be selective in deciding which elements they want to adopt as part of their own identity. In contrast, students learning an FL usually do so within the context of their own native culture, often have little opportunity to interact with members of the language community who speak the FL natively (unless they study abroad), and typically have little opportunity (or need) to participate fully in the FL society – indeed, too often the sole reason for studying the language is that it is required for graduation. An AL is learned in a context where it will function for political or technological purposes, and when its use will generally be limited to these social domains; to the extent an AL is required at all for face-to-face interaction, it is likely to be used in linguistically diverse settings which require participants to make use of a common language code for a restricted range of social functions. Examples might include use of English by a Thai speaker for international trade, an Igbo speaker in Nigeria for national-level political meetings, or a Chinese speaker for pan-Asian economic conferences.

Within the definition of communicative competence, then, the content of "what a speaker needs to know," as well as judgments of relative success in attaining that knowledge, depend on the social context within which he or she learns and is using the language.

Microsocial factors

Within a microsocial focus, our first topic will be *L2 variation*, which has received extensive attention since the 1970s from SLA researchers concerned primarily with sociolinguistics. We explore how contextual dimensions relate to variation in learner language and consider why differing varieties of an L2 may be chosen as targets of SLA even within groups who are supposedly learning the "same" language. Our second microsocial topic is *input and interaction*, where we consider how native speakers often modify their language in communicating with L2 learners, how social and cultural factors may affect the quantity and quality of input, and how cultural knowledge and prior experience are involved in processing and interpreting input. As our third topic, we examine how Vygotsky's Sociocultural Theory views interaction as the basic genesis of language itself and explore how learners negotiate meaning and fulfill pragmatic objectives even while their linguistic resources are still exceedingly limited.

Variation in learner language

One defining characteristic of L2 learner language is that it is highly variable. Some of the variability is due to changes that occur in what learners know and can produce as they progressively achieve higher levels of L2 proficiency. However, there is also considerable variation in learners' L2 production at every stage along the way that we can attribute to their social context.

One of the most important contributions of sociolinguistics (beginning with Labov 1965) has been the demonstration that much of what earlier linguists had considered unsystematic irregularity in language production can be seen to follow regular and predictable patterns, when treated as variable features. These are multiple linguistic forms which are systematically or predictably used by different speakers of a language, or by the same speakers at different times, with the same (or very similar) meaning or function. They occur at every linguistic level: vocabulary, phonology, morphology, syntax, discourse; they include both standard ("correct") and nonstandard options; and they are characteristic of *all* natural language production, whether L1 or L2. For example, native speakers of English may say: *I ate dinner* or *I ate supper* (variable vocabulary); *She was coming* or *She was comin'* (variable phonology); *She has sewed* or *She has sewn* (variable morphology); and *That is a big book* or *That a big book* (variable syntax); and they may respond to an introduction with *Hi* or *I am very pleased to meet you* (variable discourse).

Which variable feature occurs in the production of any one speaker (native or language learner) depends largely on the communicative contexts in which it has been learned and is used. Some relevant contextual dimensions are:

- *Linguistic contexts*:   elements of language form and function associated with the variable element. In the examples given above, for instance, the phonological variable [ŋ] in *coming* is more likely to be used before a word which begins with a back consonant or before a pause, and the variable [n] in *comin'* is more likely before a front consonant. The part of speech can also be a relevant linguistic context, with production of [ŋ] most frequent in one-syllable nouns such as *ring* or *song*, and [n] in the progressive form of verbs, as in *I'm workin'*.
- *Psychological contexts*:   factors associated with the amount of attention which is being given to language form during production, the level of

automaticity versus control in processing, or the intellectual demands of a particular task. In learners' production, for instance, the copula of *That is a big book* may be produced during a formal second language lesson or in a writing exercise but omitted in informal conversation even at the same point of L2 development. Similarly, the variable [ŋ] is more likely to be used by L1 or L2 speakers when they are focusing on their pronunciation in a formal setting than in casual conversation.

- *Microsocial contexts*:   features of setting/situation and interaction which relate to communicative events within which language is being produced, interpreted, and negotiated. These include level of formality and participants' relationship to one another, and whether the interaction is public or intimate. Such features interact importantly with the amount of attention that is paid to language form, as illustrated above for the probability that the copula or [ŋ] versus [n] will be produced, or that the differences among *see, saw*, and *have seen* will be consistently observed.

Macrosocial factors, which will be discussed later, may also influence linguistic variation. These include features of the larger political setting within which language learning and use takes place, including the social position and role of users (e.g. whether immigrant, international student, visiting dignitary), societal attitudes toward specific languages and multi-lingualism in general, and institutional organization (e.g. patterns of edu-cation, employment, and political participation). For example, standard and prestige L2 forms are more likely to be used by international students or diplomats while they are functioning within those social roles than by the same individuals while they are shopping in a market or visiting tourist sites.

Variation that occurs in learners' language as they develop increasing competence over a period of time is of particular interest from linguistic and psychological perspectives, as it reflects a developmental continuum. Variation that occurs in different contexts at a single point in time is of more interest from a social perspective, as it often corresponds to informal-formal features associated with linguistic **register**.

A substantial amount of research on the effect of microsocial contexts has been based on the framework of **Accommodation Theory**. Speakers (usually unconsciously) change their pronunciation and even the gram-matical complexity of sentences they use to sound more like whomever they are talking to. This accounts in part for why native speakers tend to simplify their language when they are talking to an L2 learner who is not fluent (which we will discuss below), and why L2 learners may acquire somewhat different varieties of the target language when they have different friends.

The effect of macrosocial contexts can also be seen when learners acquire different varieties of the "same" target language. Given similar linguistic, psychological, and microsocial contexts, for instance, female immigrants in the US may hear and use more standard variants than male immigrants from the same language and cultural background – in part because females are more likely to find employment in middle- or upper-class households or in service positions, while males are more likely to find employment in blue-collar occupations. Workplace stratification affects both the nature of language input and group identity.

Research in social contexts of SLA

In one study, Adamson and Regan (1991) examined the pronunciation of -ing in Cambodian and Vietnamese immigrants in the Washington, DC area. Native English-speaking men tend to pronounce -ing as -in', whereas native women are less likely to do so, perhaps because women tend to be more status conscious and want to use the more prestigious form. While the Cambodian and Vietnamese immigrants produced less -in' than native speakers overall, there is still a gender division with males producing -in' more often than females. Adamson and Regan hypothesize that the Cambodian and Vietnamese immigrant males are unconsciously attempting to sound more like native-speaking men.

Frequency of -in' according to sex of speaker		
Subjects	Sex	Overall % produced
Native speakers	Female	20
	Male	65
	Total	58
Nonnative speakers	Female	15
	Male	23
	Total	20

Adamson, H. D. and Regan, V. (1991). The acquisition of community speech norms by Asian immigrants learning English as a second language: a preliminary study. Studies in Second Language Acquisition, *13*, 1–22.

Still more effects of macrosocial contexts can be found in the variable L2 production of learners whose L1 is relatively more or less prestigious in the wider society, and in the L2 of learners who are acquiring it as an auxiliary language for indigenous technical and political functions rather than as a second language for use with its native speakers. Speakers of a prestigious L1 may carry more features of L1 pronunciation and lexical borrowings into a less prestigious L2 than they do when their L1 is less prestigious. For learners of an auxiliary language, the target language grammar may not be that of native speakers, but of educated users of the L2 in their own country (Kachru 1986); learners may not wish to identify with or fully participate in a language community for which the L2 is politically dominant. These factors are explored further when we shift to a macrosocial focus later in this chapter.

Some variation in IL production (called free variation) remains even after accounting for linguistic, psychological, and social contexts as much as possible, and it can shed particularly important insights on processes of development. Indeed, Ellis suggests "that free variation constitutes an essential stage in the acquisition of grammatical structures" (1997:19). He hypothesizes that the nature of variability changes during the process of L2 development in the following stages:

(1) A single form is used for a variety of functions.
(2) Other forms have been acquired but are initially used interchangeably (i.e. in "free variation").
(3) The variant forms begin to be used systematically (e.g. depending on the amount of attention to form or the situational context).
(4) The non-target forms are eliminated. Removal of free variability is making the IL more efficient.

Summarizing the sociolinguistic perspective, then: (1) what is acquired in L2 includes variable linguistic structures and knowledge of when to use each; (2) the process of acquisition includes progress through stages in which different types of variability are evident; and (3) reasons why some learners are more successful than others include how well they can perceive and align their own usage in accord with the target system. Considering all of the variable features which occur in IL development and use, and all of the contextual dimensions which influence their occurrence, however, we are still left with the observation made in previous chapters that the *sequence* of SLA is remarkably the same under all conditions.

Input and interaction

Language input to the learner is absolutely necessary for either L1 or L2 learning to take place, but the nature of its role is in dispute. Within the linguistic approaches discussed in Chapter 3, for instance, followers of behaviorist learning theories consider input to form the necessary stimuli and feedback which learners respond to and imitate; followers of Krashen's Monitor Model consider comprehensible input not only necessary but sufficient in itself to account for SLA; proponents of UG consider exposure to input a necessary trigger for activating internal mechanisms, but of minimal importance for many aspects of language development beyond the initial state. Within the psychological approaches discussed in Chapter 4, those working from an IP framework consider input which is attended to (i.e. intake) as essential data for all stages of language processing; those working from a connectionist framework further consider the quantity or frequency of input structures to largely determine acquisitional sequencing, though this is partially contradicted by actual frequencies. Within the social approaches surveyed in this chapter, some researchers also consider input primarily as "data" for essentially innate linguistic and/or cognitive processes, but others claim a more important role for input in determining what features of language are learned, and how. Social approaches also consider the nature and role of interaction in acquisition, and ways in which it is helpful – and perhaps necessary – for the development of advanced levels of L2 proficiency. From a social perspective, interaction is generally seen as essential in providing learners with the quantity and quality of external linguistic input which is required for internal processing, in focusing learner attention on aspects of their L2 which differ from target language norms or goals, and in providing collaborative means for learners to build discourse structures and express meanings which are beyond the current level of their linguistic competence.

Nature of input modifications

Language addressed by L1 speakers to L2 learners frequently differs in systematic ways from language addressed to native or very fluent speakers. In speech, the modified variety is called **foreigner talk**; it has the characteristics listed in 5.1 (based on Long 1996).

5.1 Characteristics of foreigner talk
Simple vocabulary, using high-frequency words and phrases
Long pauses
Slow rate of speech
Careful articulation
Loud volume
Stress on key words
Simplified grammatical structures
Topicalization (topic at the beginning, then a comment about it)
More syntactic regularity
Retention of full forms (e.g. less contraction, fewer pronouns)

While utterances by native speakers to language learners are usually grammatical, simplified input may omit some obligatory elements. For example, JoAnne Kleifgen (1986) recorded the following utterances by a native English-speaking teacher to L2 children who were engaged in an art activity:

___ *Mommy look at your work?* (deletes *does*)
___*You have Indians in Korea?* (deletes *do*)
Would you give us ___ pencil? (deletes *a*)
See, Siti's made ___ mouth real scary. (deletes *the*)
Baby sitter take_ care of baby. (deletes *-s*)

Although this teacher's modification of input to L2 learners was for the most part unconscious, she adroitly adjusted her language to individuals' level of proficiency. This includes not only the grammatical deletions that these examples illustrate, but also shorter sentences and less varied vocabulary addressed to the least proficient children. This selective modification can be considered part of her own "communicative competence," acquired as a result of many years' experience in teaching young English learners.

There is no direct evidence as to whether or not the modifications found in Kleifgen's study enhanced the children's comprehension, but we have reports that it does for older learners. When we surveyed international students at a US university to determine which professors they found easiest to understand, for example, faculty with extensive teaching experience in L2 contexts (who were more practiced in making appropriate modifications) were rated more comprehensible. Modifications with students at the university level are also generally unconscious, but they are likely to rise to an instructor's awareness when addressing classes which include both beginning and advanced L2 learners, or both limited and native speakers of the language. In such situations, I often find myself restating a point I consider important with stress on key terms as a topic indicator and then a "translation" of them with simpler vocabulary.

The types of adaptations that are found in speech to L2 learners are similar in some ways to the "baby talk" used with young children in many languages (Ferguson 1971). Some of the linguistic modifications appear to aid comprehension at early stages of learning: e.g. high frequency phrases may be memorized as chunks of speech which can be processed automatically; pauses at appropriate grammatical junctures can help listeners recognize constituent structures; a slower rate of speech allows more time for information retrieval and controlled processing; and topicalization helps in identifying what a sentence is about and what part of it contains new information. On the other hand, the common practice of speaking louder to an L2 learner (as if the person were hard of hearing) probably does no good at all, and "simplification" of sentence structure may actually impair comprehension to the extent that it reduces redundancy.

Modification of written input for L2 learners also typically includes controlled vocabulary and shorter, simpler sentence structure. In written academic texts, modifications meant to help L2 students understand what they read are essentially the same as those used in textbooks for native speakers of English. These include those listed in 5.2.

As in oral input, "simplification" of sentence structure alone is of questionable value in enhancing the comprehensibility of written text (e.g. see Floyd and Carrell 1987). More important for interpretive processing are the provision of relevant background knowledge and modifications which assist readers in focusing on important terms and concepts.

In the nature of input modifications, then, we find both similarities and differences for L1 and L2 learners. Some of the oral modifications may make acquisition easier, but all L1 and many L2 learners can succeed without them. Modifications in written input which improve comprehension are similar for L2 and L1 students, but research on their effectiveness for SLA is quite limited.

5.2 Modifications in academic texts
Frequent organization markers, such as headings and linking devices
Clear topic statements
Highlighting of key terms and inclusion of synonyms and paraphrase
Bulleted or numbered lists of main points
Elaboration of sections which require culture-specific background knowledge
Visual aids, such as illustrations and graphs
Explicit summations at regular intervals
Questions which can be used for comprehension checks

Nature of interactional modifications

Along with input, social interaction is also essential for L1 acquisition: no children can learn their initial language by merely listening to tape recordings, radio broadcasts, or television programs. In contrast, many L2 learners do acquire at least some level of competence without interacting with speakers of the target language, and for at least some highly motivated and/or talented learners, that level may be very high. For example, I recall meeting with a delegation of English L2 speakers from China not long after the end of the Cultural Revolution in that country, which had banned almost all contact with foreigners for twenty-five years. Members of the Chinese delegation reported that they learned English via language laboratory drills (notably translations of political slogans) and BBC broadcasts, and that they had not engaged interactionally in English until their (then) current trip to the USA. Some of the delegates' level of L2 proficiency was exceptionally high, so they must be considered successful learners. This observation does not argue against the helpful effects of reciprocal social interaction on SLA but does contribute to the conclusion that it is not absolutely necessary.

Interactional modifications made by L1 speakers in discourse with L2 learners appear to provide even more significant help than do the modifications of oral input which are listed above. Some useful types of modifications include those listed in 5.3, together with illustrations of each in English learning contexts (taken from personal observations).

Repetition by native speakers (NSs) of part or all of their previous utterances allows nonnative speakers (NNSs) more time for processing and an opportunity to confirm or correct perception; paraphrase by NSs allows NNSs to cast a wider net for words they recognize and may increase their vocabulary store; expansion and elaboration by NSs provide models of contextually relevant utterances which may exceed NNSs' immediate ability to produce; sentence completion and frames for substitution provide NNSs with words or chunks of language from NSs which they can use in subsequent turns of talk; and vertical constructions allow NNSs to

5.3 Interactional modifications

Ns = native speaker; NNS = nonnative speaker

Repetition

NS:	*This is your assignment for tomorrow.*
NNS:	*What?*
NS:	*This is your assignment.*

Paraphrase

NS:	*This is your assignment for tomorrow.*
NNS	*What?*
NS:	*This is homework.*

Expansion and elaboration

NNS:	*Hot.*
NS:	*Yes, it's very hot today.*

Sentence completion

NNS:	*For tell how old tree is, you count . . .*
NS:	*Rings. Tree rings.*

Frame for substitution

NS:	*How old are you?*
NNS:	*Five old are you.*

Vertical construction

NNS:	*Taki.* (name of another student)
NS:	*What did Taki do?*
NNS:	*Pencil.*
NS:	*What did Taki do with the pencil?*
NNS:	*Throw.* (makes throwing motion)
NS:	*Taki, don't throw pencils.*

Comprehension check and request for clarification

NS:	*Subtract, and write the remainder here.*
NNS:	*What is "remain"?*

construct discourse sequences beyond their current independent means (a notion associated with scaffolding, which is discussed below).

Comprehension checks and requests for clarification by NSs focus NNSs' attention on segments of sentences which are unclear, and such checks and requests by NNSs inform NSs where repetition, paraphrase, or additional background information is required. These are important devices in the **negotiation of meaning** between NSs and NNSs which help in pre-venting or repairing breakdowns in communication. Other devices include selecting topics that the other is familiar with, and switching topics to repair conversational breakdowns which do occur.

Feedback

Other types of interaction which can enhance SLA include **feedback** from NSs which makes NNSs aware that their usage is not acceptable in some way, and which provides a model for "correctness." While children rarely receive such negative evidence in L1, and don't require it to achieve full native competence, corrective feedback is common in L2 and may indeed be necessary for most learners to ultimately reach native-like levels of pro-ficiency when that is the desired goal.

Negative feedback to L2 learners may be in the form of **direct correc-tion**, including explicit statements like *That is the wrong word*; directives concerning what "cannot" or "must" be said; and explanations related to points of grammar and usage. Or the negative feedback may come as **indirect correction**, which includes several of the same interactional modification forms which were listed in 5.3, but here they have a different function. For example:

- What appears at a literal level to be a comprehension check or request for clarification may actually be intended to mean that the NNS utter-ance was incorrect.

NSS: *I can't assist class.* (Meaning 'I can't attend class.')
NS: *You can't what?* (Meaning 'You've got the wrong word. Try again.')

- Rising intonation questions by NSs which repeat part or all of a NNS's utterance ("echo" questions) often mean that the utterance was wrong. (In contrast, repetition by NSs with falling intonation usually affirms correctness.) The NS usually stresses some element in the repeated form with either meaning.

a. NNS: *John goed to town yesterday.*
   NS: *John goed to town?* (Meaning 'The word goed is wrong.')
b. NNS: *This book is hard.*
   NS: *This book is hard.* (Meaning 'You're right. It is.')

- Paraphrase of an NNS utterance by NSs may be intended merely to provide an alternative way to say the same thing without overtly suggesting that an error has been made, but what might appear to be a paraphrase is often a **recast** which substitutes a correct element for one that was incorrect.

NNS: *John goed to town yesterday.*
NS *(correcting)*:   *Yes, John went shopping.*

One potential problem for L2 learners is that they sometimes do not recognize when indirect feedback is corrective in intent. It does not help that the English phrases *OK* and *all right* (when followed by pauses) are often used as discourse markers to preface corrections and not to convey that the prior utterance is actually "OK" or "all right" in form or content. Even many experienced English teachers are not conscious of this potential source of confusion for their students, which highlights the importance and relevance of understanding L2 discourse conventions as well as vocabulary and syntax.

Intake to cognitive processing

We have already emphasized that language input may "go in one ear and out the other," and it contributes to acquisition only if it is "let in" to the mind for processing: i.e. if it becomes **intake**. According to claims made in the **Interaction Hypothesis,** the modifications and collaborative efforts that take place in social interaction facilitate SLA because they contribute to the accessibility of input for mental processing: "*negotiation for meaning,* and especially negotiation work that triggers *interactional* adjustments by the NS or more competent interlocutor, facilitates acquisition because it connects input, internal learner capacities, particularly selective attention, and output in productive ways" (Long 1996:151–52).

To summarize the interactionist perspective, then: what is acquired in L2 includes only that portion of L2 input "which is assimilated and fed into the IL system" (Ellis 1985:159); L2 is acquired in a dynamic interplay of external input and internal processes, with interaction facilitating (but not causing) SLA; and the reasons that some learners are more successful than others include their degree of access to social experiences which allow for negotiation of meaning and corrective feedback. However, reciprocal interaction as a source and stimulus for learning ignores "autodidacts" who teach themselves from books and recordings. Further, this perspective addresses in only a limited way the evidence for universal sequencing in L2 learning.

Interaction as the genesis of language

An alternative view of the role of interaction in SLA is based on **Sociocultural (S-C) Theory** (Vygotsky 1962, 1978). A key concept in this approach is that interaction not only facilitates language learning but is a causative force in acquisition; further, all of learning is seen as essentially a social process which is grounded in sociocultural settings. S-C Theory differs from most linguistic approaches in giving relatively limited attention to the structural patterns of L2 which are learned, as well as in emphasizing learner activity and involvement over innate and universal mechanisms; and it differs from most psychological approaches in its degree of focus on factors outside the learner, rather than on factors which are completely in the learner's head, and in its denial that the learner is a largely autonomous processor. It also (as noted above) differs from most other social approaches in considering interaction as an essential force rather than as merely a helpful condition for learning.

According to S-C Theory, learning occurs when simple innate mental activities are transformed into "higher order," more complex mental functions. This transformation typically involves **symbolic mediation,** which is a link between a person's current mental state and higher order functions that is provided primarily by language. This is considered the usual route to learning, whether what is being learned is language itself or some other area of knowledge. The results of learning through mediation include learners' having heightened awareness of their own mental abilities and more control over their thought processes.

Interpersonal interaction

So far we are using the term "interaction" to mean **interpersonal interaction:** i.e. communicative events and situations which occur between people. One important context for symbolic mediation is such interpersonal interaction between learners and experts ("experts" include teachers and more knowledgeable learners). Vygotsky calls the level where much of this type of mediation occurs the **Zone of Proximal Development (ZPD).** This is an area of potential development, where the learner can achieve that potential only with assistance. According to S-C Theory, mental functions that are beyond an individual's current level must be performed in collaboration with other people before they are achieved independently.

Lev Vygotsky (b. Orsha, current Republic of Belarus), 1896–1934

Social psychology

Vygotsky pioneered the notion that children learn within communities, rather than strictly as individuals. He is perhaps most famous for his discussion of the *zone of proximal development*, wherein children learn more with the support of adults around them. Because of international politics, Vygotsky's work was not available outside Russia until well after his death.

Interesting note: Vygotsky's works were banned in the Soviet Union from 1936 to 1956 because of his criticism of theories of psychology officially approved at the time, especially "Marxist psychology."

One way in which others help the learner in language development within the ZPD is through **scaffolding**. This includes the "vertical constructions" mentioned above as a type of modified interaction between NSs and NNSs, in which experts commonly provide learners with chunks of talk that the learners can then use to express concepts which are beyond their independent means. This type of mediation also occurs when peers collaborate in constructing language which exceeds the competence of any individual among them. More generally, the metaphor of "scaffolding" refers to verbal guidance which an expert provides to help a learner perform any specific task, or the verbal collaboration of peers to perform a task which would be too difficult for any one of them individually (see Bruner 1985). Very importantly, scaffolding is not something that happens *to* a learner as a passive recipient, but happens *with* a learner as an active participant.

Scaffolding

The following dialogue (from Donato 1994) is an example of Vygotsky's notion of scaffolding (within a peer group in this case, rather than from adult to child). Alone, each member of the group lacked the knowledge to produce the French equivalent of "You remembered" ("Tu t'es souvenu") in a grammatically correct form. However, each member of the group had some useful knowledge that they could all build upon until they arrived at the desired solution.

(In the classroom while preparing for a presentation the next day . . .)

Speaker 1:	. . . and then I'll say. . . *tu as souvenu notre anniversaire de mariage* . . . or should I say *mon anniversaire?*
Speaker 2:	*Tu as* . . .
Speaker 3:	*Tu as* . . .
Speaker 1:	*Tu as souvenu* . . . 'you remembered?'
Speaker 3:	Yea, but isn't that a reflexive? *Tu t'as* . . .
Speaker 1:	Ah, *tu t'as souvenu.*
Speaker 2:	Oh, it's *tu es*
. . .	
Speaker 1:	*Tu t'es souvenu.*

For L2 learners, L1 as well as L2 can provide helpful mediation. Talk between peers who are collaborating in tasks is often in their common L1, which provides an efficient (and sometimes essential) medium for problem-solving and can enhance learning of both L2 and any academic subjects students are studying in the second language. Symbolic mediation can be interactional without involving face-to-face communication: although we do not often think of it that way, reading actually involves an interaction between the individual and the author(s) of a text or book, resulting in an altered state of knowledge. Symbolic mediation need not even necessarily involve language (although it usually does) but can also be achieved with such nonlinguistic symbols as gestures, diagrams and illustrations, and algebraic symbols.

Intrapersonal interaction

In addition to interpersonal interaction, S-C Theory requires consideration of **intrapersonal interaction**: i.e. communication that occurs within an individual's own mind. This is also viewed by Vygotsky as a sociocultural phenomenon.

When reading, for example, we engage in intrapersonal as well as interpersonal activity: "we draw interactively on our ability to decode print, our stored knowledge of the language we are reading and the content schemata through which our knowledge of the world is organized" (Ellis 1999:1).

A second type of intrapersonal interaction that occurs frequently in beginning stages of L2 learning – and in later stages when the content and structure of L2 input stretches or goes beyond existing language competence – makes use of L1 resources. This takes place through translation to oneself as part of interpretive problem-solving processes.

Yet another type (which was of particular interest to Vygotsky) is **private speech**. This is the self-talk which many children (in particular) engage in that leads to the **inner speech** that more mature individuals use to control thought and behavior. While inner speech is not necessarily tied to the surface forms of any specific language, private speech is almost always verbalized in L1 and/or L2. Study of private speech when it is audible provides a "window into the mind" of sorts for researchers, through which we can actually observe intrapersonal interaction taking place and perhaps discover its functions in SLA.

I was intrigued by this possibility, and recorded children over a period of several weeks while they were just beginning to learn English (Saville-Troike 1988). I was particularly interested in finding out if the children were using English to themselves, and if so, what they were using the language for, during a period when they were generally very reluctant to try speaking out loud to others in the new language. Because private speech is generally much lower in volume than interactional speech, and often inaudible unless the observer is within a few inches of the speaker, I equipped these children with wireless radio microphones for recording purposes.

For the youngest children I recorded, English was largely something to play with. For example, three- and four-year-old Chinese L1 brothers (called *Didi* and *Gege*, meaning 'younger brother' and 'older brother' in Chinese) focused extensively on the L2 sounds and seemed to derive pleasure from pronouncing certain words. High-frequency private vocabulary items for them included *butter pecan*, *parking lot*, *skyscraper*, and *Cookie Monster*. Both children also demonstrated their attention to sound by creating new words with English phonological structure, including *otraberver*, *goch*, *treer*, and *trumble* – impossible sequences in their L1. The focus on sounds not infrequently led to a private game, as the boys chanted rhythmically or intoned words to themselves. For example:

DIDI: *Jelly bean, jelly bean. Jelly, jelly, jelly, jelly.*
GEGE: *Yucky. Yucky scoop. Scoop scoop yucky scoop. Yucky yucky yuck-yucky.*

For somewhat older children, English was used more to comment about ongoing events. They displayed a higher level of mental activity related to L2 learning by focusing on grammar as well as on the sound of their utterances. This was very clear in private pattern drills, such as those in the following examples that were produced by a five-year-old Japanese L1 boy in his kindergarten class. While saying (a) to himself, he was practicing English auxiliaries; his drill indicates he had correctly assigned *have* and *am* to the same syntactic slot, and he recognized the contraction *I'm* as equivalent to *I am*. Example (b) represents a "build-up" drill, where the same child practiced adding an object to make the sentence longer.

a. *I finished. I have finished. I am finished. I'm finished.*
b. *I want. I paper. Paper. Paper. I want paper.*

The oldest children I recorded also focused on L2 form but added self-guiding language more frequently than did the younger learners. The next example illustrates a pattern which an eight-year-old Chinese L1 girl commonly produced while writing sentences in her language workbook. She first constructed the parts to herself, then named letters as she wrote, and finally repeated the result.

I see a, elephant. E, L, E, P, H, A, N, T.
I see a elephant. I see a elephant nose?
Is in the, water. W, A, T, E, R. Water.

In addition to play, even the youngest children used private speech as intrapersonal symbolic mediation, as illustrated below in my final examples of private speech. Here, they are making use of their L1 to translate to themselves as they incorporate new language forms. (The Chinese and mixed utterances below are glossed in English.)
Didi (while watching another child who is crying):

Look? Let's stop? Stop? Stop? Stop? Stop?
Ting a.
('Stop.')

Stop?

Bu yao ku.
('Don't cry.')

Gege (while driving around on a tricycle):

Dao skyscraper Chicago.
('Go to skyscraper Chicago.')

Wo yao dao Chicago le.
('I want to go to Chicago.')

Private speech by these children provides good evidence that even when they were not interacting with others, they were not merely passively assimilating L2 input; they were using intrapersonal interaction in an active process of engagement with the input they heard, practicing to build up their competence. Similar audible evidence would be more difficult to obtain from older learners (partly because of the inhibiting effects of social constraints on talking to oneself in public), but many report repetition and experimentation strategies in their inner speech, and some report continuing private speech (often reduced to muttering) when not within hearing range of others.

Audible private speech may continue among adult learners in specialized, socially sanctioned settings where imitation or other controlled response to linguistic input is considered "normal" behavior. A low level of muttering is frequently heard in language laboratories where learners wearing headphones practice alone in cubicles, for instance, and Ohta (2001) recorded students in a language classroom as they responded to corrections and questions quietly, even when they were not being directly addressed. The social constraints that determine which type of symbolic mediation is appropriate in a specific situation underscore its nature as a sociocultural as well as a mental phenomenon.

A common intrapersonal activity that is closely related to private speech is "private writing," in which individuals record language forms and other meaningful symbols on paper in order to help store items in memory, organize thought, solve problems, or such, without intent to communicate with others. Students of language, for example, may keep personal journals or diaries of their learning experiences, jot notes in the margins of textbooks, list new words along with some mnemonic aid, write interlinear L1 translations in a text, and highlight or underline important points. Many language teachers list major topics and activities which they plan to include in a class lesson in a form of private writing, and they may add phonetic symbols to student names on their class roster which they otherwise might not remember how to pronounce.

Overall, Sociocultural Theory claims that language is learned through socially mediated activities. The S-C framework supports the view that some learners may be more successful than others because of their level of access to or participation in a learning community, or because of the amount of mediation they receive from experts or peers, and because of how well they make use of that help.

Acquisition without interaction; interaction without acquisition

There are challenges to a socioculturally oriented view of L2 acquisition, however. The following two facts are somewhat difficult to explain if we hold a strong position that social interaction is an essential *causative* force in second language learning:

(1) Some individuals are able to achieve a relatively advanced level of L2 proficiency without the benefit of any interpersonal communication or opportunity to negotiate meaning in the language with others.
(2) Some individuals engage in extensive interaction with speakers of another language without learning that language to any significant degree.

We might explain the first phenomenon by including learner engagement with text and electronic media as types of "social interaction," as well as intrapersonal communication in the form of private speech and writing, or of inner speech. Such learners would not have the benefit of scaffolding with immediate help from other humans, but corrective feedback and other potential enhancements to SLA can be provided by other means. We could still claim that live face-to-face interaction facilitates L2 learning – at least for most people, but not that it is absolutely necessary.

Explaining why some individuals apparently interact quite successfully with others while developing little or no competence in a common linguistic code requires a closer look at what other strategies are used for communication. These include:

- Background knowledge and experience which help individuals organize new information and make guesses about what is going on and what will happen next
- Understanding of the overall situation or event, including its goal, the relationships among participants, and what they expect one another to do and say
- Extralinguistic context, including physical setting and objects
- Knowledge of genre-specific discourse structures: e.g. what rules for interaction are expected in a conversation versus a lesson at school, and what sequence of actions is likely
- Gestures, facial expressions, and other nonverbal signs
- Prosodic features of tone and stress to convey emotional state

In spite of cultural differences in each of these elements, there is often enough commonality to allow at least some level of meaningful communication between people who do not speak the same language, but who are cooperative and willing to guess.

An experience I had in Taiwan illustrates how well these nonlinguistic factors can work. I had accepted a last-minute opportunity to teach English there, and I arrived in the country with no prior knowledge of Chinese. One of my first goals was to mail a letter back to my family in the USA to let them know that I had arrived safely. A student who spoke some English pointed out a post office to me, and I was on my own. The physical setting inside the building was familiar enough, with a long counter on the far side of a large, rather bare room. I knew from prior experience that I needed to buy a stamp, that the man standing behind the counter facing me must be a postal clerk who could sell me one, and that the people standing in line in front of me must be other patrons. I followed the "rule" I know of taking a place in line and waiting my turn to be served. When I reached the counter, the clerk said something in Chinese (I assume the equivalent of "May I help you?") and I asked for a stamp in English, holding out my letter and pointing to the upper right corner of the envelope where I knew that a stamp should be placed. He took the letter from me and said something else (I assume telling me the amount of money I owed, since that was what I expected to hear next in the sequence of this event). I held out a handful of Chinese coins, although I had no idea how much he had said the stamp cost or how much money I was offering; the clerk took a few and returned the rest. He said something, but seemed from facial expression and tone of voice to be satisfied, so I said "Thank you" and left. The transaction was thus successfully completed without benefit of any mutual linguistic knowledge, but making use of all of the other communicative strategies that I listed above.

Communicative events cannot be completed without a common language in the absence of familiar context and props, of course, or when nonpredictable information needs to be conveyed. Students studying in a foreign country, for example, cannot understand or express abstract concepts in academic subject fields without L2 knowledge or L1 translation; however, they may be able to function quite adequately in many social situations while still possessing only limited linguistic resources. If individuals have need and opportunity to develop increasing competence in the L2, they will do so; if they are not motivated to learn the L2, they may not – even if they have ample social opportunity.

An illustration of fairly prolonged interaction without acquisition comes from the experiences of Gege and Didi, the young Chinese brothers whom I introduced earlier with examples of their private speech. They not only talked to themselves while in the nursery school they attended, but addressed in Chinese their teachers and other children who spoke and understood only English, with sometimes surprisingly successful results:

Three-year-old Didi walked over to a teacher and showed her a broken balloon.

DIDI: *Kan. Kan. Wo zhe mei le. Kan. Kan.*
          ('Look. Look. Mine is gone. Look. Look.')
TEACHER: *Oh, it popped, didn't it? All gone.*

The teacher understood Didi's meaning because he was holding up a broken balloon for her to see, and his comment was obviously about the condition of that object.

Four-year-old Gege looked at a hose lying on the playground.

GEGE: *Zhege shi shenme guanzi a?*
          ('That is what [kind of] hose?')
TEACHER: *That's a fire hose.*

Gege's question to a different teacher was also clear because there was a notable object in the immediate setting which she could assume he was asking about.

In contrast, the following exchange was not successful:

DIDI: *Laoshi, qu na shui.*
          ('Teacher, go get water.')
TEACHER: *What do you want?*
DIDI: *He shui.*
          ('Drink water.')
TEACHER: *He shui. Um.*
DIDI: *Laoshi, qu na shui.*
          ('Teacher, go get water.')

In this case, Didi was trying to get the teacher to understand that he wanted to have a drink of water. Didi's attempts to convey his message included repetition and paraphrase, and the teacher even repeated his Chinese utterance *He shui* in an apparent effort to understand it, or to elicit clarification. She understood from his tone of voice that he wanted something, but this attempt at communication failed because no contextual cues were available to identify the object he wanted.

My final example in this section shows that children can also make use of nonlinguistic cues for negotiation of coherent interaction between themselves. In this event, English-speaking Michael (also four years old) approached a playhouse in the nursery school yard and correctly interpreted Gege's repeated utterance in Chinese as a directive to come inside, which he rejected. Gege then "softened" his invitation for Michael to come in with a paraphrase, which Michael agreed to. Although in this exchange neither child understood what the other was saying, they successfully negotiated entry to a social event that subsequently yielded several minutes of sustained cooperative play.

GEGE: *Yao jinlai cai yao kai.*
        ('[If you] want to come in, then open [the door].')
        Yao jinlai cai yao kai.
        ('[If you] want to come in, then open [the door].')
MICHAEL: *I don't have to.*
GEGE: *Ni yao bu yao jinlai?*
        ('Do you want to come in?')
MICHAEL: *Okay.*
        [He enters the playhouse.]

The strategy that was shared by Chinese- and English-speaking four-year-olds in this exchange was probably the use/interpretation of paraphrase as having a "softening" effect. The sheer persistence of Gege in maintaining verbal interaction may also have been interpreted by Michael as a "friendly" overture, regardless of what Gege actually said or meant.

In due time, Didi and Gege became aware that others could not understand them. Indeed, when interviewed in Chinese, Gege stated this realization explicitly and said that he intended to learn English. Over the next few years, Didi and Gege became fluent English speakers, even dominant in English to the extent that they had problems communicating in Chinese – but that is another story. The illustrative case of *non-acquisition* here concerns the other participants in these events. Although the nursery school teachers and other children interacted successfully with Didi and Gege for several months before English became a common language, none of them learned even a single word of Chinese as a result of the interaction. The teachers and playmates relied completely on context, nonverbal signals, and internal information to infer meaning. They had the opportunity to learn, but neither need nor motivation.

Macrosocial factors

We now shift to consideration of macrosocial factors in looking at how social contexts affect SLA, drawing primarily on the frameworks of the **Ethnography of Communication** and **Social Psychology**. These broader societal approaches in research and theory allow exploration of issues such as how identity, status, and values influence L2 outcomes, and why. The macrosocial factors we will consider are at several levels in the ecological context of SLA:

- Global and national status of L1 and L2
- Boundaries and identities
- Institutional forces and constraints
- Social categories
- Circumstances of learning

At a global and national level, influences on SLA involve the power and status of learners' native and target languages, whether overtly stated in official policies or covertly realized in cultural values and practices. Social boundaries that are relevant to SLA may coincide with national borders, but they also exist within and across them as they function to unify speakers as members of a language community and to exclude outsiders from membership; influences on SLA at this level often involve the relationship between native and target language groups, as well as the openness and permeability of community boundaries. Within nations, institutional forces and constraints often affect the use and knowledge of L2 in relation to such things as social control, political and religious practices, and economic and educational opportunities. Age, gender, and ethnicity are factors of social group membership which may potentially be relevant to SLA. Finally, circumstances of learning can influence SLA, such as learners' prior educational experiences, whether the L2 learning process is informal or formal, and (if formal) the type of educational model learners have access to and the pedagogical orientation of their teachers and administrators.

Global and national status of L1 and L2

Languages have power and status at global and national levels for both symbolic and practical reasons. An important symbolic function of language is political identification and cohesion. We see this in the USA, for example, where English is generally accepted as the single national language, and most people consider it important for national unity that all citizens be able to use one language. Immigrants who come from other language backgrounds are expected to add English as a requirement for citizenship, for participation in US democratic processes, for economic mobility, and for access to education and other social services. Maintenance of indigenous and immigrant languages other than English is not widely encouraged and is often actively discouraged. Indeed, pride in ethnicity along with associated language use can be seen as very threatening to the dominant group, and as a symbol of disunity and separatism; to speak a language other than English may be considered somehow unpatriotic and "un-American." In sum, learning English is expected, and the teaching of English as an L2 to immigrants is encouraged and/or mandated by state and federal agencies. In contrast, state and federal support for learning other languages is sporadic and generally ineffectual.

The symbolic function of language for political identification and cohesion is even more important for countries that are in the process of nation-building. For example, establishing the official use of Hebrew was symbolically important to the creation of Israel, even though few early citizens spoke it natively. Massive efforts were made to teach Hebrew as an L2 to all immigrants, and there were social sanctions against the use of Yiddish or other languages which might rival Hebrew for ethnic identification or religious functions. Efforts have also been made to spread knowledge and use of Irish and Welsh as L2s for purposes of national identity, but these have not been as successful.

Second languages have also served political functions in times of conquest and empire-building: e.g. the Norman Conquest brought French L2 to Great Britain, colonial expansion brought English L2 to Africa and Asia and French L2 to Africa, and post-World War II domination by the Soviet Union brought Russian L2 to much of Eastern Europe. These three examples also illustrate the highly diverse outcomes which may follow periods of linguistic spread. The linguistic absorption of the Norman conquerors left behind a residue of French vocabulary embedded in English – no longer as elements of a second language, but integrated in English native speech. With the end of British colonial rule in Africa and Asia, English remained in some of the newly independent nations for auxiliary or official functions. In Nigeria and India, for instance, English was selected as the official national language (in India along with Hindi) because it was widely used and accessible, although not native to any major group of citizens (and thus ethnically neutral). In contrast, the role of Russian L2 has been of sharply waning importance as Ukrainian, Kyrgyz, Kazakh, and other languages of former USSR constituent republics have become symbols of nationalism. Indeed, the situation has become inverted, as many native Russian speakers living in the newly independent countries have recognized the need to add those national languages to their own linguistic repertoires: to learn them as L2s.

We see both historically and in the present that the need for L2 learning at a national level is strongest when groups from other language backgrounds immigrate to a country without prior knowledge of its official or dominant language, and when the official or dominant language shifts because of conquest, revolution, or other major political change. Need for L2 learning at a global level is motivated largely by control of and access to resources in areas of commerce and information/technology transfer. Opportunities as well as motivation for learning a particular L2 often depend on its relative power or status, whether symbolic or practical; this usually cannot be separated from the relative economic or military power or status of the society that it represents. For this reason, interest in learning Chinese as an L2 can be predicted to increase as the economic status of China grows. Where knowledge of a particular language confers few visible economic or social benefits, there will be little motivation for acquiring it as an L2.

Boundaries and identities

Part of the identity function of language is accomplished by creating or reinforcing national boundaries, but linguistic boundaries often also exist within or across national borders. They serve both to unify speakers as members of one language community, and to exclude outsiders from insider communication. The function of unification is illustrated by the official use of Hebrew in Israel and English in Nigeria as part of the process for establishing those nation-states. In contrast, the function of exclusion can be illustrated by the refusal of the Spanish conquerors in Mexico to teach the Castilian language to the native Indian population, or of the Mongol conquerors of China to make their language accessible to the Chinese. Language communities may also reinforce their boundaries by discouraging prospective L2 learners, by holding and conveying the attitude that their language is too difficult – or inappropriate – for others to use. When artificially created national borders transect language areas (as is the case for most former colonial territories or the Southwestern USA), social and political tensions may lead to discrimination against minority language speakers, and to enforced teaching of the dominant language.

Crossing a linguistic boundary to participate in another language community, and to identify or be identified with it, requires learning that language. It is both a necessary tool for participation and a badge which allows passage. Full participation also commonly requires learning the culture of that community and adapting to those values and behavioral patterns: i.e. acculturation. Whether or not this occurs depends largely on group motivation.

We considered the concept of motivation in Chapter 3 as a difference among individuals which accounts for why some are more successful L2 learners than others, but motivation is also profoundly influenced by external social factors. Social psychologists who study SLA emphasize the effects of motivation on whether groups of immigrants or ethnic minorities integrate culturally and linguistically into the dominant society. The same general motivational factors account for why dominant group members often do *not* learn a minority language at all, or not too well if they do not want to be identified with the minority community. Wallace Lambert (1991:220) suggests this is why many English L1 students in Canada's French L2 immersion programs showed a limit on how much French they acquired even after years of study that began in childhood (and why some even regressed in their pronunciation of French when they reached high school).

John Schumann (1978) identifies other group factors that affect SLA outcomes negatively in his Acculturation Model. For example, factors that are likely to create social distance between learner and target groups, limit acculturation, and thus inhibit L2 learning are: dominance of one group over the other, a high degree of segregation between groups, and desire of the learner group to preserve its own lifestyle. English speakers in the Southwestern USA often live and work side by side with Spanish speakers for years without acquiring more than a few words of the language, and

Spanish speakers in Paraguay who employ Guarani speakers as servants in their homes rarely learn more than a smattering of Guarani.

Institutional forces and constraints

Within the bounds of nations and communities, social institutions are systems which are established by law, custom, or practice to regulate and organize the life of people in public domains: e.g. politics, religion, and education. Many of these involve power, authority, and influence related to SLA; the forces and constraints which most concern us here are language-related social control, determination of access to knowledge, and other instances of linguistic privilege or discrimination.

The most obvious form of linguistic social control takes the form of official or unofficial policies that regulate which language is to be used in particular situations. For example, use of the national language is often required in political meetings and is sometimes required even for lower-level bureaucratic functions such as applying for permits of various kinds or negotiating for social services. A high level of fluency in the national language is typically required for election or appointment to political office, which tends to reinforce the power of some groups over others because of the language they speak. On the other hand, to the extent that political officeholders need to represent (or at least get votes from) speakers of other languages, competence in those languages may also be valued, and perhaps mandated. For example, presidential election campaigns in the USA recently have featured candidates' orating in Spanish (often poorly) as well as in English in regions of the country which have strong blocs of Spanish L1 voters, in spite of the de facto national status of English-only. Use of even a few words or phrases in Spanish is intended to carry the symbolic message that the candidate is concerned about that segment of the population. Conversely, in Bolivia and Guatemala, Spanish was until recently spoken natively by only a minority, but their economic status and the institutionalization of Spanish as the official language enabled them to maintain control of the respective Quechua/Aymara and Mayan L1 majorities.

Looking at language-related social control in the domains of law and social services, we can see that language policy may result in blatant discrimination, especially if a trial defendant does not understand the language of the court, or if the officially designated language of "service" is not one in which some of those being "served" are fluent. This is likely to have a particularly negative impact on immigrants in countries where there is no provision for official communication in minority languages. As a side-effect, differences in multilingual competence within immigrant families can lead to disintegration of the traditional family structure, as children who are learning the dominant language at school become translators and brokers for their parents in service encounters, inverting the power structure and undermining parental authority.

Access to education may also be limited for minority language speakers, since entry to those institutions often requires applicants to display competence in "proper" language usage. In some multilingual societies, this means that linguistic competence may be recognized only insofar as it is demonstrated in the official or prestigious language of the dominant group; the potential for discrimination is multilayered, since access to knowledge of the language which is required for social opportunities may itself be prevented at an earlier level by financial barriers. For example, admission to universities and professional schools in some countries requires prior study of a foreign language (often English), with the necessary quality and quantity of language instruction available only in exclusive preparatory academies. These in turn may require prior language study which is not offered by public education, but only to children whose parents are wealthy enough to send them to private schools. Thus wealth and social status may determine opportunities for acquisition of an L2.

Access (or barriers) to language instruction may also be motivated for other political reasons. The riots of the 1970s in Soweto, South Africa, for example, were motivated in part as protests to a language policy which would not provide basic elementary education in English, a policy that was perceived as keeping the Black population in the region from acquiring the unification and international voice which English would provide, and that Afrikaans would not. More recently, differential access to knowledge and power through a second language has been reported by Palestinians in Israel who say that limited opportunities to develop advanced English skills in their high schools block admission to better universities in the country because the entrance examinations require knowledge of English.

An unintentional international outcome of providing advanced-level education in English, on the other hand, has perhaps been inhibiting access to knowledge in some academic areas. There are contemporary concerns about the power position of English as the international language for scholarly conferences and publications, for example, since this status clearly privileges individuals in many disciplines who have received higher education in English-medium universities.

Although the acquisition of an L2 has been treated neutrally or positively as an additive gain from linguistic and psychological perspectives, from a social perspective it may be problematic for several reasons. Acquisition of a dominant L2 may lead to actual loss or attrition of a minority L1, potentially creating alienation from the L1 group for the individual, and the ultimate disappearance of the minority language itself. Also, acquisition of technical knowledge through the medium of an L2 may render the learner unable to express that knowledge in his or her L1. For example, native speakers of Arabic, Chinese, and other languages who study linguistics in an English-speaking country may return to their home countries and find themselves ill-equipped to make the subject accessible to others in the national language or to relate to traditional language scholars.

Social categories

People are categorized according to many socially relevant dimensions: e.g. age, sex, ethnicity, education level, occupation, and economic status.

Such categorization often influences what experiences they have, how they are perceived by others, and what is expected of them. When they are L2 learners, members of different social categories frequently experience different learning conditions, and different attitudes or perceptions from within both native and target language communities. Therefore, this is another level we need to consider in the macrosocial context of SLA.

Age is an example. We considered age as a biological factor affecting L2 learning in Chapter 4, but it is social as well. Young L2 learners are more likely than older learners to acquire the language in a naturalistic setting as opposed to a formal classroom context. They are more likely to use the L2 in highly contextualized face-to-face situations rather than decontextualized academic ones, or ones which initially involve reading and writing. It is not certain whether these social factors favor SLA by children over older learners, but they make different requirements and involve different learning tasks.

Some aspects of the social setting within which SLA takes place may particularly disadvantage lower age groups. Young immigrant children who are submerged in L2 dominant environments appear ultimately to do less well both in L2 learning and in academic content learning through the medium of L2 than do children who immigrate after receiving basic education in their native language and begin L2 learning at an older age. For instance, Gonzalez (1986) has shown both in Illinois and California that immigrant students from Mexico who attended school in Mexico for two years prior to coming to the US had higher reading scores in English by the sixth grade than did Spanish L1 peers who began school in the USA. In short, students with two years' *less* instruction in English did better in English than those who had two years' more instruction in the USA. Similar findings are reported by Cummins (1981) for Japanese immigrant students in Canada.

The likely explanation for such findings is complex, and we should beware of simplistic one-dimensional interpretations. Development of cognitive and academic competence in their L1, which Mexican children acquire in Mexico and Japanese children in Japan, may have a significant effect in promoting the transfer of these skills into English and enabling them to succeed in American or Canadian English-medium schools. At the same time, however, these children also have not faced the early negative expectations or pressures for assimilation in and out of school that their peers often do in a predominantly English-speaking setting, which may have adversely affected the level and quality of their instructional experience. In another famous case, Finnish children attending school in Sweden, where they were viewed negatively as members of a minority group, did less well than Finnish children in Australian schools, where they were viewed positively as Scandinavians.

Biological factors which generally favor a younger age for SLA can also be overridden by contexts in which older learners succeed in SLA to the level of being able to "pass" for a native speaker (even in pronunciation) when social motivation is strong enough. For example, research conducted with couples in "mixed" English L1–German L1 marriages suggests that age of first exposure to a new language is less important for predicting ultimate ability than the age when learning the L2 *really* becomes important to the learners, and when they take active responsibility for that learning (Piller 2002).

Another example is sex, which we also considered in Chapter 4 as a biological factor in learning. This, too, is a social category. We can see that different attitudes and learning conditions which are experienced by males and females may advantage one group over the other for SLA in different ways in different societies, but neither group has an innate advantage. For example, young male children of migrant farm laborers appear to be more fluent in Spanish L1 and better learners of English L2 than their female age-mates. The boys in a study which I conducted had been allowed to play outside in the labor camps with other children prior to attending school, while the girls had been kept inside both because of their responsibility to care for younger siblings and for their own safety. While the early limitations on their opportunity for social interaction were generally overcome with subsequent experience, the girls were at an initial disadvantage for language learning. On the other hand, girls were advantaged over a male peer for L2 learning in a classroom that was studied by Willett (1995). The girls were allowed to sit together, collaborate productively, and support one another; the boy was kept apart from other boys because of gender-related differences in his behavior, and he was not allowed to seek help from bilingual peers.

Different learning conditions for males and females are not limited to children. Some female students who enroll in study-abroad programs while in college report having less opportunity than male students to immerse themselves in foreign language and cultural experiences, which may inhibit development of L2 skills. This may be because there are more restrictions on unsupervised activities for females, or because female students tend to avoid situations in which they might encounter sexual harassment (see Polanyi 1995).

Ethnic category may have influence on SLA primarily because of socially constructed attitudes from within native and target communities as a result of historic or current intergroup relations related to social boundaries and identities. These attitudes determine to a significant degree what input L2 learners will be exposed to and make use of, as well as the nature of their interaction with native speakers and other learners of the target language.

The relationship between people assigned to different ethnic categories is usually characterized along one of two dimensions when the different categories coexist in heterogeneous societies: perceived horizontal distance between the groups, or relative power and prestige of one over the other. Members of ethnic groups who perceive themselves to have much in common are more likely to interact, and thus are more likely to learn the other's language. Miller (2000) reports that ethnicity is one of the factors involved in perceptions of difference in her study of migrant high school students in Australia. She found that fair-haired Europeans who physically resembled their Australian classmates established friendships and assimilated more readily than did differently appearing students from Asia. Other factors potentially contributing to perceptions of social distance include religion and cultural background, along with patterns of behavior that are considered appropriate for interaction with strangers or new acquaintances. In my own research with younger students (e.g. Saville-Troike 1984), I observed that children from South America and the Middle East as well as from Europe appeared to establish friendships with American children more readily than did children from China, Japan, and Korea. I would attribute this to relative cultural congruence of interaction patterns rather than to physical appearance.

Perceptions that members of one ethnic category are more, or less, privileged than another are determined in large part by which group is politically and economically dominant in a multiethnic society, which is also often the one that has majority status. Two outcomes of SLA related to this dimension are the types of bilingualism which may result from contact (Lambert 1974; Gardner 2002): additive bilingualism, where members of a dominant group learn the language of a subordinate group without threat to their L1 competence or to their ethnic identity; or subtractive bilingualism, where members of a subordinate group learn the dominant language as L2 and are more likely to experience some loss of ethnic identity and attrition of L1 skills – especially if they are children. There are many other social variables contributing to "additive" versus "subtractive" outcomes, including (for immigrant groups) the degree of opportunity for continued contact with their country of origin, the composition of families (e.g. whether they include grandparents or other elderly relatives), and whether the L1 continues to fulfill an institutional function such as the practice of religion.

Wallace Lambert (b. Nova Scotia), 1922–present

Social psychology

Wallace Lambert's diverse education and experiences explain his success as a researcher in the complex and sensitive area of bilingualism and biculturalism. Lambert (1974) differentiated between *additive and subtractive bilingualism*. Lambert is also well known for his work on motivation with Gardner (see Gardner 1985 for a summary). In addition, Lambert is known for his work in Matched Guise studies (Lambert, Hodgson, Gardner, and Fillenbaum 1960). These studies investigate listeners' reactions to bilingual speakers who read a passage in two languages. The listeners are not told that the same person is speaking and are asked to make judgments about the person reading each passage, thus possibly revealing their personal biases or attitudes towards the group they imagine the speaker to belong to.

Interesting note: During his student years, Lambert was involved with psychiatric social work, served in the army, studied psychology, sociology, and anthropology in three different countries (Canada, the United States of America, and France).

Circumstances of learning

The final macrosocial factors in the ecological context of SLA that we will consider are *circumstances of learning*. We begin with learners' prior educational experiences. These are part of the larger social context within which SLA takes place because learning begins with children's first experiences with the families into which they are born, the communities to which they belong, and the cultural environment within which they live. By the time children begin their formal education at the age of five or six, they have already internalized many of the basic values and beliefs of their native culture, learned the rules of behavior which are considered appropriate for their role in the community, and established the procedures for continued socialization. They have learned how to learn.

We already noted in Chapter 3 that learner differences in cognitive styles and learning strategies are at least partly based in these experiences. The difference between field-dependent (FD) and field-independent (FI) cognitive styles, for example, correlates with how children are raised. Findings on this subject are somewhat speculative, but FD styles appear to be related to the more cooperative settings of rural residence, FI to more competitive urban circumstances; and FD seems to be related to lower economic categories and FI to more affluent. Cultural values for some cognitive styles over others also play a role.

A clear example of culture-based learning strategies is seen in the superior capacity for rote learning among Asian students who have had more experience with teaching methods that involve memorization. Chinese students score significantly higher than Europeans and Americans on tests that measure memory for numbers, which reflects ways they have learned to learn in the course of earlier schooling. This advantage is lost if Chinese students are schooled in Europe or America, which proves that their achievement is based on prior educational experience and not genetic makeup. Chinese students learning English as an L2 may learn more effectively and efficiently through memorization, while this approach may not work as well for students less accustomed to this learning strategy.

Another fundamental difference in situational circumstances is whether L2 learning is informal versus formal, or naturalistic versus instructed. Informal/naturalistic learning generally takes place in settings where people contact – and need to interact with – speakers of another language. This can be because they live in a multilingual society, their circle of family and friends is multilingual, and/or their lifestyle involves international travel and residence for business or pleasure. Formal/instructed learning generally takes place in schools, which are social institutions that are established in accord with the needs, beliefs, values, and customs of their cultural settings.

L2 learners who are majority L1 speakers often have access only to foreign language programs which offer the L2 as an academic subject and give little opportunity for students to develop full communicative competence. In social contexts where multilingualism is highly valued and expected, however, program options are more likely to include other subjects such as history or science additionally taught in the L2, immersion programs with all instruction in the L2, or two-way bilingual programs in which students who speak different native languages attend classes together, learn each other's language, and learn subject matter through both languages. Where economic resources permit, options may also include study-abroad and student-exchange programs.

Minority L1 speakers who receive formal L2 instruction within the L2 speech community typically have quite different experiences. To begin with, because second language instruction for minorities generally takes place in educational institutions that are situated in and controlled by the dominant social group, teaching methods and materials may conflict with ways minority students have already learned to learn. Social attitudes toward ethnic boundaries and identities influence whether students are segregated from L2 peers or have integrated learning experiences. Social attitudes toward the value and validity of students' L1 largely determine whether instructional goals include multilingual competence, with L2 added while L1 is maintained and enriched, or there is a complete transition to L2. Most so-called "bilingual" programs in US schools provide instruction in the L1 only as a temporary expedient until students can be transitioned entirely into L2, after which the L1 is abandoned.

No individual factors in the macrosocial context of SLA can be isolated from others. Circumstances of learning are related to the nation that the learner lives in and its history, culture, and geopolitical position, and to social and economic categorizations within the society, which in turn are related to historical, institutional, and political forces and constraints, all of which are related to and reflect or determine the status of the languages involved. All of these factors powerfully influence the microsocial contexts of learning, determining who does and does not have opportunities for L2 input and interaction and of what sort, and what the outcomes of L2 learning are likely to be. The individual learner often has few or no choices in the matter of whether an L2 will be available for formal study, what language it will be, how it will be taught and at what levels, the level of proficiency that will be expected or required, and what the consequences or advantages of learning or not learning will be. The accident of one's birth may determine what L2s will be available or expected for informal acquisition, and what value or significance they will have in affecting one's life chances. These various factors are beyond the control of the individual, but whether options are available or not, one's L1 and possible L2(s) can have profound effects on the course of one's life.

Chapter summary

Learning a second language for communicative purposes requires knowledge and skills for using it appropriately, as well as knowing aspects of linguistic forms and how they are organized. Taking a social perspective, in this chapter we have seen ways in which L2 interpretation and production are influenced by contextual factors, how the nature of social interaction may facilitate or inhibit L2 acquisition, and how outcomes of learning may be determined by the broad ecological context of SLA. The L1 we are born into, and our success or failure in acquiring a particular L2, whether through formal or informal means, can profoundly influence the entire trajectory of our lives.

We have explored the effects of microsocial contexts that we see primarily within the communicative events which learners experience, including who they interact with about what, and how the negotiation of meaning is accomplished in various settings. We have also explored the effects of macrosocial contexts in accounting for language power and prestige, group boundary and identity issues, institutional forces and constraints, and other circumstances which affect learning.

We have now viewed SLA from three disciplinary perspectives: linguistic, psychological, and social. As these perspectives provide different foci and different insights, their multiple lenses bring us closer to the goal of a holistic understanding of second language learning.

Activities
Questions for self-study

1. Match the following terms to their corresponding examples:

1.	auxiliary language	a.	A French person studies German for six years because the school system requires it.
2.	foreign language	b.	A Chinese family immigrates to Canada and studies English so as to enter the school systems and the work force.
3.	second language	c.	In India, native speakers of Tamil learn English to participate in official Indian governmental proceedings.

2. Variation in second language can occur for linguistic, psychological, or social reasons. Match the following communicative contexts to the corresponding description(s) of second language variation. Two responses have more than one possible answer, so consider multiple options and explain your reasoning for each match.

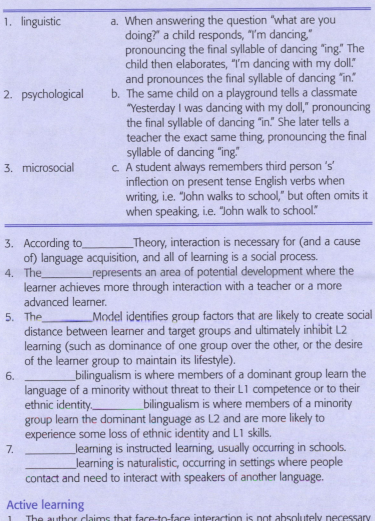

1. linguistic

    a. When answering the question "what are you doing?" a child responds, "I'm dancing," pronouncing the final syllable of dancing "ing." The child then elaborates, "I'm dancing with my doll." and pronounces the final syllable of dancing "in."

2. psychological

    b. The same child on a playground tells a classmate "Yesterday I was dancing with my doll," pronouncing the final syllable of dancing "in." She later tells a teacher the exact same thing, pronouncing the final syllable of dancing "ing."

3. microsocial

    c. A student always remembers third person 's' inflection on present tense English verbs when writing, i.e. "John walks to school," but often omits it when speaking, i.e. "John walk to school."

3. According to_____Theory, interaction is necessary for (and a cause of) language acquisition, and all of learning is a social process.

4. The_____represents an area of potential development where the learner achieves more through interaction with a teacher or a more advanced learner.

5. The_____Model identifies group factors that are likely to create social distance between learner and target groups and ultimately inhibit L2 learning (such as dominance of one group over the other, or the desire of the learner group to maintain its lifestyle).

6. _____bilingualism is where members of a dominant group learn the language of a minority without threat to their L1 competence or to their ethnic identity._____bilingualism is where members of a minority group learn the dominant language as L2 and are more likely to experience some loss of ethnic identity and L1 skills.

7. _____learning is instructed learning, usually occurring in schools. _____learning is naturalistic, occurring in settings where people contact and need to interact with speakers of another language.

Active learning

1. The author claims that face-to-face interaction is not absolutely necessary for second language acquisition. What do you think? Support or refute this claim based on your own experience.

2. Communicative competence is defined as "what a speaker needs to know to communicate appropriately within a language community." How is this different from pure linguistic competence? Do you believe linguistic competence is sufficient for effective communication, or do you agree that communicative competence is necessary? Provide real-life examples to support your viewpoint, combined with theoretical explanations from the chapter.

3. Subtractive bilingualism is defined as having members of a minority group learn the dominant language as L2, where they are more likely to experience some loss of ethnic identity and L1 skills. What are the challenges to maintaining ethnic identity and L1 skills while learning an L2 in the L2 setting? Is it possible to be a minority group in an L2-dominant setting and experience more of an additive bilingualism, where the L1 skills and identity are maintained? Support your answer with your own experiences and the experiences of people you know.

4. Considering your own learning, or the learning of someone you know well, do you believe in scaffolding and the Zone of Proximal Development? Describe examples in your own life when you are the learner in need of scaffolding, and when you are the more advanced learner or teacher providing a learner with more opportunity for development.

Further reading

Saville-Troike, M. (2003). *The Ethnography of Communication: An Introduction* (Third Edition). Oxford: Blackwell.

  This text introduces the basic concepts of the ethnography of communication, one important one being communicative competence. Chapter 2, "Basic terms, concepts and issues" specifically defines and explains communicative competence (pp. 18–22), along with other central ideas, such as communicative functions and units of analysis.

Bialystok, E. & Hakuta, K. (1994). *In Other Words: The Science and Psychology of Second-Language Acquisition*. New York: Basic Books.

  Chapter 5, "Self," and Chapter 6, "Culture," present discussion of social factors in second language acquisition.

Ellis, R. (1999). *Learning a Second Language through Interaction*. Amsterdam: John Benjamins.

  Along with several former students, Ellis reports on the role of interaction in second language learning. While some language learning may take place without interaction, Ellis openly supports the notion that most learners get their input from interaction, and that input from interaction will be more readily available to learners in the acquisition process.

Lantolf, J. P. (ed.) (2000). *Sociocultural Theory and Second Language Learning*. Oxford: Oxford University Press.

  This book contains many perspectives on using Vygotsky's theories (i.e. private speech, activity theory, scaffolding, and the zone of proximal development) in diverse areas of second language learning.

Pinker, S. (1994). *The Language Instinct*. New York: William Morrow and Company.

  Chapters 12 and 13 offer discussion of the social aspects of language acquisition and language learning.

McKay, S. L. & Hornberger, N. H. (eds.) (1996). *Sociolinguistics and Language Teaching*, Cambridge: Cambridge University Press.

  Part I, "Language and society," discusses how aspects of society influence perception of languages and language varieties and motivation to learn or not learn certain languages. Chapter 1 treats how the larger social setting can influence an individual's motivation regarding language study. Chapter 2 presents multilingualism in society, showing how different purposes are attributed to different languages. Chapter 3 discusses the use of English in a global context. Chapter 4 examines language planning undertaken to solve perceived problems of communication between members of a society.

6 Acquiring knowledge for L2 use

CHAPTER PREVIEW

KEY TERMS

Pragmatic competence

Academic competence

Interpersonal competence

Cohesion

Genre

Bottom-up processing

Top-down processing

Context

Schemas

Speech acts

Contextualization cues

Communication strategies

In this chapter, we continue our consideration of the acquisition of **communicative competence** by examining the knowledge that is needed for second language use. After beginning with an overall characterization of communicative competence, we will see that we must distinguish between (1) knowledge that must be learned in order to fulfill academic functions and (2) knowledge required for interpersonal functions. Areas of knowledge needed are then categorized and prioritized according to traditional levels of language (vocabulary, morphology, phonology, syntax, discourse), and according to activity type (reading, listening, writing, speaking). This chapter thus brings together and integrates the elements of SLA study that we have been exploring within separate linguistic, psychological, and social frameworks in the previous chapters.

Competence and use

The definition of communicative competence introduced in Chapter 5 is broadly inclusive in scope: "everything that a speaker needs to know in order to communicate appropriately within a particular community." This construct combines the knowledge of language which defines linguistic competence, knowledge of the specific components and levels of a language, and knowledge that is required for their appropriate use in communicative activities. Accounting for competence in this broader sense also requires considering "encyclopedic" cultural knowledge concerning the content of what is written or talked about, and recognizing the social significance of the context within which language use takes place. Knowledge of culture includes content, context, and linguistic elements in important respects, as well as an understanding of the wider societal structures and practices that influence norms and conventions of language interpretation and usage. The relationship of these domains is represented in 6.1.

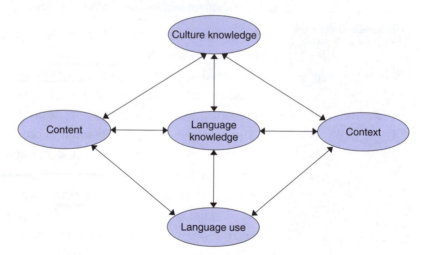

6.1
Relationship of domains
of communicative
competence

The ability to use language appropriately includes pragmatic competence. This can be defined as what people must know in order to interpret and convey meaning within communicative situations: knowledge that accounts for "the choices they make, the constraints they encounter in using language in social interaction, and the effects their use of language has on other participants in the act of communication" (Crystal 1997a:301).

The relationship of knowledge among domains of content, context, culture, language form and structure, and language use is dynamic, interactive, and constitutive. It would be a mistake to think of language use merely as the product of the other domains, since use plays an essential role in their very creation, maintenance, and change.

The knowledge that an L2 learner begins with includes everything that he or she has previously acquired as part of his or her general cognitive development and prior social experience, as well as in his or her acquisition of L1. This prior knowledge partly explains the advantages that older L2 learners such as college students typically have over children in expressing and understanding the information content of L2 writing and speech, in perceiving writer/speaker intent, and in fulfilling interactional and instrumental goals of communication. It also accounts in part for the interference which may occur when prior knowledge of content, context, and culture (as well as L1 linguistic elements) is inappropriately applied to situations of L2 use.

This chapter addresses aspects of commmunicative competence from the perspectives of the three basic questions which have organized this book. We focus here particularly on *what* knowledge of language is required for different types of language use, *how* activities in L2 reading, listening, writing, and speaking are achieved, and *why* learners reach different levels of proficiency in language use.

Academic vs. interpersonal competence

L1 competence ideally involves the broad repertoire of knowledge which people need to communicate appropriately for many purposes within their native language community. L2 competence is typically, perhaps unavoidably, much more restricted, especially when SLA takes place in a foreign language setting. For most people, their second language often serves a much more limited range of needs than their first language, depending on the situation they are in. For example, native speakers of English in the USA might learn Spanish L2 because their jobs require engaging in cross-national sales and services, or because they are in social service roles which involve daily communication with native Spanish speakers, or because they have academic interests in New World history and need access to archival records and scholarly publications that are available in Spanish. Native speakers of Chinese in China, on the other hand, might need to learn English L2 to prepare for an influx of English-speaking visitors to China for Olympic games, to serve on international committees that use English as a common language for proceedings, or to pursue graduate degrees in an English-dominant country. Native speakers of Turkish might learn German L2 to engage in information exchange on technological topics, to provide guide services for German tourists in Turkey, or to work for a company in Germany. Each of these motivations for learning an L2 entails very different combinations of linguistic and cultural knowledge and different levels and types of proficiency.

Priorities for L2 use

In considering the purposes for which people learn second languages, we must make a distinction between at least two fundamental types of communicative competence: academic competence and interpersonal competence. Academic competence would include the knowledge needed by learners who want to use the L2 primarily to learn about other subjects, or as a tool in scholarly research, or as a medium in a specific professional or occupational field. Learners with such a goal should concentrate above all on acquiring the specific vocabulary of their field or subject area, and on developing knowledge that enables them to read relevant texts fluently in that subject area. If language learners plan to study the subject at an L2-medium university, beyond specific vocabulary knowledge and reading ability, they must also put a high priority on processing oral L2 input during lectures and class discussions: i.e. on developing the ability to engage successfully in academic listening. Further, they are likely to need proficiency in L2 academic writing in order to display their knowledge on examinations that may be required for university admission and to earn academic degrees. Many students need to develop L2 writing proficiency for the academic purposes of producing term papers or theses, and researchers may need to do so for publishing articles for international information exchange. Developing L2 academic reading, listening, and writing proficiency, however, does not necessarily require fluent speaking ability, particularly for learners studying the L2 in a foreign language context.

Interpersonal competence encompasses knowledge required of learners who plan to use the L2 primarily in face-to-face contact with other speakers. As with academic competence, vocabulary is the most important level of language knowledge for these learners to acquire, although the domains of vocabulary involved are likely to be very different. Knowledge which enables them to participate in listening and speaking activities merit the highest priority for interpersonal contexts; they must be able to process language rapidly "online" (without the opportunity to review or revise text that is possible in reading and writing), as well as possess strategies for achieving clarification and negotiation of meaning during the course of face-to-face interaction. Depending on the situation, the level of language to be used may be formal or informal. Writing and reading activities are required in some interpersonal situations, but speaking and listening are much more likely to play dominant roles in interpersonal production and interpretation.

The contrast in priorities for L2 communicative activities depending on academic versus interpersonal needs is shown in 6.2. The key differences are that reading is typically much more important for academic than for interpersonal needs, and that speaking is usually much more important for interpersonal than for academic purposes.

6.2 Priorities for L2 activities	
Academic competence	Interpersonal competence
1. Reading	1. Listening
2. Listening	2. Speaking
3. Writing	3. Reading
4. Speaking	4. Writing

6.3 Classification of activities involving language use		
	Written mode	Oral mode
Receptive	Reading	Listening
Productive	Writing	Speaking

As shown in 6.3, the four areas of activity involving language use that are listed in 6.2 may be classified along two dimensions: as receptive versus productive, and as conveyed by written versus oral modes of communication. The activities that have highest priority in academic competence are receptive (reading and listening), which function primarily in processing input; the activities with highest priority for interpersonal competence are oral (listening and speaking), which function in processing both input and expression. While all four areas of communicative activity draw on an overlapping pool of L2 knowledge at different language levels, they are independent to some extent. Development of receptive ability must normally precede productive ability in any language, but beyond that basic sequence, order of L2 development along these dimensions depends on social circumstances. It is possible for learners to develop a relatively high degree of proficiency for engaging in receptive activities along with only very limited ability for production, or a high degree of proficiency for engaging in either written or oral activities without well-developed ability to engage in activities in the other mode. Many fluent bilinguals around the world are illiterate in one or both of their languages. Learners' academic and interpersonal competence which underlie their ability to engage in these activities usually develop to different degrees, and there is no necessary reason for one type to precede or outpace the other. It is known, however, that literacy (and schooling) in the L1 facilitates acquisition of competence in an L2 under conditions of formal instruction.

Components of language knowledge

Linguists have traditionally divided language into the following five components for purposes of description and analysis (as listed in Chapter 3):

- vocabulary (lexicon)
- morphology (word structure)
- phonology (sound system)
- syntax (grammar)
- discourse (ways to connect sentences and organize information)

Even the most highly educated adult native speakers can never expect to have mastery of *all* the potential resources of a community's language, and such an expectation for the vast majority of any L2 learners would be completely unrealistic. Especially in contexts where a second language is going to be needed for only a limited range of functions, deciding on priorities for *what* needs to be learned is an important step for teachers and learners to take.

Determining the specific L2 needs of any group of learners involves identifying what subset of linguistic elements is associated with the varieties (or **registers**) of a language that are used in particular situations. In recent years, much of this task has been carried out using computerized analyses of "corpora," or large collections of written and spoken texts (e.g. Biber, Conrad, and Reppen 1998). Such **corpus linguistic analysis** can be especially useful in determining the relative frequency of different vocabulary items and grammatical patterns as a basis for deciding what needs to be taught for specific purposes.

Vocabulary

As we have already noted, **vocabulary** (or **lexicon**) is the most important level of L2 knowledge for all learners to develop – whether they are aiming primarily for academic or interpersonal competence, or for a broader scope of communicative competence that spans the two. There is a core of high-frequency words in a language that everyone needs to learn, but beyond that, which specific vocabulary elements learners are most likely to need depends on whether the L2 is going to be used primarily for academic or interpersonal functions.

The core vocabulary in every language includes **function words,** a limited set of terms that carry primarily grammatical information. For example, in English the most frequently used words include: determiners *the*, *that*, *this*; prepositions *to*, *of*, *for*; conjunctions *and*, *but*; pronouns *I*, *it*, *he*, *she*, *you*; and auxiliary verbs *is/was/be*, *have/has/had*. The most frequently used words in spoken (but not written) English also include interjections *yeah*, *oh*; contractions *it's*, *that's*, *don't*; and verbs expressing personal opinion or feeling *know*, *like*, *think*. Compilations of the fifty most common words in written versus spoken English are listed in 6.4.

English words that occur with high frequency in a wide range of academic (but not interpersonal) contexts include modifiers such as *analytical*, *explanatory*, and *implicit*, as well as names for scientific concepts such as *data*, *hypotheses*, and *correlation*. Other general academic vocabulary items from written texts have been compiled in the *University Word List* (Xue and Nation 1984). A subset of these words is reproduced in 6.5. Many technical terms must be learned for any specialized field, such as *lexicon*, *morphology*, *phonology*, and *discourse* for linguistics. Beginning students in a field (whether L1 or L2 speakers) typically encounter such subject-specific terms during introductory coursework along with the concepts they represent. Part of the vocabulary challenge for advanced L2 students and scholars in a field is learning L2 labels for concepts they may have already acquired in their L1. Some of these will be recognized even without learning, since common scientific and technological terms increasingly tend to be borrowed from one language to another. But this is not always the case, and differences can create additional difficulties for learners from different L1s. For example, English *linguistics* is *la linguistique* in French, and *la linguística* in Spanish, but *Sprachwissenschaft* in German and *yuyanxue* in

6.4 Fifty most frequent words in written and spoken English

Rank	Written	Spoken	Rank	Written	Spoken
1	the	the	26	by	we
2	to	I	27	me	he
3	of	you	28	her	do
4	a	and	29	they	got
5	and	to	30	not	that's
6	in	it	31	are	for
7	I	a	32	an	this
8	was	yeah	33	this	just
9	for	that	34	has	all
10	that	of	35	been	there
11	it	in	36	up	like
12	on	was	37	were	one
13	he	is	38	out	be
14	is	it's	39	when	right
15	with	know	40	one	not
16	you	no	41	their	don't
17	but	oh	42	she	she
18	at	so	43	who	think
19	his	but	44	if	if
20	as	on	45	him	with
21	be	they	46	we	then
22	my	well	47	about	at
23	have	what	48	will	about
24	from	yes	49	all	are
25	had	have	50	would	as

Written data from Cambridge International Corpus (CIC); spoken data from CANCODE (from McCarthy and Carter 1997:23-24)

Chinese. Obviously going between English and French or Spanish is easier in the field of linguistics than between any of these languages and German or Chinese.

On the other hand, "everyday" vocabulary and expressions are most likely to be very different in unrelated languages, since they are rarely borrowed. Thus while English *good* is *gut* in German, it is *bon* in French, *bueno*

6.5 General Academic Word List (Nation and Waring 1997:16).				
accompany	formulate	index	major	objective
biology	genuine	indicate	maintain	offer
comply	hemisphere	individual	maximum	passive
deficient	homogeneous	job	modify	persist
edit	identify	labour	negative	quote
feasible	ignore	locate	notion	random

in Spanish, and *hao* in Chinese. However, similarities in borrowed or commonly inherited words can sometimes contain unexpected traps for the learner, as German *gross* means simply 'large,' and Spanish *largo* means 'long,' while *embarazada* in Spanish means 'pregnant.' Thus, ironically, learning the L2 vocabulary for ordinary informal interpersonal interaction sometimes poses more difficulties than learning the technical vocabulary for an academic or scientific field.

Interpersonal situations can be subdivided into those which have primarily affective (interactional) purposes, and those which are task-oriented (transactional). Each specific context determines priorities for vocabulary learning beyond the most frequent core. Beyond common greetings, leave-takings, invitations, refusals, and warnings, the necessary vocabulary and phraseology is likely to differ drastically between, say, going on a swimming party at the beach and following instructions on how to repair an automobile engine. And social context may dictate register differences as great as *How are you today?* vs. *How're ya doin'?* or *I'm fine, thank you* vs. *Just great* or some current slang-determined response. Regional differences are likely to be greatest at the informal interactional level, and least at more formal and more academic levels. Differences between national varieties of a widespread language may affect even relatively technical transactions, as the names for car parts famously differ between British and American English, and the meanings of food terms may differ between Spain and Latin American countries.

Besides individual vocabulary items (single words and compounds), other lexical elements which vary in frequency by domain include idioms, metaphors, and other multiple word combinations that commonly occur together (collocations). These "chunks" of language are typically memorized as holistic units, and often without recognition of individual words or analysis of how they are combined. Some of those reported in English academic speech (e.g. occurring in class lectures and discussion) are *bottom line*, *the big picture*, *take at face value*, and *a ballpark guess*. Others serve organizational functions, signaling logical connections between segments of classroom discourse or a change of focus: e.g. *go off on a tangent*, *on that note*, and *train of thought* (Simpson and Mendis 2003). Though such expressions are seldom taught in language lessons, their appropriate interpretation may be significant for establishing coherence in L2-medium subject area instruction. The most frequent multiple-word combinations in English interpersonal speech include greetings and other formulaic routines, and such discourse fillers, hedges, or smoothers as *you know*, *kind of*, and *never mind*.

Vocabulary knowledge is acquired to different degrees, with learners first recognizing words they see or hear, then producing them in limited contexts, and ultimately (perhaps) fully controlling their accurate and appropriate use. L2 speakers may never acquire complete knowledge of some words that nevertheless become part of their productive repertoire. Among the last types of word knowledge to be mastered are collocational behavior (what words go together), metaphorical uses, connotations associated with synonyms, and stylistic register constraints (see Nation 1990).

The number of words that L2 speakers learn, as well as the degree of their vocabulary knowledge, depends on their ability to "pick up" this information from contexts (both oral and written) in which the words are used as well as from explicit instruction. The following types of knowledge contribute to effective use of context for vocabulary learning (Nagy 1997):

- *Linguistic knowledge*:   syntactic information; constraints on possible word meanings; patterns in word structure; meanings of surrounding words.
- *World knowledge*:   understanding of the concepts which the words represent; familiarity with related conceptual frameworks; awareness of social associations.
- *Strategic knowledge*:   control over cognitive resources.

Beyond knowledge of words, fluent use of language requires a level of automaticity that allows processing their structures and meanings in real time. This is an incremental achievement upon which effective engagement in all language activities ultimately depends.

Morphology

L2 learning at the level of morphology (or word structure) can be very important for vocabulary development as well as for achieving grammatical accuracy. This level is highly significant for learning English, for instance, where thousands of words are formed by compounding smaller words (e.g. *wind* + *shield* = *windshield* [British *windscreen*]) or by adding prefixes and suffixes (called derivational morphology) that can create new meanings (e.g. *un-* + *kind* = *unkind*) or change part of speech (e.g. *friend* [noun] + *-ly* = *friendly* [adjective]). Again using English as an example, words used for academic communication (especially in writing) are characteristically longer than words used for interpersonal communication (especially in speech), and using them requires knowledge of such word-forming elements and processes. Commonly encountered affixes in scientific terms are the suffix *-ology* 'study of' (*sociology*, *psychology*, *biology*), and the prefix *bio-* 'life' (*biology*, *biodiversity*, *biochemical*) or *geo-* 'earth' (*geography*, *geology*, *geomorphism*). Suffixes may convert adjectives to verbs or nouns, verbs to nouns, nouns to adjectives or verbs, and adjectives to adverbs, as in *divers-ifi-cation-al-ly* or *operat-ion-al-ize-abil-ity*. (In fact, learning to compute the meaning of such complex forms automatically is part of the L2-like experience of getting a college education even for native speakers.)

Grammatical accuracy in many languages requires knowledge of the word parts that carry meanings such as tense, aspect, and number (called **inflectional morphology, or inflections**), as in English *kicked*, *coming*, and *books*. Researchers from both linguistic and cognitive perspectives have focused considerable attention on how these are acquired (discussed in Chapters 3 and 4). The process is an especially interesting target of study in SLA because errors at the level of morphology often persist even many years after individuals have learned substantial vocabulary and mastered most elements of L2 syntax.

Inflectional morphology, and related phenomena like gender and number agreement (in Romance languages, German, or Russian) may long remain problematic for L2 learners in part because the information these carry is often redundant in actual contexts of language use, and thus not essential for the interpretation of meaning (especially in face-to-face interaction). The logical unnecessariness of most inflectional morphology is shown by the fact that languages like Chinese and Thai dispense with it almost entirely. However, in those languages which have it – and this includes all European languages – accuracy in production of morphology is usually expected as part of advanced academic language competence, and in the interpersonal competence of L2 speakers who want or need to project an image of being well educated, or who want to be fully accepted as an in-group member.

Phonology

Mastery of the L2 sound system was considered the first priority for teaching and learning during the middle of the twentieth century (as expressed in the writing of Fries 1945; quoted in Chapter 3). This level of language received much less attention during the second half of the century as major interests in linguistic theory shifted from phonology to syntax, and with general acceptance of the **Critical Period Hypothesis,** which claims that learners past the age of puberty are in all probability unable to achieve native-like pronunciation in any case – no matter how much effort is spent on the learning task. In recent years, however, there has been renewed interest in phonological perception and production from linguistic, cognitive, and social perspectives, and (for at least some contexts of use) renewed emphasis is now being placed on pronunciation in teaching second languages.

As a component of academic competence, proficiency in phonological perception is required for listening if learners are studying other subjects through the medium of L2, and at least intelligible pronunciation is needed for speaking in most educational settings. A much higher level of proficiency in production is required if researchers or students are using the second language to teach others or for participating orally in professional conferences, but the relative priority of pronunciation otherwise remains low compared to vocabulary and syntax.

As a component of interpersonal competence, proficiency in phonological perception and intelligible production are essential for successful spoken communication, but a significant degree of "foreign accent" is acceptable in most situations as long as it is within the bounds of intelligibility. Native or near-native pronunciation is usually needed only when learners want to identify socially with the L2 language community for affective purposes, or when their communicative goals require such identification by hearers. With many US and British business firms establishing telephone-based service centers in other parts of the world, for instance, employees in those countries may need to master even specific regional features of American or British English as part of their job training in order to create the illusion for customers that calls are being answered domestically.

The following aspects of the sound systems are likely to differ for L1 and L2 (see Chapter 3):

- Which speech sounds are meaningful components of the phonological system (phonemes)
- Possible sequences of consonants and vowels (phonotactics)
- Which speech sounds can and cannot occur in combination with one another, in which syllable and word positions
- Intonation patterns (stress, pitch, and duration)
- Rhythmic patterns (pauses and stops)

Transfer from L1 to L2 phonology occurs in both perception and production, and is thus a factor in both listening and speaking. Trubetzkoy ([1939]1958) characterized perception of L2 speech sounds as being "filtered" through the phonological system of L1, which acts like a "sieve." Particularly at early stages of acquisition, L2 learners are likely to perceive L2 pronunciation in terms of the L1 phonemic categories which have already been established.

The types of potential mismatch between L1 and L2 systems have been characterized as contrasts in phonemic correspondences (Haugen 1956), as shown in 6.6.

This contrastive model predicts that English L1 speakers will have difficulty perceiving and producing Spanish L2 distinctions between *pero* 'but' (with a flapped /ř/) and *perro* 'dog' (with a trilled /r̄/) because English does

6.6 Types of phonemic correspondences		
	Examples	
Type	L1	L2
divergent	English /r/	Spanish /ř/ and /r̄/
convergent	English /i/ and /I/	Italian /i/
new	English –	German /x/; Navajo /ɣ/
similar	English /t/	Spanish /t/

not distinguish between flapped and trilled variants of /r/; learning Spanish requires acquiring a *divergent* distinction for English speakers. Italian L1 speakers will have difficulty with the English L2 distinction between *meet* /mit/ and *mitt* /mIt/, because Italian does not have a meaningful distinction between those two vowels. In the other direction, Spanish L1 speakers who are learning English L2 and English L1 speakers who are learning Italian L2 might initially overdifferentiate target phonemes /r/ and /i/, respectively, but *convergence* – essentially ignoring the differences – is called for as part of the SLA process. As is evident, convergence is always far easier than divergence in L2 learning.

New phonemes are likely to be perceived as having features of the L1 speech sound which is the closest correspondent: German *ich* /ix/ 'I' is heard as /ik/ by the English learner, and Navajo *hogan* /hoɣan/ 'house' is heard as /hogan/, because the English phonemic system does not include sounds that are represented by the symbols /x/ and /ɣ/, and /k/ and /g/ are their nearest equivalent. The *similar* type of correspondence, as English /t/ and Spanish /t/, is not likely to be problematic for listening but contributes to a "foreign accent" in speaking; English /t/ is pronounced with the tongue making contact further back on the gum ridge than Spanish /t/, which is produced with the tongue against the back of the teeth.

Transfer can also be found for other aspects of phonological systems, including syllable structure. An initial consonant cluster such as the /sk/ in English *school* is not permitted in Spanish syllable structure, as mentioned earlier, so a Spanish L1 speaker may pronounce the word as two syllables, /es-kul/, to fit the Spanish pattern. Conversely, English speakers may find it difficult to pronounce /ts/, which is a common sequence at the end of words in English, as in *cats*, when it occurs at the beginning of words as in German *zehn* '10.' Intonation often conveys important elements of meaning such as speaker intent which can be lost or misidentified across languages, and patterns of stress in words and phrases, which provide information for segmenting speech into grammatical units, may not be perceived or produced accurately. English speakers, who are accustomed to reducing vowels in unstressed syllables to an indistinct schwa, may create confusion in Spanish by failing to distinguish between the final unstressed vowels of *hermano* 'brother' and *hermana* 'sister.' L1 speakers of European languages, who use differences in voice pitch primarily for sentence or phrase intonation, find it challenging to perceive and produce distinctive tones necessary for distinguishing individual words in Chinese.

As we saw in Chapter 3, contrastive analysis of L1 and L2 does not account for all learner errors, and many problems which are predicted do not emerge. The approach has been most reliable for predicting L1 influence on L2 acquisition of phonology, however, and remains useful for explaining nonnative perceptual patterns (e.g., there are contrastive outlines of over twenty languages published as a guide for English teachers in Swan and Smith 2001).

The concept of phonemes as "bundles" of distinctive features (e.g. Chomsky and Halle 1968) is also still relevant in accounts of why L2 speech sounds are perceived in terms of L1 categories. On this account, each phoneme in a language consists of a unique "bundle" of distinctive features which make it perceptibly different from other phonemes to speakers of that language. The possible set of features is a universal; those features which distinguish phonemes in any L1 or L2 are a subset. Some analysts argue that it is these features, rather than the phonemes per se, which influence perception (see Brown 2000).

Another aspect of perception and production of speech segments which has received considerable attention is voice onset time (VOT), which is related to the location of a phoneme boundary and to identification of initial stop consonants. The location of boundaries for multilinguals often involves compromise, with a VOT value between L1 and L2. This process is often found to be not so much simple transfer from L1 to L2 as restructuring of acoustic-phonetic space to encompass both systems (Leather and James 1996).

In contrast, yet another effect that is found is one of exaggeration, where learners sometimes maximize a difference between L1 and L2. For example, Flege (1980) found that an Arabic L1 speaker produced a greater duration contrast between /p/ and /b/ in English L2 than do English L1 speakers (although Arabic does not have a similar /p/–/b/ distinction), and Gass (1984) reported an Italian L1 speaker maximizing the phonetic contrast between Italian /b/ and English /p/ when producing English L2: "learners first identify *that* there is something to learn and then work out the details, which in many cases involves the maximization of the features of the new element and contrast" (Gass 1996:328). Individual, sociolinguistic, and sociocultural factors can also have a major impact on L2 phonology; these were discussed in Chapters 4 and 5.

Syntax

Depending on the theoretical linguistic perspective one takes (Chapter 3), acquiring the syntax of another language may be seen as an issue of internalizing new construction patterns, generative rules, different parameters for innate principles, or collocational probabilities and constraints. Whatever the analysis, the process begins with recognizing that sentences are more than just combinations of words, and that every language has specific limits and requirements on the possible orders and arrangements of elements. Contrastive analysis helps us anticipate some of the problems and difficulties – or lack thereof – that we may face in trying to acquire another language.

A first step is realizing that certain aspects of language are universal, but how they are expressed may vary greatly. All languages have structures for making statements, asking questions, and denying assertions. Sentences in all languages consist of a subject and a predicate, and predicates consist of a verb, or a verb and one or two objects, plus other possible phrases expressing such things as time, place, frequency, manner, goal, source, or purpose. But the order of elements, and degree of flexibility in their order, may differ radically. Using *S* for subject, *V* for verb, and *0* for object, linguists classify languages according to the typical order in which these components occur, e.g.

S V O   *English, Chinese, French, Russian*
S O V   *Japanese, Turkish, Persian, Finnish*
V S O   *Irish, Welsh, Samoan, Zapotec*

(German is unusual in having a mixed system, since the word order is SVO in main clauses and SOV in subordinate clauses.)

While these orders are statistically most common, most languages have ways to vary the basic order to some extent for various reasons, including focus, information structure, and style. Some languages, like English or Japanese, are fairly rigid insofar as allowing variation in order; others such as Russian or Latin are extremely flexible. In English, for example, the SVO order is often essential in distinguishing subjects and objects: in *William hit Peter*, we know from the order that William initiated the action and that Peter was the one injured; if the order is reversed to *Peter hit William*, we make the opposite inference. In a language like Russian or German, however, case markers on the noun or article indicate subject or object function, so any order is possible since the information will still be evident (in this way morphology and syntax interact).

English as it was spoken a thousand years ago (Old English) was more like Russian or Latin, as this sentence shows:

Se cyning seah ðone bisceop.
('The king saw the bishop.')

Since the form of the definite article (*se* vs *ðone*) identified whether the noun was subject (nominative case) or object (accusative case), the order could be switched without changing the basic meaning:

ðone bisceop seah se cyning.
Se cyning ðone bisceop seah.
ðone bisceop se cyning seah.

Modern English has lost this flexibility, since the invariant form of *the* no longer reflects the function of the noun in the sentence.

Note, however, that word order in Old English was not completely free, since the position of the article could not be switched with the noun. Just as we cannot say

*King the saw bishop the.

the order of these words could not be switched either. Just so, even in very flexible languages, the order of elements *within* constituent phrases may be quite rigid:

English	Japanese
in Tokyo	Tokyo *de*
*Tokyo in	**de* Tokyo

English speakers are familiar with the concepts of grammatical gender and number, which determine the choice of pronouns, and whether the noun is marked for singular or plural:

Singular		Plural	
the boy	he/him	the boys	
the girl	she/her	the girls	they/them
the tree	it/it	the trees	

In German, as was formerly the case in English, the form of the article must agree both in gender and number with the noun, and additionally may indicate whether the noun phrase is used as subject, object, or modifier (genitive):

Singular	Plural
der Arm 'the arm'	die Arme 'the arms'
die Reise 'the trip'	die Reisen 'the trips'
das Kind 'the child'	die Kinder 'the children'

English speakers will predictably have difficulty with this (something our linguistic ancestors took for granted!), whereas German speakers learning English face a much easier task, since they can simply ignore the need for article agreement. Speakers of Russian, Chinese, and Japanese, on the other hand, will find even this simplified *the* very difficult to master, since these languages lack an exact equivalent.

English speakers acquiring a Romance language (French, Spanish, Italian) must learn to categorize all nouns into two genders, rather misleadingly labeled "masculine" and "feminine," and to select articles to agree in gender and number with the noun, as well as to show this agreement in adjectives (and to place most adjectives *after* rather than before the noun):

Masculine	Feminine
el edificio blanc*o*	*la* casa blanc*a*
los edificios blanc*os*	*las* casas blanc*as*

While speakers of these languages face a simpler task in acquiring this aspect of English:

the white building	the white house
the white buildings	the white houses

they conversely must learn when *not* to use the definite article:

I always enjoy the rap music.

For Chinese speakers, and speakers of most Asian languages, having to mark plurals on nouns in English will be a challenge, since this is not done in these languages, which also do not distinguish gender (except artificially in writing) or subject/object function in pronouns:

English	Chinese
he/him	ta
she/her	ta
it/it	ta

English speakers, on the other hand, while finding Chinese pronouns simple to acquire (though they must, conversely, learn *not* to use them much of the time), will have to internalize a completely different system of gender, one based primarily on the *shape* of things, e.g.:

English	Chinese	
a book	yiben shu	(collection of objects)
a table	yizhang zuo	(flat object)
a pen	yizhi bi	(long, thin object)

Other differences between English and some other languages include whether any movement of words in the sentence is required to form yes/no and Wh-questions, how passives are formed, where and how negation is marked (and whether "double negatives" are required, as in Romance languages), and how time and perspective are marked in the verb system.

These are only a few examples of the kinds of grammatical issues that face speakers of different L1s acquiring an L2, just within simple sentences. But academic competence requires processing much longer and more complicated sentences than does interpersonal competence. Academic sentences are often grammatically complex, involving various types of subordination. In addition, passive constructions are much more likely to be used in order to foreground objects and results and to background agents of actions (or omit them entirely, as in the present passive sentence). The general need to provide specific content information in academic discourse results in different forms of linguistic expansion and elaboration, including (in many European languages, for example) the use of more prepositional phrases and relative clauses to modify nouns. The impersonal nature of much academic writing and speaking, especially in European languages, leads to the use of more abstract expressions, emphasizing states rather than expressing actions.

One way this is achieved in English is through the use of nominalizations, by which whole sentences are transformed into fillers for noun phrase positions. E.g.

Edison invented the phonograph.	==> Edison's invention of the phonograph
Caesar conquered Gaul.	==> Caesar's conquest of Gaul
I analyzed the report.	==> My analysis of the report
Someone constructed the Sphinx.	==> The construction of the Sphinx
Bacteria exist in the mouth.	==> The existence of bacteria in the mouth
The war was widely opposed.	==> Wide opposition to the war

This process allows several simple sentences to be combined into one, and increases the density of information transmitted. E.g.

Scientists were working in a laboratory.
The laboratory was in Chicago.
Scientists discovered something.
Bacteria exist in the mouth.
This is what they discovered.
Someone reported this event last month.
==> The discovery of the existence of bacteria in the mouth by scientists in a laboratory in Chicago was reported last month.

Here six sentences are condensed into one, reducing the number of words from thirty to twenty one, but at the expense of increasing the syntactic complexity of the resulting sentence, and introducing the abstract nouns, *discovery* and *existence*, which may be less familiar to some readers, who may not know how to process the relations of other words to these, and who may not realize that the complex construction can be deconstructed back to simpler sentences.

In contrast, grammatical structures used for interpersonal functions are much more likely to be short, simple sentences. Often they are not complete sentences at all, but fragments like *OK*, *Right*, and *Me too*. Contracted forms such as *I'm*, *it's*, and *don't* are common, and questions and directives are more frequent sentence types. Language used for affective purposes often serves to express a speaker's point of view rather than to transmit referential information; this functional difference accounts for a high frequency of such verb constructions as *is going to*, *is supposed to*, *needs to*, and *wants to* (Scheibman 2002), and verbs like *know*, *think*, and *say* (see 6.4).

Because many of the grammatical structures common to interpersonal communication are different from those found in written academic texts, even the development of considerable fluency for everyday interactive purposes does not guarantee that a learner will acquire the syntactic knowledge that is necessary for the advanced literacy that full academic competence requires. Nor does proficiency in processing the formal, complex structures of academic writing guarantee a learner's ability to participate appropriately in informal conversations which are characterized by sentence fragments and contractions, rapid give-and-take, and "everyday" vocabulary. Beyond very basic common structures, the syntactic knowledge required for either domain requires extensive input that is specific to the intended context of use.

Discourse

Linguistic elements at the level of discourse function beyond the scope of a single sentence. At a microstructural discourse level these include sequential indicators, logical connectors, and other devices to create cohesion. At a macrostructural discourse level we go beyond linguistic elements to knowledge of organizational features that are characteristic of particular genres, and of interactional strategies. Both microstructural and macrostructural levels are sensitive to the relationship between language forms and the communicative situations within which they are used, requiring an essential interface of linguistic knowledge with content, culture, and context.

Sequential indicators are linguistic elements that connect phrases, clauses, or longer units of written or spoken text to signal the order in which events take place. In English they may be set off with a comma or pause, as in the following example (which is a paraphrase of the preview to this chapter):

First, we will consider an overall characterization of communicative competence. *Then,* we will distinguish between knowledge that is required for academic versus interpersonal functions. *Next,* we will categorize and prioritize areas of knowledge according to traditional levels of language. *Finally,* we will explore aspects of communicative competence in relation to activity type.

Other common indicators of temporal sequence in English include *before–after*, and *yesterday–today–tomorrow*. An overlapping set of elements indicates spatial sequence and may also be used to delineate items in a list (often in order of priority or relative importance).

Logical connectors occur between clauses or other grammatical constituents to indicate such relations between them as cause–effect (e.g. *because*; *as a result*; *consequently*) contrast (e.g. *however*; *on the other hand*), and addition of information (e.g. *furthermore*; *moveover*). Academic written English typically prefers overt verbal expression of the connections, but many other languages (e.g. Chinese and Korean) often prefer to express such relationships by juxtaposition of clauses rather than with added linguistic elements. Use of overt logical connectors is an aspect of English L2 which is problematic for many learners.

Cohesion devices link one element of discourse to another, integrating them into a unified text. They include many of the sequential indicators and logical connectors that are listed above, but also such ties as pronominal and

6.7 Types of cohesion in English	
Reference	
• Pronominals	*he, they*
• Demonstratives; articles	*this, the*
• Comparatives	*same, other*
Substitution	
• Nominal substitutes	*one, all*
• Verbal substitutes	*do, likewise*
• Clausal substitutes	*so*
Ellipsis	
• Nominal ellipsis	*(omissions at subsequent mention)*
• Verbal ellipsis	
• Clausal ellipsis	
Conjunction	
• Additive	*and, as well as*
• Adversative	*yet, but, however*
• Causal	*so, it follows*
• Temporal	*then, in the end*
• Continuative	*of course, anyway*
• Intonation	
Lexical	
• Same item	*mushroom–mushroom*
• Synonym or near synonym	*the ascent–the climb*
• Superordinate	*a new Jaguar–the car*
• "General" item	*the rafters–those things*
• Collocation	*boy–girl, north–south*

lexical reference, substitution, and ellipsis. The most frequently cited typology of English devices is by Halliday and Hasan (1976).

Some of these devices are illustrated in the following paragraph:

Students who acquire second languages *do so*[1] in many social contexts. For example, *they*[2] may *learn L2s*[3] in formal classrooms, or [   ][4] in informal interaction with native speakers. *Language learners*[5] may profit from *either setting*[6], *but*[7] *of course*[8] not *all*[9] will have equal success. *In the end*[10], motivation *as well as*[11] aptitude *and*[12] opportunity is *a critical variable*[13].

[1]Substitution for *acquire second languages*
[2]Pronominal reference for *students who acquire second languages*
[3]Synonym for *acquire second languages*
[4]Ellipsis for *they may learn L2s*
[5]Synonym for *students who acquire second languages*
[6]Substitution for *formal classrooms* and *informal interaction*
[7]Adversative
[8]Continuative
[9]Substitution of quantifier for elided *language learners*
[10]Temporal
[11]Additive
[12]Additive
[13]Superordinate for *motivation, aptitude,* and *opportunity*

Both academic and interpersonal domains involve conventionalized categories and types of discourse, called **genres**. Different genres are typically characterized by having different functions within a language community, involving different classes of participants (speakers/writers and audience), addressing different topics, and requiring different language styles and organization. Academic genres include research papers, lectures, and book reviews; interpersonal genres include conversations, service encounters (e.g. ordering food in a restaurant), and letters. Genres are "conventionalized" categories of discourse in the sense that knowledge of their nature and regularities is shared by members of a language community as part of the cultural component of communicative competence.

L2 learners of a language often have to learn new organizational features for a relevant genre as well as new linguistic elements when they wish to join the community that uses it. For example, academic research reports that are written in English commonly follow the following sequence (see Swales 1990):

(1) Statement of the problem under investigation and its potential significance
(2) Specific research questions or hypotheses
(3) Review of related research
(4) Description of data collection and analytic procedures
(5) Presentation of findings
(6) Discussion of results
(7) Conclusion (often including mention of limitations and suggestions for future research)

There is variability in the pattern by discipline (e.g. academic reports differ somewhat depending on whether they are situated in the physical sciences, social sciences, or humanities), but an English-speaking researcher in any subject area would consider it "odd" if a report presented findings before describing data-collection procedures, and a report which deviated significantly from disciplinary conventions of organization would probably not be accepted in fulfillment of an academic thesis requirement or be published by a professional journal. An example of cultural differences in the organizational pattern of this academic genre is that a

Chinese scholar is likely to omit the review of related research, whether writing in Chinese L1 or English L2 (Taylor and Chen 1991). Contrastive Rhetoric is an area of research that compares genre-specific conventions in different languages and cultures, with particular focus on predicting and explaining problems in L2 academic and professional writing (see Connor 1996 for a survey of research topics and findings).

Examples of conventional features that L2 learners must acquire for interactional genres include politeness and turn-taking strategies for conversations. Some general (and perhaps universal) rules for politeness have been suggested, such as "Do not impose" and "Help the other person save face" (Traugott and Pratt 1980), but similar communicative behaviors may be interpreted differently in different cultures. Essentially the same act may be perceived as "friendly" in one setting but "rude" in another (e.g. asking a casual acquaintance about their religious or political views, or whether they have children). Appropriate conversational turn-taking in some cultures involves interruptions, overlaps, or simultaneous speaking; some cultures require several seconds of silence before another speaker may begin, with a shorter interval again considered "rude" or overly aggressive.

Transfer of politeness and turn-taking conventions from L1 to L2 in cases where such contrasts exist may not interfere with expression and interpretation of the referential content of messages but can contribute to instances of serious misunderstanding of speaker intent and message tone. Comparative research on interactional genre with particular focus on such factors can be found in the domain of Intercultural Communication (e.g. see Scollon and Scollon 2001).

Development of the ability to use elements of L2 discourse appropriately is not unlike the development of other elements of interlanguage. It takes place gradually and systematically, and many errors in production can be attributed to either transfer of L1 knowledge in using the L2 or to developmental patterns within the L2 (e.g. Ellis 1997). And as with the other elements, the nature and amount of input to learners largely determines the degree of proficiency that they will attain. The development of academic discourse competence requires reading and hearing an ample number of academic texts within meaningful contexts, and it benefits from feedback on the appropriateness of written production. Development of interpersonal discourse competence requires opportunity for social interaction and the input and feedback that it produces.

Receptive activities

The labeling of reading and listening as "receptive" (as opposed to "productive") activities does not imply that L2 learners perform them passively and without effort. Learners must actively participate in creating meaning from L2 input, or else writing remains merely marks on paper and speech remains only a stream of noise that people emit through their mouths. We saw examples in Chapter 5 of children and adults who failed to learn a single word of another language even after extended opportunity to do so when they lacked need or motivation. Successful SLA requires active engagement.

Comprehension of written or spoken language involves both bottom-up and top-down processing. Bottom-up processing requires prior knowledge of the language system (i.e. vocabulary, morphology, phonology, syntax, and discourse structure) and interpretation of physical (graphic and auditory) cues. Knowledge of vocabulary is needed to recognize words and to understand what they mean; knowledge of morphology is needed to interpret complex lexical elements, as well as to perceive grammatical information that is carried by inflections; knowledge of phonology is needed to recognize spoken words, to segment speech into grammatical units, and to relate written symbols to their spoken form; knowledge of syntax is needed to recognize how words relate to one another, and how they are constituted as phrases and clauses; knowledge of discourse structure is needed to interpret stretches of language that are longer than a single sentence.

We can generally assume that sufficient prior linguistic knowledge – except perhaps vocabulary – is automatically (and unconsciously) available to L1 and to highly skilled L2 speakers for interpretation of meaning, but the language knowledge of L2 learners is often insufficient for comprehending written or spoken input. At early stages of learning, bottom-up processing is limited to visual or auditory recognition of the limited set of words and word combinations that have been acquired thus far, and of simple grammatical sequences. When L2 input significantly exceeds these limits, understanding is likely to be fragmentary.

Top-down processing can compensate for linguistic limitations to some extent by allowing learners to guess the meaning of words they have not encountered before, and to make some sense out of larger chunks of written and oral text. For both L1 and L2 speakers, top-down processing utilizes prior knowledge of content, context, and culture, which were shown in 6.1 to be essential components of communicative competence.

Content knowledge is background information about the topic that is being read about or listened to; new information is perceived and interpreted in relation to this base. For example, when early reading in an academic text is related to subject matter that L2 learners have already studied in their L1, that prior content knowledge provides a "scaffold" for understanding new terms and integrating new information in a coherent conceptual framework. Indeed, L2 learners may sometimes know more about the topic of a text than do L1 speakers, and thus be able to make considerable sense of what they read or hear in spite of gaps in their comprehension of specific words and grammatical structures.

Context knowledge includes information learned from what has already been read or heard in a specific text or situation, as well as an understanding of what the writer's or speaker's intentions are, and the overall structure of the discourse pattern being used; it allows prediction of what is likely to follow, and how the information is likely to be organized.

Culture knowledge subsumes content and context in many ways but also includes an understanding of the wider social setting within which acts of reading and listening take place. Precisely because this knowledge is taken for granted by the writer of the text being read (and often by the teacher in an instructional situation as well), it is rarely expressed explicitly, so that its

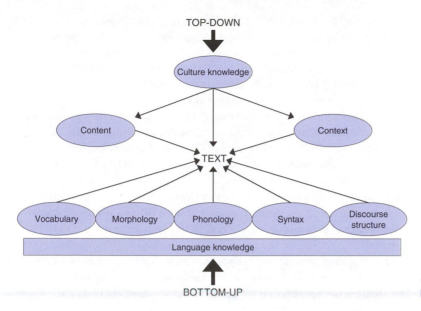

TOP-DOWN

BOTTOM-UP

6.8
Receptive processing

role in the process of understanding (or conversely, the failure to understand) is rarely recognized. While we can generally assume that many social dimensions of culture knowledge are automatically available to L1 speakers who grow up as members of the native speech community, they are often not within the background experience of foreign language learners.

All types of pre-existing knowledge that readers and listeners bring to the interpretation of text contribute to their **schemas**, or the mental structures that map the expected patterns of objects and events. These types of knowledge are represented in 6.8.

Reading

Reading is the most important area of activity for individuals to engage in for the development of L2 academic competence, and it is important as well for interpersonal functions and for merely "getting along" in any literate society. For many learners, reading is the primary channel for L2 input and a major source of exposure to associated literature and other aspects of the L2 culture. In the case of a language that is used for wider communication (such as English), reading also provides significant input related to technological developments, world news, and scientific discoveries. Reading ability (literacy) in general is needed not only for access to printed resources such as books and journals but may also be needed for access to computers and the Internet. Non-academic situations which require reading range from those which involve interpreting directions on signs and product labels to those which involve receiving news from friends in letters or e-mail.

Grabe (1991) reviews research on fluent academic reading in terms of six component abilities and types of knowledge that are involved in the activity.

(1) *Automatic recognition ability*. Automatic (as opposed to conscious) word perception and identification is necessary for fluency. There is also some

evidence that lower-level automaticity is important (e.g. at feature and letter levels), as well as automatic recognition of syntactic structures.

(2) *Vocabulary and structural knowledge.* Fluent reading requires a large recognition vocabulary (some estimates range up to 100,000 words) and a sound knowledge of grammatical structure.

(3) *Formal discourse structure knowledge.* Good readers know how a text is organized, including (culture-specific) logical patterns of organization for such contrasts as cause–effect and problem–solution relations.

(4) *Content/world background knowledge.* Good readers have both more prior cultural knowledge about a topic and more text-related information than those who are less proficient.

(5) *Synthesis and evaluation processes/strategies.* Fluent readers evaluate information in texts and compare it with other sources of knowledge; they go beyond merely trying to comprehend what they read.

(6) *Metacognitive knowledge and comprehension monitoring.* Fluent readers have [unconscious] knowledge about knowledge of language and about using appropriate strategies for understanding texts and processing information. Monitoring involves both recognizing problems that occur in the process of interpreting information in a text, and awareness of non-comprehension.

Fluency in reading takes time to develop in either L1 or L2, but it is an essential aspect of academic competence. Most L2 learners have already learned to read their L1 and thus do not need to begin acquiring this ability anew: there is significant transfer of knowledge and ability from reading in one language to reading in another. The basic concept of deriving meaning from abstract written/printed symbols is the same in most languages, and the same top-down strategies for making inferences, using prior knowledge, and reasoning are applicable. Indeed, level of L1 reading ability is a very strong predictor of how successful students will be in learning to read L2. This is true even when the L1 is represented in a different symbolic writing system (or **orthography**), as when L1 readers of Japanese or Hebrew transfer reading skills to English L2 (e.g. Saville-Troike 1984). Content knowledge which is applied in the top-down processing of texts is not language-specific for the most part. Concepts that are learned through the medium of one language still exist in the mind when access to them is triggered through the medium of another. (Of course it is always possible that differences might exist in the structure or content of a concept as it was learned in an L1 and as it is presented or assumed in the L2; the conflict, which may go unnoticed, can lead to misunderstanding or confusion. This conflict can exist as well between varieties of an L1, particularly in the application of vocabulary labels.)

Developing fluency in reading requires acquiring sufficient knowledge of the new language elements (especially vocabulary, but also grammar and discourse structure) for these to be recognized and interpreted automatically, without conscious attention. Achieving automatic recognition requires extensive practice: as is true in many other fields of activity, one learns to read by reading.

Purposeful academic reading is possible even during the beginning and intermediate states of L2 learning, since reading for different purposes does not necessarily require the same level of background linguistic knowledge nor automaticity. Grabe (2002) lists the following functions for reading in academic settings, which are listed here in order of their likely difficulty for L2 learners (from least to most difficult):

- *Reading to find information*:   scan or search text for a specific topic, word, or phrase
- *Reading for general understanding*:   get the main ideas and at least some supporting ideas and information
- *Reading to learn*: understand the main ideas and store meanings and supporting details in a coherent organizational frame
- *Reading to critique and evaluate*:   in addition, reflect on text content, integrate it with prior knowledge, and judge quality and appropriateness of texts in relation to what is already known about the topic

Even a relative beginner can scan text for a specific topic or word, and intermediate L2 learners can comprehend the main ideas and get some supporting information, but reading to learn and critical/evaluative reading are generally achieved only at advanced levels of SLA (though knowledge of discourse/textual schemas and common technical vocabulary can sometimes enable even a relative novice to gather useful information from a text in another language which utilizes a similar orthography).

Beginning L2 reading

Learners whose L1 is written in a different orthographic system from their L2 need to be able to recognize symbols in the target language as an early step, although they may learn to recognize a number of words by their appearance as whole units before they can identify constituent parts. Different types of writing systems are illustrated in 6.9: alphabetic, syllabic, and logographic. The sentences given in English (Roman), Lao, and Greek alphabets, Japanese syllabary, and Chinese logographic characters have approximately the same meaning, 'She went to the market.' English

6.9 Writing systems of the world			
Alphabets	English	She went to the market.	
	Lao	ລາວໄປຕລາດ	law pa:i thala:t
			she go market
	Greek	πιγε στιν αγορα	pighe stin aghora
			he/she.went to.the market
Syllabary	Japanese	かのじょがマーケットにいきました	kanojo ga maketto ni ikimashita
			she nom. market to went
Logographic	Chinese	她去了市场	ta qu le shi.chang
			she go perfect market

L1 learners of Spanish or French L2 share the same Roman alphabet and thus already know the symbols that are used to represent the consonant and vowel sounds of those languages. In contrast, English L1 learners of Lao and Greek or Korean must learn rather different sets of alphabetic symbols to relate to consonants and vowels in those languages; learners of Japanese must learn different sets of symbols to relate to larger syllabic (consonant + vowel) units; and learners of Chinese must learn a logographic system in which symbols (or a sequence of two or more symbols) relate holistically to word meanings. The task is made more difficult when the "same" symbols take different forms in print and handwriting, in upper and lower case (as in the Roman and Cyrillic alphabets), or in initial and final word position (as in Hebrew and Arabic alphabets), and when they occur in both "simplified" and "unsimplified" variants (as in Chinese characters). Another difference in writing systems which may be encountered at an early stage is *directionality* (e.g. whether print is to be decoded left to right, right to left, or top to bottom, and which part of a book is the "front").

Learning a new system of graphic representation also requires learning to recognize and interpret new conventions of punctuation. Punctuation provides information about the scope of grammatical constituents within sentences and how they are related, and often signals aspects of meaning that are carried by intonation in spoken language. There are also different conventions for whether punctuation should be used at all, and whether blank spaces should occur between words. (For example, Thai and Lao do not make use of such spaces, and Chinese characters are all equally spaced, regardless of their relation to one another.)

Depending on how much prior oral knowledge of the L2 that learners have before starting to read, rate of progress through beginning stages will vary greatly. Learners who are literate in their L1 and who already recognize a substantial amount of L2 vocabulary and basic grammatical structures can expect to extract a significant amount of information from written L2 text as soon as they can process its graphic representation. Learners who begin reading L2 without some (prior or simultaneous) exposure to the oral form of the language may be more limited in what they can process (depending on the similarity in the writing systems and the amount of identifiably related vocabulary). Even so, early introduction of reading can be advantageous. The rate of learning (especially of vocabulary) is generally enhanced by having visual as well as auditory input; background knowledge about the topic helps beginners guess meanings of unknown words in context and further enhances incidental learning.

What is acquired in beginning L2 reading is essentially learning how to relate knowledge of different levels of language to graphic representation, along with developing the ability to compensate for limitations in linguistic knowledge through top-down processing. How this is accomplished is largely by transfer of L1 reading processes; transfer is greatly facilitated by selection of content topics which learners have already experienced.

Academic reading

Advanced reading ability in both L1 and L2 is usually required to extract detailed information from L2 texts on science, technology, and other subject matter involving both linguistic and nonlinguistic prerequisite knowledge. Prerequisite L2 linguistic knowledge includes:

- A large recognition vocabulary of both basic and subject-specific terms, including their meaning, graphic representation, and probability of occurrence with other lexical items.
- Complex sentence structures, along with punctuation conventions that contribute to syntactic processing.
- Organization features at the sentence level which identify elements that are in focus and distinguish old and new information.
- Organization features at the discourse level, such as how texts are structured and how information is organized (Grabe 2002).

Development of advanced academic reading proficiency requires extensive exposure to written text. Because vocabulary, grammar, and discourse structures differ in the kind of language used for academic versus interpersonal purposes, and in written versus oral channels, academic text material provides the most appropriate source of language input for this purpose. Texts about subjects in the target content area ensure exposure to maximally relevant vocabulary selection and additionally add to the background knowledge that readers can use in top-down processing for meaning. Explicit instruction about language structure is useful in achieving advanced academic reading proficiency in an L2, especially if the instruction includes focus on the more complex grammatical forms that characterize this writing and on ways in which information is organized that may differ from L1 texts. Exclusive focus on conversational L2 usage and simplified written text does not adequately prepare learners to accomplish advanced academic goals.

Once advanced reading proficiency has been attained, it can often be maintained at a high level without help from a teacher and even if there is minimal opportunity for exposure to face-to-face interaction or other sources of continuing L2 input.

Listening

Listening accounts for most of the language input for L1 acquisition by children, but L2 learners often have much less opportunity to hear the target language and therefore receive proportionally less input via this channel. Listening is a critically important activity, however, both for learners who want or need to participate in oral interpersonal communication and for learners who want or need to receive information from such oral sources as lectures and media broadcasts.

One way to classify listening tasks is on a continuum from reciprocal to non-reciprocal communication (Lynch 1998). Participation in face-to-face interpersonal interaction is at the reciprocal end of this continuum, and listening to radio or TV news broadcasts is at the non-reciprocal end.

Listening to academic lectures or conference presentations has the potential to be relatively more or less reciprocal depending on whether listeners have the opportunity to ask questions of the speaker and participate in discussion. Reciprocal communication requires learners to speak as well as to listen, and to collaborate in the negotiation of meaning. Non-reciprocal communication places heavier requirements on the listener for processing input and constructing meaning "online" or in real time, without being able to request repetition or clarification.

Another way to classify listening activities is according to whether they require general or selective listening (Nida 1953). General listening requires only that listeners get the general gist of the message, while selective listening requires perception and comprehension of important details. The latter type of task is common for academic lectures in which students are expected to note facts such as names, places, and dates, but also occurs in reciprocal interpersonal conversations such as when the listener is invited to be in a certain place at a particular time.

The theory of SLA most commonly used to account for listening phenomena is **Information Processing** (see Chapter 4). The first stage is **input**, or perception which requires noticing relevant auditory cues. This requires much more conscious attention and effort for L2 reception than for L1, especially in early language learning. The next stage is **central processing,** involving both the bottom-up and top-down factors which were discussed above. Bottom-up processing must be under a high degree of attentional control until components of L2 knowledge become automatic, and many linguistic cues to meaning are inaccessible because of learners' limited store of phonological, lexical, and grammatical information. Limits are also imposed by the mental "working space" required for conscious processing, which leaves relatively little capacity for new information and higher order thought. Top-down factors such as prior content knowledge and expectations may already be automatized and available for integration, even at early levels of L2 learning. While this generally facilitates comprehension, the unconscious and automatic access that listeners have to prior knowledge of content, context, and culture may be inappropriate in the L2 situation and could account for some misunderstanding. In addition to potential inappropriate transfer of prior knowledge in top-down processing, interference in bottom-up processing commonly results from transfer from a listener's L1 phonological system, as discussed earlier in this chapter.

Beginning L2 listening

Speech in a foreign language is initially perceived as merely a stream of noise. The first step in making sense of what people say is recognizing patterns in recurring sequences of sounds and attaching meaning to them. This begins the process of segmenting the stream of speech into meaningful units: sounds that form words, words that form phrases, and phrases that constitute clauses or sentences. Segmenting speech requires not only perceiving sound, but noticing patterns in relation to a context which allows interpretation. As we have seen, this requires the active engagement of learners.

Beginning L2 learners can begin to create sense from auditory input most easily if:

- They know in advance what the speaker is going to be talking about.
- Key words and phrases are learned as recognition vocabulary elements before they are encountered in connected speech.
- Speakers pause frequently at boundaries between parts of sentences.
- Auditory messages are supported by visual images (including writing).
- The communicative situation is a reciprocal one that allows the listener to seek repetition and clarification, or to ask the speaker to slow down.

Many nonlinguistic factors also influence comprehensibility in beginning L2 listening. Interference can be caused by:

- Poor signal quality (such as static or sound distortion)
- Background noise
- Any distraction of the listener's attention
- Affective features such as anxiety (see a review of factors in Lynch 1998)

Speaker pronunciation is also a factor that influences listener comprehension. Many learners report that they find it easier to understand L2 utterances produced by speakers of their own L1 than by native speakers of the L2, presumably because the speakers' accent is closer to their own phonological perceptual system. However, research on this topic suggests that familiarity with the accent is even more important (Flowerdew 1994). In universities where different native regional varieties of speech are found among instructors (as well as different nonnative accents), students can improve their comprehension by tape-recording classroom proceedings for subsequent "ear-tuning" (or familiarization), as well as for providing opportunities for review of linguistic structures and content. Replay of recorded L2 speech helps learners "work out what is being said as a prerequisite to understanding what is being meant" (Lynch 2002:47). Considered within the Information Processing approach to SLA, repetition can enhance noticing and contribute to automatization, by facilitating faster processing of input, and the ability to process longer segments in "working memory." Video-recording television programs of different genres, especially programs which provide simultaneous closed captioning (or movies with subtitles) can also provide a useful source for listening practice.

Academic listening

Academic listening requires much of the same L2 linguistic knowledge as was listed above for academic reading: a large recognition vocabulary of both basic and subject-specific terms; complex sentence structure; and organizational features at sentence and discourse levels that distinguish new from old information and highlight important content. In addition, academic listening often requires ability to process pronunciation by speakers of different native and nonnative varieties of the language which can be especially challenging for L2 learners. Tape-recording lectures and other relatively non-reciprocal listening activities is useful for advanced as well as beginning students in such contexts, both for "ear-tuning" and for content review. It often takes several weeks for even advanced L2 learners to understand all of the input they need from lectures and other oral events if they have not had recent extensive experience with listening activities; recordings allow for recovery of information that might otherwise be lost, and for recontextualization of key vocabulary that has been noted for subsequent definition or elaboration.

As with reading, development of advanced academic listening proficiency requires extensive exposure to oral, academic text. Unlike reading, listening proficiency can usually not be maintained at a high level without continuing L2 oral input.

Productive activities

Productive activities for language use involve essentially the same top-down and bottom-up processes as those for reception. Production (like comprehension) of written or spoken language requires prior knowledge of vocabulary, morphology, phonology, syntax, and discourse structure to access words and combine them into phrases, clauses, and longer units of text. The relatively limited knowledge of L2 learners at early language learning levels can cause problems in production (as well as interpretation) of meaning, although productive and receptive abilities are in some ways independent of one another. In top-down processing, prior knowledge of content is the substance of information that a writer or speaker wishes to communicate; knowledge of context accounts for writers' and speakers' ability to select from potential linguistic options those which are appropriate to a specific communicative situation, including what should (or should not) be written or said next; prior knowledge of culture includes cultural conventions for language use.

Writing ordinarily presumes ability to read (even if only to interpret or review what one has produced), and speaking usually occurs in contexts which also involve listening and in which appropriateness of what is said requires understanding of what others have said and prediction of how they will respond. The knowledge of language that can be accessed for production is only a subset of what may be used for interpretation of language that is used by others; i.e. receptive competence always exceeds productive competence.

Writing and speaking differ from reading and listening in referring primarily to constructing one's own linguistic forms rather than interpreting what others write or say. Key differences between the two productive activities are that (1) writing is typically addressed to readers and speaking to listeners (though written text may be read aloud, and spoken text may be transcribed and read later), (2) writing usually allows time for planning and editing of production while speaking is often unplanned and requires "online" or "real-time" processing, and (3) writing is more likely than is speaking to be disassociated from the immediate time and place of production and from a specific audience. Some L2 learners consider writing to be the easier of these two skills to acquire because it allows them time to consciously access and edit language elements at different levels, but many learners find speaking easier at least in part because it allows them to seek clarification and other types of interactional support from cooperative partners in communication.

Writing

Writing is the most important productive activity for L2 learners to develop if they will use the language for academic purposes, or in certain types of service functions (e.g. providing reports to supervisors or clients). Writing is a common medium for testing knowledge in much of the world – including knowledge of the L2 itself, even within instructional programs that emphasize oral production. L2 speakers who pursue degrees in L2-medium universities typically must display a high level of writing proficiency through standardized entrance examinations and writing samples that are evaluated by admissions committees. Once enrolled in programs, such students must complete papers and other written assignments for many of their classes, and essay examinations are commonly used to judge student progress. Graduate degrees usually require writing extended texts (theses or dissertations), and many disciplines expect advanced students and graduates to publish their work in L2-medium journals and books.

Many professions and occupations also require a high level of L2 proficiency in writing for purposes of formal correspondence or for preparing applications and reports, whether the written texts address L1-speaking individuals and institutions or target speakers of different native languages in multilingual settings. Advanced L2 ability is also required for journalistic and creative purposes when writers wish to reach a wider audience.

Functions of L2 writing may include composing informal letters and e-mail if learners want or need to communicate with speakers of the language outside of an immediate interactional context, and daily life in some highly literate societies may necessitate at least limited L2 writing ability. However, L2 writing tasks outside of academic and professional situations typically do not have the same demanding standards for accuracy in production as do the more formal contexts of academic writing.

In addition to fulfilling academic and interpersonal functions, the process of writing itself is potentially important because of how it may contribute to successful L2 learning. We saw in an earlier discussion of Information Processing (Chapter 4) that meaningful language output facilitates SLA in several ways (e.g. Swain and Lapkin 1995). These notably include:

- Generating input.
- Enhancing fluency by furthering development of automaticity through practice.
- Helping learners notice gaps in their own knowledge as they are forced to visibly encode concepts in L2 forms, which may lead them to give more attention to relevant information.

- Allowing learners to test hypotheses they have formulated as part of their developing linguistic systems, with opportunity for monitoring and revision.
- Providing opportunities for others to comment on problems and give corrective feedback.

Because writers must express ideas without recourse to objects and events in their own immediate physical environment or that of their reader(s), or to gestures and other nonverbal means of communication, and without reliance on immediate feedback or hearer cooperation to fill in gaps, writing can potentially push learners closer to the limits of their current level of linguistic knowledge than can speech. We have already seen from a **functional** approach to SLA (Chapter 3) that increased reliance on language structure over situational context to express meaning characterizes progressive change in learners' interlanguage systems. It seems likely that pushing the limits of linguistic knowledge in written production contributes to SLA by stimulating syntactic development.

The need for interaction of other domains of communicative competence with language knowledge is evident when we consider some of the steps that are involved in proficient writing:

- Formulating mental concepts that are to be expressed centrally requires **content knowledge**.
- Recognizing what content will be relevant for intended readers, and what will be shared versus new information, requires **context knowledge**.
- Constructing text within socially defined conventions of expression (including selecting linguistic forms and organization patterns that are appropriate for the topic, purpose, and audience) also requires other aspects of **culture knowledge**.

As in the receptive activities of reading and listening, knowledge of content, context, and culture can partially compensate for limited knowledge of L2 language elements in writing. However, writing is probably the most dependent of the four language activities on linguistic knowledge.

Beginning L2 writing

As is the case for developing reading ability, learners whose L1 is represented in a different orthographic system from the L2 need to learn symbols for encoding the target language as an early step in acquisition. Adding ability to use a new alphabetic system (as when an English L1 speaker is learning to write Thai or Arabic), a new syllabic system (e.g. Japanese), or a new logographic system (e.g. Chinese) requires extensive practice to develop automaticity. Some learners begin with the low-level task of copying (even tracing over) words and phrases that they recognize by sight, or recording graphically something that they hear spoken. Knowledge of what symbols should be used to represent specific words is part of vocabulary knowledge, along with the meaning, pronunciation, and grammatical features of words.

Transfer of effective language-specific writing processes that have been acquired in L1 to L2 is not possible until a threshold level of L2 structural knowledge has been reached. However, the content knowledge for formulating concepts to be expressed and the context knowledge for deciding relevance and appropriateness are not language-specific and thus may be accessed even when knowledge of L2 linguistic elements is very limited. More complex thinking can be involved in composition if these domains are initially associated with L1 linguistic structure and then encoded (insofar as possible) into L2. This allows attention to be focused on content and context (since L1 linguistic forms can be accessed automatically), and then shifted consciously to L2 forms of expression.

Many L2 learners feel more secure if they are given a model to follow in early stages of writing, so that they only need to make minimal linguistic changes and substitutions in what someone else has produced to construct their "own" text. At a very early level, for instance, they might be asked to revise the account of an event to include multiple participants rather than a single participant, or to change the time frame from present to past. This type of tightly controlled writing exercise was popular when behaviorism was the dominant theory of SLA and "free" writing was thought to present occasions for production errors and thus "bad" habit formation. Controlled writing exercise has some value in developing automaticity in accessing and producing mechanical elements, but it does not push learners to the limits of their current level of linguistic knowledge in a way that is likely to benefit interlanguage development, and it may create an overreliance on following models which inhibits individual expression at later stages of development. A few students remain so dependent on following models in L2 writing that they approach or cross the border of "plagiarism" when they are in settings where more independence and originality are mandated.

Academic writing

Effective academic writing requires considerable knowledge of linguistic elements at levels of vocabulary, morphology and syntax, mechanics of orthographic representation and punctuation, and conventions related to style and organization of presentation that are appropriate for the target genre. Command of a relatively formal register is needed, and accuracy in production is usually very important. The activity has received a great deal of attention in recent years from perspectives of Contrastive Rhetoric (mentioned above in the section on Discourse), needs assessment (e.g. Leki and Carson 1997), and the relationship between L2 academic writing research and pedagogy (e.g. Swales and Feak 1994). Courses exclusively devoted to academic L2 writing are now commonly offered in universities and language institutes, and many teacher training programs schedule a methods course which focuses on this activity. Assessment of writing is also now included in standardized tests of language proficiency, including the TOEFL Test of Written English and the British Council's IELTS writing sub-test, as well as in general tests such as the Graduate Record Examination (GRE).

The relatively formal register needed for most academic writing may conflict with the relatively informal register that is often emphasized in "communicative" language teaching. This underlines the need for teachers and students to consider *why* an additional language is needed before determining priorities for *what* must be learned. It is probably in the best interest of most English L2 learners of the world to aim for a formal register before an informal one (neither is inherently more difficult). It is perfectly possible (as the experience of generations of language learners around the world has shown) to become proficient in writing a language well with little experience in either hearing it or speaking it.

Speaking

Speaking (in conjunction with listening) is a very important area of activity for L2 learners if they will be using the language for interpersonal purposes, whether these are primarily social or instrumental. There is need for speaking in virtually all situations where L2 learners participate in the L2 speech community: tourists generally need to ask directions and seek information about hotels and entertainment; immigrants need to shop for goods, seek services, and describe symptoms in case of health problems; foreign students and other temporary residents need to negotiate transactions for housing, utilities, and currency exchange, as well as to express themselves in an academic or professional speech genre.

The language knowledge involved in bottom-up processes for speech production includes appropriate vocabulary, features of pronunciation, grammatical patterns that will convey intended meaning, and understanding of discourse structures that will provide cohesion and coherence within a conversation or other spoken communicative event. The top-down processes simultaneously involved in speech production require content knowledge about a topic, cultural knowledge that informs determination of proprieties and provides macrosocial context for expression, and knowledge of microsocial context such as the significance of the immediate communicative activity, speaker role and relationship to addressees, and appropriateness conditions (e.g. what must be said, what may be said, and what should be left unsaid).

As with listening, speaking tasks can be classified on a continuum from reciprocal to non-reciprocal communication. Participation in face-to-face interpersonal interaction is at the reciprocal end of this continuum, and delivering lectures or conference presentations is close to the non-reciprocal end. Reciprocal communication requires learners to listen as well as to speak, and to collaborate in the negotiation of meaning. Unlike listening, non-reciprocal spoken communication places lighter requirements on the speaker for processing "online" or in real time than reciprocal, since there is usually time for preplanning. Indeed, the L2 learner may even read aloud a paper which has been written beforehand.

A linguistic approach to SLA that is commonly used to account for speaking phenomena is Functionalism (Chapter 3), which considers the development of learner language to be motivated and furthered by interactive language use. Psychological approaches (Chapter 4) explain L2 speaking proficiency largely as degree of automaticity in processing. A major social approach relates to L2 variation (Chapter 5), which explores how contextual dimensions influence quality of learner language production. From this social perspective, fluency and accuracy in speech activities may be attributed to how much attention the speaker is paying to linguistic form, intellectual demands of a task, level of formality, setting of interaction (e.g. public or private), and relationship of speaker and addressee, as well as to linguistic contexts.

Speech acts

An important concept for SLA which was originated in the field of philosophy (Searle 1969) is that language use accomplishes speaker goals by means of utterances which request something, apologize, promise, deny, express emotion, compliment, complain, and so forth. Utterances which fulfill such functions are called **speech acts**, and they constitute most of what is said by people in the course of interpersonal communication. The same acts can be accomplished in the use of any language with others who understand that language, but the actual forms and conventions that can be used are of course language-specific. Learning how to perform these acts in the L2 is central to language learning, and knowing when to deploy them is basic to what we have called **pragmatic competence**.

A variety of linguistic forms may be selected to accomplish any one speaker goal, with appropriate choice for a particular situation requiring cultural and contextual knowledge. For example, a student who wishes to borrow another student's notes to study for a test might say (in English):

Give me your notes.
Please let me make a copy of your notes.
You are a much better note-taker than I. Would you help me prepare for this test?
Could I take a little peek at your notes before the test?

Appropriate selection from among these and other possibilities depends on the relative social status of the speaker and addressee, the closeness or distance of their relationship, and the degree of imposition the request involves. Conditions do not receive the same weight in different cultures and do not receive the same interpretation, so the appropriate L2 selection of linguistic form is not a simple translation from what would be appropriate in L1. Acquisition of this aspect of L2 communicative competence requires adding new knowledge of culture and context. (Research methods, findings, and implications of Speech Acts for the study of SLA are surveyed in Cohen 1996.)

Other aspects of speaking competence

Other aspects of communicative competence which need to be acquired especially for successful participation in conversational speech activities include the following:

Knowledge of conversational structure. Possible differences in rules for turn-taking were discussed above in the section on Discourse: some languages consider interruptions, overlaps, and simultaneous speaking to be appropriate; some consider a period of silence between speakers to be a necessary condition for "polite" interaction. There are also linguistic and cultural differences in the sequence in which turns of talk are expected to occur (e.g. according to age or social status), and in production of **back-channel signals** (e.g. verbal or nonverbal indications by a listener of comprehension or lack of it). Conversational structure also involves rules for topic maintenance and shift, and for which utterances should be tied as **adjacency pairs** (e.g. whether a question should be immediately followed by a response, or a compliment by an acknowledgment, and especially what response or acknowledgment is appropriate or inappropriate).

Knowledge of contextualization cues. **Contextualization cues** (Gumperz 1977) are elements of communication that allow people to express and interpret meaning beyond the referential meaning that the surface structure of messages provides. Cues may involve any of the linguistic knowledge we have considered, including speaker selection of vocabulary and pronunciation, prosody (intonation and stress), and rhythmic patterns (pauses and stops). Beyond this level, they involve sociocultural knowledge that matches linguistic forms to culture-specific expectations and allows appropriate interpretation of meaning within the contexts of use. People rely on such cues to make inferences about what is not explicitly said, and to identify speakers' expressive overtones. Because knowledge of contextualization cues depends on cultural and communicative experience, this is a potential minefield of significant misunderstanding for L2 learners and others they are interacting with. Successful acquisition is most likely to be realized in situations where learners have opportunity for feedback from culturally sensitive native speakers, since the cues cannot be described abstractly and are elusive targets for formal instruction.

Knowledge of communication strategies. A final aspect of communicative competence we will consider here is learner knowledge of how to compensate for limitations in their L2 linguistic resources, or **communication strategies**. This includes knowledge of how to assess and repair misunderstanding, how to make use of interlocutor collaboration, and how to sustain interpersonal interaction. The basic problem that the strategies address may be formulated for early stages of SLA as: "how do you manage to communicate when you have limited command of a language?" (Bialystok 1990:vi). Use of the term "strategies" implies that means of remediation for the problem may be conscious and intentional, although they need not be.

The types of strategies that were suggested by Elaine Tarone (1977), along with a brief description of each, is given in 6.10. Knowledge of communication strategies is particularly important for early L2 learners who want and need to participate in speaking activities because they allow talk to continue in a situation when it might otherwise cease. Continuation of talk, in turn, provides learners with more input, more practice, and more opportunity for collaborative construction of meaning.

6.10 Typology of communication strategies		
1 Avoidance		
	(a) Topic avoidance	Avoiding reference to a subject for which the learner lacks necessary vocabulary
	(b) Message abandonment	Giving up on a topic because it is too difficult to talk about
2 Paraphrase		
	(a) Approximation	Using a word that is not correct, but that refers to a similar object or event
	(b) Word coinage	Making up a new word or phrase to describe an object or event
	(c) Circumlocution	Describing an object or event instead of using an appropriate vocabulary item
3 Conscious transfer		
	(a) Literal translation	Translating word for word from the L1
	(b) Language switch	Inserting L1 words or phrases into L2
4 Appeal for assistance		Asking a native speaker, looking a word up in a dictionary, or consulting some other authority
5 Mime		Using gestures or other nonverbal means to refer to an object or event

Chapter summary

Second language communicative competence involves both knowledge of linguistic elements and the knowledge that is required for appropriate L2 use in different contexts. In this chapter, we have surveyed the integrated roles of linguistic, cognitive, and social knowledge in the interpretation and expression of meaning; we have looked in more depth at components of language knowledge that must be accounted for in academic and interactional competence; and we have explored what knowledge accounts for learner ability to participate in L2 activities and how it is acquired.

What must be acquired in learning an L2 can vary as much as the goals for learning. It is possible to develop fluent reading ability in an L2 with only a limited awareness of its pronunciation or rules for appropriate social use, though a knowledge of grammar and vocabulary are determinative. At the other extreme, the achievement of fluent speaking as interactional ability can take place without a knowledge of reading and writing, but again the role of grammar and vocabulary are significant. However, the grammatical forms and structures as well as the vocabulary needed for successful informal interpersonal communication can be vastly different from those required for advanced academic study, using the L2 as a medium for learning complex content and writing to meet academic requirements. Curricula for teaching L2 should be differentiated according to the relevant goals of learning, since a "one-size-fits-all" approach, such as a purely communicative approach, may do a serious disservice to learners whose primary need is to develop academic reading, writing, and listening skills.

Learning an L2 can be facilitated or made more difficult by degrees of similarity or difference between L1 and L2 phonology, grammar, vocabulary, system of writing, and rules for social use. A Japanese or Korean speaker already familiar with borrowed Chinese characters will find it easier to gain fluency in reading and writing Chinese than will an English speaker familiar only with the Roman alphabet (even though all three languages are equally unrelated to Chinese). Conversely, while an English speaker will find the acquisition of French or Spanish facilitated by similar alphabets and numerous shared vocabulary (particularly in more advanced technical and academic fields), as well as grammatical parallels, a Chinese, Japanese, or Korean learner of English or French will find them equally daunting since there are few recognizable cognates and the alphabets are equally unfamiliar.

Learners of an L2 for academic purposes need to focus on building receptive processing ability in listening and reading, though this can be greatly aided by using familiar content knowledge to help interpret the linguistic input. L2 learners with primarily interpersonal interactional goals need to develop very different abilities, emphasizing rapid online processing of often highly elliptical and sometimes fragmented speech, as well as a different core of "everyday" vocabulary and rules for appropriate social usage which may be encoded in subtle or obvious lexical and intonational ways.

Activities
Questions for self-study
1. ———— competence encompasses knowledge required of learners who will use the L2 mostly in face to face contact with other speakers, whereas ———— competence encompasses the knowledge required of learners who will use the L2 mostly as a tool for learning, research and scholarly exchange.
2. Receptive activities, such as ———— and ————, function primarily in processing input. The ability for productive activities, such as ————and ————, usually follows the development of receptive ability.

3. Halliday and Hasan (1976) discuss types of cohesion (reference, substitution, ellipsis, conjunction and lexical) used in English. Read the following paragraph and underline all the cohesion devices used. Then classify each device per Halliday and Hasan's typology.

   Second language communicative competence involves both knowledge of linguistic elements and the knowledge that is required for appropriate L2 use in different contexts. In this chapter, we have surveyed the integrated roles of linguistic, cognitive, and social knowledge in the interpretation and expression of meaning; we have looked in more depth at components of language knowledge that must be accounted for in academic and interactional competence; and we have explored what knowledge accounts for learner ability to participate in L2 activities and how it is acquired.

4. Bottom-up processing requires prior knowledge of the language system. List at least one way that processing involves each of the following levels of language: vocabulary, morphology, phonology, syntax, and discourse.

5. Top-down processing utilizes prior knowledge of essential components of communicative competence (content, context, and culture). List at least one way for each that content, context, and culture help with top-down processing.

6. List at least three conditions under which beginning L2 learners are most likely to be capable of making sense out of auditory input.

Active learning

1. Two types of communicative competence are academic competence and interpersonal competence. In your own studies of an L2, which one of these was stressed? Thinking of your goals for that L2, was it the right one for you? Give examples from your life to explain why.

2. The level of L1 reading ability is a very strong predictor of success in L2 reading ability. Has this been true in your life? What is your attitude toward reading in L1 versus in L2? Why do you feel this way?

3. Grabe lists the following four functions of reading in academic settings on p. 38: reading to find information, reading for general understanding, reading to learn, and reading to critique and evaluate. Which of these functions do you use in your L2? Which ones are more and less challenging for you? More or less interesting? Why?

4. Listening, speaking, reading and writing are seen as essential activities for L2 use in an academic context, and often in interpersonal communication as well. Do you feel any of these skill areas are stronger in your own L2 use? Why do you think that is?

5. We have seen thus far that some L2 learners have a higher degree of success than others. Taking into consideration linguistic, psychological and social factors, what do you see as most crucial to the success of L2 learning? Why?

Further reading

Hinkel, E. (ed.) (1999). *Culture in Second Language Teaching and Learning*. Cambridge: Cambridge University Press.

   Part I, "Culture, interaction and learning," contains three chapters relevant to competence and use of L2 in the classroom. Chapter 1 discusses some implications of interaction between teachers and students of different cultural backgrounds. Chapter 2 treats the learning of a second culture from a cognitive perspective. Chapter 3 also explores interactions between people of different cultural backgrounds, specifically studying if and when L2 speakers understand certain implications of conversation in the target language.

Rose, K. R. & Kasper, G. (eds.) (2001). *Pragmatics in Language Teaching*. Cambridge: Cambridge University Press.

In this volume, Rose and Kasper have concentrated on the question of the viability of teaching and testing pragmatics, with studies all relating to pragmatics in second language teaching and testing (including sections on the theoretical and empirical background of pragmatics, issues in classroom-based learning of pragmatics, the effects of instruction in pragmatics, and testing pragmatics).

Saville-Troike, M. (1996). The ethnography of communication. In S. L. McKay & N. H. Hornberger (eds.), *Sociolinguistics and Language Teaching* (pp. 351–82). Cambridge: Cambridge University Press.

Saville-Troike presents Dell Hymes' (1966) notion of the ethnography of communication, including discussion of appropriate situations to use different registers and features of language, and different areas of competence necessary for successful L2 communication.

Bialystok, E. & Hakuta, K. (1994). *In Other Words: The Science and Psychology of Second-Language Acquisition*. New York: Basic Books.

Bialystok and Hakuta's final chapter, "Last word," treats the fact that the learners' diverse experiences and goals produce different results in their L2 acquisition. Further, their differences in goals and outcomes cannot be classified as more or less successful, only different.

Swan, M. & Smith, B. (eds.) (2001). *Learner English: A Teacher's Guide to Interference and Other Problems*. Cambridge: Cambridge University Press.

This book offers insight on common characteristics of English as it is learned and produced by native speakers of a variety of other languages.

Celce-Murcia, M. & Olshtain, E. (2000). *Discourse and Context in Language Teaching: A Guide for Language Teachers*. Cambridge: Cambridge University Press.

Part 1 presents background in discourse analysis and pragmatics in discourse analysis. Part 2 covers some components of language knowledge with chapters on phonology, grammar, and vocabulary. Part 3 treats receptive and productive activities, with chapters on listening, reading, writing, speaking, and an epilogue about the integration of these four areas.

Flowerdew, J. (ed.) (1994). *Academic Listening: Research Perspectives*. Cambridge: Cambridge University Press.

While this text is not geared towards beginners to the field of SLA, this seminal volume presents original research on academic listening in a second language from various perspectives (ethnography, discourse analysis, application of theory to pedagogy).

McKay, S. L. (1996). Literacy and literacies. In S. L. McKay & N. H. Hornberger (eds.), *Sociolinguistics and Language Teaching*, pp. 421–45. Cambridge: Cambridge University Press.

This article presents literacy as an individual skill and a social construct, and it recognizes the multiple kinds of literacy possible and valued in different communities and aspects of communication.

Hinkel, E. (ed.) (1999). *Culture in Second Language Teaching and Learning*. Cambridge: Cambridge University Press.

Part II of this edition focuses on how culture influences writing. Chapter 4 questions whether nonnative speakers of English should learn to write according to the Western norms underlying Anglo-American academic writing (such as Aristotelian logic). In Chapter 5, the author uses quantitative research to present how L1 and L2 users try to create a sense of objectivity and credibility in their academic writing. Chapter 6 is an ethnographic report of how culture is treated in ESL writing classrooms.

7 L2 learning and teaching

CHAPTER PREVIEW

WHAT exactly does the L2 learner come to know? *HOW* does the learner acquire L2 knowledge? *WHY* are some learners more successful than others? While there are some significant differences of opinion, and while there is much yet to discover, there is also much that we now know about SLA. Our review of answers to these questions will be followed by a discussion of what we know about the most advanced state of L2 learning (or "near-native" competence), including what features are likely to be mastered last, and how ultimate achievement levels relate to individual and social goals. The chapter concludes with a brief set of important implications for L2 learning and teaching that we may draw from the findings we have summarized here.

Integrating perspectives

Linguistic, psychological, and social perspectives on SLA all address the basic *what*, *how*, and *why* questions that we have been considering throughout this book, but as we have seen, they have each tended to focus primarily on one question over the others. These disciplinary perspectives are listed in 7.1, along with the priorities that scholars working within them have generally set in relation to SLA.

7.1 Disciplinary priorities			
	Linguistic	Psychological	Social
1	What?	How?	Why?
2	How?	Why?	What?
3	Why?	What?	How?

There are significant differences of opinion within each perspective as well as between them, depending on subdisciplinary orientations. Still, it is possible at this stage in the development of SLA theory and research to report some answers to our questions with considerable confidence. For others, we should remain more tentative. I will integrate findings from the three perspectives as much as possible, but I give greatest weight to linguistic contributions in answer to *what*, to psychological contributions in anser to *how*, and to social contributions in answer to *why*.

What exactly does the L2 learner come to know?

- *A system of knowledge about a second language* which goes well beyond what could possibly have been taught. There is significant overlap with first language knowledge, especially (1) in underlying rules or principles that languages have in common and (2) in the potentials of language to make meaning. The L2 system is never exactly like the learner's L1, however, nor is it ever exactly the same as that of its native speakers.
- *Patterns of recurrent elements* that comprise components of L2-specific knowledge: vocabulary (lexicon), morphology (word structure), phonology (sound system), syntax (grammar), and discourse (ways to connect sentences and organize information). The amount of overlap with L1 knowledge depends on the genetic or typological relationship of the two languages and on whether there has been borrowing or other influence between them. Exactly which elements are acquired within each of these components depends in large measure on learner motivation and on other circumstances of learning.
- *How to encode particular concepts in the L2*, including grammatical notions of time, number of referents, and the semantic role of elements (e.g. whether subject or object).

- *Pragmatic competence*, or knowledge of how to interpret and convey meaning in contexts of social interaction.
- *Means for using the L2* in communicative activities: listening, speaking, reading, writing. Many learners develop only an oral channel (listening, speaking), or only a written channel (reading, writing), without the other; neither channel is a necessary precondition for the other, though they may reinforce one another. Minimally, language learning requires means for participation in at least one receptive activity (listening or reading); otherwise, necessary input for SLA would not be available.
- *How to select among multiple language systems*, and how to switch between languages in particular social contexts and for particular purposes. What is acquired thus includes a system of knowledge about how to process multiple languages: understanding of multilingual language processing is also highly relevant to our understanding of how languages are learned.
- *Communicative competence: all of the above*, plus social and cultural knowledge required for appropriate use and interpretation of L2 forms. Inclusion and definition of communicative competence as a goal or outcome of L2 learning is highly variable, depending on macrosocial contexts of learning (discussed in Chapter 5) as well as on linguistic, psychological, and interactional factors.

A basic disagreement among different linguistic perspectives comes in considering whether the system of knowledge about a second language is primarily (1) an abstract system of underlying rules or principles, (2) a system of linguistic patterns and structures, or (3) a means of structuring information and a system of communication. This disagreement stems from different assumptions about the nature of language and language study that arise from different theoretical approaches. These differing assumptions yield different questions to be explored, different methods of inquiry, and different interpretations of findings. Resolution of the disagreement is not likely in our lifetimes, and perhaps it would not even be desirable. I have suggested that we recognize these differences as being like different views we get of Mars through seeing it with different color filters. They complement one another and all are needed to gain a full-spectrum picture of the multidimensional nature of SLA.

Looking to future directions, neurolinguists in particular have made important advancements in exploration of what is being acquired in a physical sense: specifically, changes in the architecture of the brain that accompany SLA. Although this line of inquiry is far from new, there is much that is not yet known, and findings thus far have not been well integrated with those of scholars who take different approaches to the study of L2 phenomena. Modern brain-imaging capabilities, especially as they are applied to greater numbers of L2 learners and at progressive stages in their L2 development, offer exciting prospects for future discovery.

How does the learner acquire L2 knowledge?

- *Innate capacity.* While there is disagreement over whether capacity for language learning is basically different from learning any other complex domain of knowledge, it is clear that some innate capacity must be posited to account for learning. Language learners are not merely passive recipients of "stimuli." There is a creative force involved in language development (and other domains of learning) which must be an innate endowment.
- *Application of prior knowledge.* The initial state of L2 includes knowledge of L1 (and Language in general), and the processes of SLA include interpretation of the new language in terms of that knowledge. There is also application of what has been acquired as part of general cognitive development, as well as of all prior social experience.
- *Processing of language input.* The critical need for L2 input in SLA is agreed on, although its roles in acquisition receive differential definition and weight in accounts from alternative perspectives and orientations. The processing of input in itself is a necessary factor in acquisition.
- *Interaction.* Processing of L2 input in interactional situations is facilitative, and some think also causative, of SLA. Benefits come from collaborative expression, modified input, feedback (including correction), and negotiation of meaning. SLA is likely to be greatly inhibited if learners are isolated from opportunities for use. Social perspectives generally hold that SLA benefits from the active engagement of learners in interaction, or participation in communicative events.
- *Restructuring of the L2 knowledge system.* SLA occurs progressively through a series of systematic stages. Development of L2 knowledge does not manifest itself in a smooth cline of linguistic performance, but rather in one which sometimes shows abrupt changes in the interlanguage system. This indicates reorganization takes place from time to time during the process of SLA, presumably as perceived L2 input cannot be accommodated within the learners' existing system of knowledge. This restructuring is a creative process, driven by inner forces in interaction with environmental factors, and motivated both by L1 knowledge and by input from the L2.
- *Mapping of relationships or associations* between linguistic functions and forms. L2 acquisition (like L1 acquisition) involves increasing reliance on grammatical structure and reduced reliance on context and lexical items. This development is driven by communicative need and use, as well as by awareness of the probability that a particular linguistic form represents a particular meaning.
- *Automatization.* While simplistic notions of habit formation are no longer accepted as explanations for language acquisition, frequency of input as well as practice in processing input and output are widely recognized determinants of L2 development. Frequency and practice

lead to automaticity in processing, and they free learners' processing capacity for new information and higher-order performance needs. Automatization is an incremental achievement upon which efficient and effective engagement in all language activities ultimately depends.

A basic disagreement within both psychological and linguistic perspectives comes in considering language learning as primarily a process of acquiring (1) language-specific systems of rules, (2) very general principles with options to be selected, or (3) increasing strength of associations between linguistic forms and meaning. Again, this disagreement derives from very basic differences in theoretical orientations and is not likely to be resolved.

Looking to future directions, the growing recognition of the complex nature of SLA, and of individual and situational differences, promises acceptance of more complex answers to the question of how language is learned. Scholars may not need to decide whether general or language-specific learning forces are involved in SLA, for example, but how types of learning complement each other and interact.

Why are some learners more successful than others?

- *Social context.* An early activity in this book asked you to identify yourself as a good or poor second language learner, and to speculate why that is so. Most of you probably gave reasons which relate to social context and experience, and you were quite right. Features of social context which affect degree of success include the status of L1 and L2, boundary and identity factors within and between the L1 and L2 speech communities, and institutional forces and constraints. These macrosocial factors influence L2 learning primarily because of their impact on attitude and opportunity. They also determine whether the L2 is being learned as a second language, a foreign language, an auxiliary language, or a language for specific purposes.
- *Social experience.* Quantity and quality of L2 input and interaction are determined by social experience, and both have significant influence on ultimate success in L2 learning. Because social variables are complex and often impossible to control, there is very little experimental evidence to support this conclusion. However, correlational and anecdotal evidence abounds, and it is quite convincing.
- *Relationship of L1 and L2.* All languages are learnable, but not all L2s are equally easy for speakers of particular L1s to acquire. Knowledge of L1 is an important component of all L2 competence in its initial state, but the genetic, typological, and historical relationships of L1 and L2 will yield differential possibilities for positive transfer of parameter settings and surface-level features, including vocabulary and writing system. This remains an underexplored area of SLA, but there is little question that it is significant.

- *Age.* There is a common belief that children are more successful L2 learners than adults, but as we noted (Chapter 4), the evidence for this is equivocal. Younger learners generally have an advantage in brain plasticity, in not being so analytical, in (usually) having fewer inhibitions and weaker group identity, and in having more years to learn the language before ultimate proficiency is judged. Older learners generally have an advantage in learning capacity, in analytic ability, in pragmatic skills, in greater knowledge of their L1, and in real-world knowledge. It is possible for older learners to achieve near-native competence in an L2, but less likely.
- *Aptitude.* Learners differ in capacity to discriminate and process auditory input, to identify patterns and make generalizations, and to store linguistic elements in memory. We may conclude that aptitude is an important predictor of differential success in L2 learning, but it is not completely deterministic.
- *Motivation.* Motivation largely determines the level of effort which learners expend at various stages in their L2 development, and it is often a key to ultimate level of proficiency. No particular type of motivation (e.g. integrative or instrumental) appears to have any inherent advantage over the other in terms of L2 achievement.
- *Instruction.* Quality of instruction clearly makes a difference in formal contexts of L2 learning, although this book has not attempted to evaluate teaching methods. What is known from linguistic, psychological, and social perspectives on SLA, however, does not strongly support any one instructional approach over others, despite the claims of proponents. The array of social circumstances and individual learner factors which we have explored indeed suggests that there can be no one "best" method that will fit all, and a combination of different methods is undoubtedly the wisest approach.

Basic disagreement remains in the definition of relative "success" in L2 learning. Without common criteria for evaluation, drawing general conclusions is very difficult, since the definition of criteria for "success" (along with determining questions to be explored, appropriate methods of assessment, and interpretations of findings) depends on theoretical orientation. Any answers to this question must be considered within the disciplinary framework in which it is posed. From a social perspective, it becomes particularly problematic when "success" is measured only in relation to native speaker norms, since there are significant ethical issues to consider when this is used as a determining factor in access to educational and economic advancement.

Looking to future directions, we can anticipate more relativistic criteria for the definition of "success," and even more consideration of the complex interaction of social, psychological, and linguistic criteria in research on L2 learning. A crucial element for guiding developments in this direction is the recognition of SLA as a necessarily interdisciplinary field of study.

Approaching near-native competence

The judgment that L2 learners have approached or achieved "near-native" or "native-like" competence means that there is little or no perceptible difference between their language performance and that of native speakers. Because one's L2 system is never exactly the same as the native speaker's (even if we cannot readily perceive differences), most of us would not consider the final state of L2 development to be completely "native," although we may allow for some rare exceptions.

The most likely level of linguistic production to retain some identifiably "foreign" feature is pronunciation, especially if L2 learning began after the age of twelve or so. Next most likely is that learners will have to select from a more limited lexical repertoire than do native speakers of the same educational level, will not use words with the same probability of occurrence in the same phrasal units (e.g. collocations), and will not recognize connotations and allusions which require cultural information and experience. Native interpretation of variability is also unlikely ever to be acquired in L2, including the social meaning of variants and appropriate choice for different registers. For example, while the English adjective *big* may be perfectly "correct" semantically and grammatically, it may sound "odd" in written academic contexts where a native speaker would use *large, major, great, considerable, significant,* or some other synonym.

Among the last grammatical forms to be mastered in English L2 are the choice of complements to follow specific verbs (e.g. the use of *for . . . to* after *like,* as in *I like for her to sing* but not after *enjoy,* as in **I enjoy for her to sing*), article selection (*the, a,* or nothing) before nouns, and appropriate use of prepositions. The residual nature of these problems cannot be explained in terms of order of exposure or frequency of input, since articles and prepositions are among the first words encountered and have the highest frequency in the language. I cannot find convincing evidence to account for this phenomenon, but I believe that these errors remain persistent in large part because they resist conscious, "logical" treatment. When nonnative uses of articles and prepositions are pointed out to them, advanced English L2 students may ask why one form rather than another is used. The only genuinely valid answer, "Because it is," appeals to grammaticality judgments that are based on a level of intuition which few L2 learners can be expected to attain.

Older L2 students who do approach "near-native" competence almost surely have benefitted from extensive and varied input, feedback which includes some correction and focus on grammatical form, and very high levels of motivation. At the same time, we must recognize that many intelligent, hard-working, highly-motivated students will not approach this level of competence.

It is important for language teachers, in particular, to accept the fact that "native-like" production is neither intended nor desired by many learners whose goals for L2 use do not include identification with native speakers of the language nor membership in its native speech communities. Indeed, adopting this goal may be considered "imperialistic" in many social and political settings (discussed in Chapters 3 and 5), and in any case, is certainly unrealistic for most beginning learners beyond the stage of puberty. To be valid, criteria for assessing relative L2 achievement must take into account the needs, goals, and circumstances of second language learners.

Implications for L2 learning and teaching

Although we have seen that knowledge of L2 goes well beyond what can be consciously learned and taught, we have also seen that (unlike L1) L2 acquisition usually requires intentional effort, and that a number of individual and social factors strongly affect ultimate outcomes. We cannot control most of these factors, but recognizing them can contribute to efficiency and effectiveness in second language development. As a starting point, our findings about SLA suggest the following general guidelines for L2 learning and teaching:

- Consider the goals that individuals and groups have for learning an additional language.
- Set priorities for learning/teaching that are compatible with those goals.
- Approach learning/teaching tasks with an appreciation of the multiple dimensions that are involved: linguistic, psychological, and social.
- Understand the potential strengths and limitations of particular learners and contexts for learning, and make use of them in adapting learning/teaching procedures.
- Be cautious in subscribing to any instructional approach which is narrowly focused or dogmatic. There is no one "best" way to learn or teach a second language.
- Recognize achievement in incremental progress. And be patient. Learning a language takes time.

Chapter summary

We conclude this book as we began, with an emphasis on the importance of taking multidisciplinary and interdisciplinary perspectives into account if we are to gain a full-spectrum picture of the processes involved in SLA. Linguistic perspectives have focused primarily on *what* is learned; psychological perspectives on *how* this knowledge is acquired; and social perspectives on *why* some learners are more successful than others. An integrated view across perspectives gives us a realistic impression of the complexity of processes and conditions involved in SLA, and it offers us a more complete and balanced understanding of these factors, and of their multiple interactions.

Answer guide to questions for self-study

Chapter 1
1. 1-B, 2-C, 3-D, 4-A
2. competence
3. performance

Chapter 2
1. Page 8 of Chapter 2 lists seven possible reasons.
2. phonemes
3. 1-C, 2-A, 3-B
4. L1-innate capacity
   L2-L1, world knowledge, interaction skills, possibly innate capacity
5. Input is necessary for both L1 and L2; social interaction is necessary for L1.
6. a. Children begin to learn their L1 at the same age, and in much the same way, whether it is English, Bengali, Korean, Swahili, or any other language in the world.
   b. If children had to actually learn the abstract rules of language, then only the smartest would ever learn to talk, and it would take several years more to learn L1 than it actually does.
   c. Children master the basic phonological and grammatical operations in their L1 by age five or six, regardless of what the language is.
   d. Children can understand and create novel utterances; they are not limited to repeating what they hear around them.
   e. There is a cut-off age for L1 acquisition, beyond which it can never be complete.

7. The internal focus seeks to account for speakers' internalized, underlying knowledge of language. The external focus emphasizes language use, including the functions of language which are realized in learners' production at different stages of development.

Chapter 3
1. a. Languages consist of recurrent elements which occur in regular patterns of relationships. Language is created according to rules or principles which speakers are usually unconscious of using if language was acquired in early childhood.
   b. Sequences of sounds or letters do not inherently possess meaning. These symbols of language have meaning because of a tacit agreement among the speakers of a language.
   c. Each language reflects the social requirements of the society that uses it. Although humans possess the potential to acquire an L1 because of their neurological makeup, that potential can be developed only through interaction with others in the society. We use language to communicate with others about the human experience.
2. 1-C, 2-D, 3-A, 4-B
3. 1-E, 2-C, 3-F, 4-B, 5-A, 6-D
4. fossilization
5. Performance is actual use of language in a specific instance, whereas competence is

the underlying knowledge of language we possess.

6. communication
7. a-IUO, b-FUO, c-NUO, d-FUO, e-IUO, f-NUO

Chapter 4

1. 1-B, 2-C, 3-A
2. speak; audio input
3. 1-B, 2-C, 3-A
4. Learners must notice or pay attention to input to make it available for processing. This kind of "noticed input" is called intake.
5. output
6. connectionist
7. integrative; instrumental

Chapter 5

1. 1-C, 2-A, 3-B
2. 1-A; it is more common to pronounce final "ing" as "ing" when it precedes a vowel or a pause in speech, and more common to pronounce it "in" when it precedes consonant sounds.
   1-C; the student may be fully aware of the grammatical rule but be unable to pronounce the consonant cluster in the final syllable of "walks" (/ks/).
   2-B; the child may use her language monitor more around her teacher.
   2-C; writing and speaking, being different cognitive activities, may be processed differently by this student.
   3-B; the child is unconsciously aware of a social difference between speaking with her classmate, a peer, and her teacher, a figure of authority.
3. Sociocultural
4. Zone of Proximal Development
5. Acculturation
6. additive; subtractive
7. formal; informal

Chapter 6

1. interpersonal; academic
2. listening and reading; speaking and writing
3. Second language communicative competence involves (1) both knowledge of linguistic elements (2) and the (3) knowledge (4) that is required for appropriate L2 use in different contexts. In this chapter, we have surveyed the integrated roles of linguistic (5) [ ], cognitive (5) [ ], (2) and social (3) knowledge in the interpretation (6) [ ] (2) and expression of meaning; (7) we have looked in more depth at components of language (3) knowledge (4) that must be accounted for in academic (8) [ ] (2) and interactional competence; (2) and (7) we have explored (9) what (3) knowledge accounts for learner ability to participate in L2 activities (2) and how (10) it is acquired.

    (1) Reference: *both*
    (2) Conjunction: *and*
    (3) Lexical: repetition of *knowledge*
    (4) Reference: *that*
    (5) Ellipsis: omission of *knowledge*
    (6) Ellipsis: omission of *of meaning*
    (7) Lexical: repetition of *we have __ed*
    (8) Ellipsis: omission of *competence*
    (9) Reference: *what*
    (10) Reference: *it*

4. *vocabulary*: needed to recognize words and to understand what they mean.
   morphology: needed to interpret complex lexical elements, as well as to perceive grammatical information that is carried by inflections.
   phonology: needed to recognize spoken words, to segment speech into grammatical units, and to relate written symbols to their spoken form.
   syntax: needed to recognize how words relate to one another, and how they are constituted as phrases and clauses.
   discourse: needed to interpret stretches of language that are longer than a single sentence.

5. *Content* knowledge is background knowledge about the topic that is being read about or listened to; new information is perceived and interpreted in relation to this base. *Context* knowledge includes information learned from what has already been read or heard in a specific text or situation, as well as an understanding of the writer's

or speaker's intentions and an overall understanding of the discourse pattern being used. It allows prediction of what is likely to follow, and how the information is likely to be organized. *Culture* knowledge includes an understanding of the wider social setting of the text. Because this knowledge is usually taken for granted by the writer or speaker, and the instructor in a classroom setting, this knowledge is rarely discussed explicitly. For that reason, it may not be available to L2 learners who did not grow up in that culture.

6. Five possible answers are listed on page 161 of this chapter.

Glossary

academic competence: The knowledge needed by learners who want to use the L2 primarily to learn about other subjects, or as a tool in scholarly research, or as a medium in a specific professional or occupational field.

Accommodation Theory: A framework for study of SLA that is based on the notion that speakers usually unconsciously change their pronunciation and even the grammatical complexity of sentences they use to sound more like whomever they are talking to.

acculturation: Learning the culture of the L2 community and adapting to those values and behavior patterns.

Acculturation Model: Schumann's (1978) theory that identifies group factors such as identity and status which determine social and psychological distance between learner and target language populations. He claims these influence outcomes of SLA. Also known as **Acculturation Theory**.

acquisition: Krashen's term for a subconscious process of SLA involving an innate language acquisition device (LAD) that is similar to the process which accounts for children's L1, in opposition to **learning**, which is conscious. "Acquisition" and "learning" are used as synonyms in this book.

additive bilingualism: The result of SLA in social contexts where members of a dominant group learn the language of a minority without threat to their L1 competence or to their ethnic identity.

adjacency pairs: Segments of conversational structure in which certain speech acts are tied together in a necessary sequence (such as question and answer, or compliment and acknowledgment).

affective filter: Krashen's notion of a mechanism that allows or restricts the processing of input. When the affective filter is "up" (because the learning is taking place on a conscious level, or because individuals are inhibited), input is not processed as well.

affective strategies: Means for learning an L2 that are related to individuals' feelings.

aptitude: An individual set of characteristics which correlates with success in language learning.

associative memory capacity: Potentials and constraints on how linguistic items are stored, and on how they are recalled and used in output. These determine appropriate selection from L2 elements that are stored and ultimately determine speaker fluency.

Audiolingual Method: An approach to language teaching that emphasizes repetition and habit formation. This approach was widely practiced in much of the world until at least the 1980s.

automatic processing: After an initial stage of **controlled processing**, automatic processing is a stage in learning that requires less mental "space" and attentional effort on the learner's part.

automatization: The activation and retrieval of certain elements in memory whenever appropriate input is perceived.

auxiliary language: A second language that learners need to know for some official functions in their immediate sociopolitical setting, or that they will need for purposes of wider communication, although their first language serves most other needs in their lives.

back-channel signals: Verbal or nonverbal indications by a listener of comprehension or lack thereof.

basic variety: A stage in development at which L2 learners have constructed an interlanguage grammar consisting of infinitival verbs and during which there is increasing use of grammatical relators such as prepositions. This is as opposed to the earlier stage where largely nominals and adjectives are used, but seldom verbs, to organize utterances. Many learners may be able to express themselves adequately at this stage in some contexts, and not all continue development beyond this level.

Behaviorism: The most influential cognitive framework applied to language learning in the 1950s. It claims that learning is the result of habit formation.

bilingualism: The ability to use two languages.

bottom-up processing: Achieving interpretation and production of language meaning through prior knowledge of the language system and of physical (graphic and auditory) cues.

Broca's area: An area in the left frontal lobe of the brain that is responsible for the ability to speak.

case marker: A grammatical marker that indicates the function of a word in a sentence, such as whether it is an agent or object.

central processing: The heart of the **Information Processing** framework, where learning occurs as learners go from **controlled** to **automatic processing** and reorganize their knowledge.

child grammar: Grammar of children at different maturational levels that is systematic in terms of production and comprehension.

cognitive strategies: Means for learning an L2 that make use of direct analysis or synthesis of linguistic material.

cognitive style: An individual's preferred way of processing: i.e. of perceiving, conceptualizing, organizing, and recalling information.

cohesion: Linguistic marking of links between elements of a text. These provide unity and consistency of thought, logic, and structure.

collocation: A combination of words that commonly occur together, including idioms and metaphors.

communication strategies: Learner techniques of compensating for limitations in their L2 linguistic resources, such as repairing misunderstanding or sustaining interpersonal interaction.

communicative competence: A basic tenet of sociolinguistics defined as "what a speaker needs to know to communicate appropriately within a particular language community" (Saville-Troike 2003).

communicative contexts: Different contexts in which variable features in language may appear: linguistic, psychological, microsocial, and macrosocial.

competence: Underlying knowledge of language.

competition Model: A functional approach to SLA which assumes that all linguistic performance involves "mapping" between external form and internal function.

compound bilingualism: Organization of two languages in the brain as a fused or unified system.

comprehensible input: Krashen's term for input that is understood.

Connectionism: A cognitive framework for explaining learning processes, beginning in the 1980s and becoming increasingly influential. It assumes that SLA results from increasing strength of associations between stimuli and responses.

connection strengths: The probabilistic associations formed and strengthened when learners are exposed to repeated patterns in units of input and extract regularities from them during processing.

Constructionism: An approach to SLA formulated within Chomsky's Minimalist Program that considers interlanguage development as the progressive mastery of L2 vocabulary along with the morphological features (which specify word form) that are part of lexical knowledge.

content: Knowledge of background information about the topic that is being read about or listened to.

context: Knowledge based on what has already been read or heard in a specific text or situation, as well as an understanding of what the writer's or speaker's intentions are, and the overall structure of the discourse pattern being used.

contextualization cues: Elements of communication that allow people to express and interpret meaning beyond the referential meaning which the surface structure of the message provides.

Contrastive Analysis (CA): A linguistic approach to SLA that involves predicting and explaining learner problems based on a comparison of L1 and L2 to determine linguistic similarities and differences.

contrastive rhetoric: An area of research that compares genre-specific conventions in different languages and cultures, with particular focus on predicting and explaining problems in L2 academic and professional writing.

controlled processing: An initial stage of the learning process that demands learners' attention.

coordinate bilingualism: Organization of two languages in the brain as parallel linguistic systems, where L1 and L2 are independent of one another.

corpus linguistic analysis: Analysis of large collections of written and spoken texts to determine the relative frequency of different vocabulary items and grammatical patterns. Often used as a basis for deciding what needs to be taught for specific purposes.

creative construction: The subconscious creation of a mental grammar that allows speakers to interpret and produce utterances they have not heard before.

critical period: The limited number of years during which normal L1 acquisition is possible.

Critical Period Hypothesis: The claim that children have only a limited number of years during which they can acquire their L1 flawlessly; if they suffered brain damage to the language areas, brain plasticity in childhood would allow other areas of the brain to take over the language functions of the damaged areas, but beyond a certain age, normal language development would not be possible. This concept is commonly extended to SLA as well, in the claim that only children are likely to achieve native or near-native proficiency in L2.

cue strength: A part of **form–function mapping** where learners detect cues in language input which are associated with a particular function and recognize what weight to assign each possible cue.

cues: Linguistic signals that are associated with a particular semantic or grammatical function.

culture: Knowledge that subsumes **content** and **context** information in many ways, but also includes an understanding of the wider social setting within which acts of communication take place.

declarative knowledge: Isolated facts and rules. Processing of this knowledge is usually relatively slow and under attentional control.

deductive processing: A **top-down** approach that begins with a prediction or rule and then applies it to interpret particular instances of input.

derivational morphology: Prefixes and suffixes that are added to words to create words with new meanings.

developmental errors: Also known as **intralingual errors**, they are inaccurate utterances that represent incomplete learning of L2 rules or overgeneralizations.

direct correction: Explicit statements about incorrect language use.

discourse: The linguistic unit which is larger than a single sentence and involves ways of connecting sentences, organizing information across sentence boundaries, and structuring storytelling, conversation, and interaction in general.

Error Analysis (EA): An approach to SLA that takes an internal focus on learners' **creative construction** of language. It is based on description and analysis of actual learner errors in

L2, rather than on idealized linguistic structures attributed to native speakers of L1 and L2 (as in **Contrastive Analysis**).

errors: Inappropriate utterances which result from learners' lack of L2 knowledge. Corder (1967) contrasts these with **mistakes**.

Ethnography of Communication: A framework for analysis of language and its functions that was established by Hymes (1966). It relates language use to broader social and cultural contexts, and applies ethnographic methods of data collection and interpretation to study of language acquisition and use.

external focus: Focus for the study of SLA that emphasizes language use, including the functions of language that are realized in learners' production at different stages of development.

feedback: Information that is provided to learners about whether or not their production and interpretation of language is appropriate. This may be in the form of direct correction, or it may take more indirect forms.

field-dependent (FD): A **learning style** characterized by a global and holistic mode of processing new information.

field-independent (FI): A **learning style** characterized by a particularistic and analytic mode of processing new information.

final state: The outcome of L1 and L2 learning, also known as the stable state of adult grammar.

first language/native language/mother tongue (L1): A language that is acquired naturally in early childhood, usually because it is the primary language of a child's family. A child who grows up in a multilingual setting may have more than one "first" language.

foreign language: A second language that is not widely used in the learners' immediate social context, but rather one that might be used for future travel or other cross-cultural communication situations, or one that might be studied as a curricular requirement or elective in school with no immediate or necessary practical application.

foreigner talk: Speech from L1 speakers addressed to L2 learners that differs in systematic ways from language addressed to native or very fluent speakers.

formal L2 learning: Instructed learning that takes place in classrooms.

form–function mapping: Basic to SLA, a process that involves correlating external form and internal function.

fossilization: A stable state in SLA where learners cease their interlanguage development before they reach target norms despite continuing L2 input and passage of time.

free variation: Variation in interlanguage that is not accounted for by linguistic, psychological, or social contexts.

function: A term with several meanings in linguistics. See **Structural Function** and **Pragmatic Function**.

function words: A limited set of terms that carry primarily grammatical information. These words form part of the core vocabulary in every language.

functional (models of linguistics): Approaches that are based on **Functionalism**.

Functionalism: A linguistic framework with an external focus that dates back to the early twentieth century and has its roots in the Prague School of Eastern Europe. It emphasizes the information content of utterances and considers language primarily as a system of communication. Functionalist approaches have largely dominated European study of SLA and are widely followed elsewhere in the world.

Functional Typology: A functional approach that involves classification of languages and their features into categories (or types; hence "typology") with a major goal being to describe patterns of similarities and differences among them, and to determine which types and patterns occur more or less frequently or are universal in distribution.

function-to-form mapping: A functional approach which has been applied to the description and analysis of interlanguage. One of its basic concepts is **grammaticalization**.

genres: Conventionalized categories and types of discourse.

Government and Binding (GB) Model: An earlier name for Chomsky's **Principles and Parameters** framework.

grammaticalization: A developmental process in which a grammatical function (such as the expression of past time) is first conveyed by shared extralinguistic knowledge and inferencing based on the context of discourse, then by a lexical word (such as *yesterday*), and only later by a grammatical marker (such as the suffix -*ed*).

grammatical sensitivity: See **inductive language learning ability**.

hemisphere: One half of the brain. The left half is called the left hemisphere; the right half is called the right hemisphere.

humanistic (approaches): Efforts to explain learning from a psychological perspective that began to influence SLA teaching and research in the 1970s. They consider emotional involvement in learning, as well as biological differences associated with age, sex, and modes of processing.

Identity Hypothesis (L1 = L2): The claim that processes involved in acquisition of L1 and L2 are the same.

idiom: A fixed expression of two or more words that is interpreted as a single lexical unit.

indirect correction: Implicit feedback about inappropriate language use, such as clarification requests when the listener has actually understood an utterance.

inductive language-learning ability: Capacity of the brain to process segmented auditory input and to perceive structure, identify patterns, make generalizations, recognize the grammatical function of elements, and formulate rules. Also called **grammatical sensitivity**.

inductive processing: A **bottom-up** approach to interpretation and production that begins with examining input to discover some pattern and then formulates a generalization or rule that accounts for it. It may then in turn be applied deductively.

inflection: A linguistic element that adds or changes grammatical meaning when added to a word (such as its tense, aspect, and number).

inflectional morphology: Word parts that carry meanings such as tense, aspect, and number.

informal L2 learning: SLA that takes place in naturalistic contexts.

information organization: How sentences and larger linguistic units are structured as a means for conveying information from speaker/writer to hearer/reader.

Information Processing (IP): A cognitive framework which assumes that SLA (like learning of other complex domains) proceeds from **controlled** to **automatic processing** and involves progressive reorganization of knowledge.

initial rate (of learning): The speed at which new L2 material is learned early in the L2 learning process, where, contrary to popular belief, older learners have an advantage over young children in SLA.

initial state: The starting point for language acquisition; it is thought to include the underlying knowledge about language structures and principles that are in learners' heads at the very start of L1 or L2 acquisition.

innate capacity: A natural ability, usually referring to children's natural ability to learn or acquire language.

inner speech: Vygotsky's term for the unvocalized self-talk that many adults use to control their own thought and behavior.

input: Whatever sample of L2 learners are exposed to.

instruction: Explicit teaching, often in school settings.

instructed L2 learning: Synonym for **formal L2 learning**.

instrumental motivation: Perception of a practical value for learning an L2, such as increasing occupational opportunities, enhancing prestige and power, accessing scientific and technical information, or passing a course in school.

intake: Input which is attended to.

integrative motivation: Interest in learning an L2 because of a desire to learn about or associate with the people who use it, or because of an intention to participate in or integrate with the L2-using speech community. Affective factors are dominant.

Interaction Hypothesis: The claim that modifications and collaborative efforts which take place in social interaction facilitate SLA because they contribute to the accessibility of input for mental processing.

interactional (purpose): Interpersonal goals in communication that are primarily affective.

Intercultural Communication: Interactional processes that take place between people who come from different cultural backgrounds.

interference: Inappropriate influence of an L1 structure or rule on L2 use. Also called **negative transfer**.

Interlanguage (IL): Intermediate states or interim grammars of learner language as it moves toward the target L2. See **learner varieties**.

interlingual errors: Errors that result from **negative transfer** of L1 to L2. Contrast with **intralingual errors**.

internal focus: Focus for the study of SLA that is based primarily on the work of Noam Chomsky and his followers. It sets the goal of study as accounting for speakers' internalized, underlying knowledge of language, rather than the description of surface forms as in earlier **Structuralism**.

interpersonal competence: Knowledge required of learners who plan to use the L2 primarily in face-to-face contact with other speakers.

interpersonal interaction: Communicative events and situations that occur between people.

intonation: Patterns of tone or pitch levels over a stretch of speech.

intralingual errors: Errors in L2 that are not due to interference from L1. These are also sometimes termed **developmental errors**, meaning that they represent incomplete learning of L2 rules or overgeneralization of them. Contrast with **interlingual errors**.

intrapersonal interaction: Communication that occurs within an individual's own mind, viewed by Vygotsky as a sociocultural phenomenon.

language acquisition device (LAD): A metaphor used by Chomsky to refer to children's **language faculty**. Extended to adult SLA by Krashen and others.

language community: A group of people who share knowledge of a common language at least to some extent.

language dominance: Multilingual speakers' relative fluency in one over another of their languages.

language faculty: Term used by Chomsky for a "component of the human mind" that accounts for children's innate knowledge of language.

language for specific purposes: Restricted or highly specialized second languages, such as *French for Hotel Management* or *English for Academic Purposes (EAP)*.

lateralization: Differential specialization of the two halves of the brain. For example, the left hemisphere becomes specialized for most language activity, many believe during a **critical period** for language development.

learner language: Synonym for **interlanguage**.

learner varieties: A term used by Klein and Perdue to refer to **interlanguage**.

learning: Krashen's term for conscious SLA. Contrasts in his usage with **acquisition**, which is unconscious.

learning strategies: The behavior and techniques that individuals adopt in their efforts to learn L2.

learning style: Characteristics of L2 learners that include a combination of personality traits and **cognitive style**.

lemmas: Within **Processability Theory**, lemmas are words that are processed without carrying any grammatical information or being associated with any ordering rules.

lexicon: The component of language that is concerned with words and their meanings.

library language: A second language that functions as a tool for further learning, especially when books or journals in a desired field of study are not commonly published in the learner's L1.

linguistic competence: The underlying knowledge that speakers/hearers have of a language. Chomsky distinguishes this from **linguistic performance**.

linguistic performance: The use of language knowledge in actual production.

logical problem of language acquisition: The question of how children achieve the final state of L1 development with ease and success when the linguistic system is very complex and their cognitive ability is not fully developed.

macrosocial (focus): An emphasis within the social perspective that is concerned with effects of broad cultural, political, and educational environments on L2 acquisition and use.

markedness: A basis for classification of languages according to whether a specific feature occurs more frequently than a contrasting element in the same category, is less complex structurally or conceptually, or is more "normal" or "expected" along some dimension (rendering it "unmarked" as opposed to "marked" in that respect).

Markedness Differential Hypothesis: Eckman's (1977) claim that unmarked features in L1 are more likely to transfer to L2, and that marked features in L2 will be harder to learn.

Mentalism: An approach that puts emphasis on the innate capacity of the language learner rather than on external factors of language learning.

metacognitive strategies: Strategies for learning an L2 that attempt to regulate language learning with conscious planning and monitoring.

metaphor: An expression which involves the substitution of a similar but figurative element of language for a literal one, such as *love is a river* instead of *love is a long process*.

microsocial (focus): An emphasis within the social perspective that is concerned with the potential effects of different immediately surrounding conditions of language use on SLA, including specific social contexts of interaction.

Minimalist Program: The internally focused linguistic framework that follows Chomsky's **Principles and Parameters** model. This framework adds distinctions between lexical and functional category development, as well as more emphasis on the acquisition of feature specification as a part of lexical knowledge.

mistakes: Inappropriate language production that results from some kind of processing failure such as a lapse in memory. Corder (1967) contrasts these with **errors** and does not include them within Error Analysis procedures.

monitor: A store of conscious knowledge about L2 that is a product of **learning** (in Krashen's usage) and is available for purposes of editing or making changes in what has already been produced.

Monitor Model: An approach to SLA introduced by Krashen (1978) that takes an internal focus on learners' **creative construction** of language.

monolingual competence: Knowledge of only one language.

monolingualism: The ability to use only one language.

Morpheme Order Studies: An approach to SLA introduced by Dulay and Burt (1974) that focuses on the sequence in which specific English grammatical morphemes are acquired. Claims are made for a **natural order**.

morpheme: The smallest unit of language that carries lexical or grammatical meaning; often part of a word.

morphology: The composition of words in different languages and the study of such systems generally.

motivation: A need and desire to learn.

Multidimensional Model: An approach to SLA which claims that learners acquire certain grammatical structures in developmental sequences, and that those sequences reflect how learners overcome processing limitations. Further, it claims that language instruction which targets developmental features will be successful only if learners have already mastered the processing operations which are associated with the previous stage of acquisition.

multilingual competence: "The compound state of a mind with two [or more] grammars" (Cook 1991:112).

multilingualism: The ability to use more than one language.

naturalistic L2 learning: Synonym for **informal L2 learning**.

natural order: A universal sequence in the grammatical development of language learners.

negative evidence: Explicit correction of inappropriate utterances.

negative transfer: Inappropriate influence of an L1 structure or rule on L2 use. Also called **interference**.

negotiation of meaning: Collaborative effort during interaction that helps prevent or repair breakdown of communication between native and nonnative speakers, like comprehension checks and clarification requests.

Neurolinguistics: The study of the location and representation of language in the brain, of interest to biologists and psychologists since the nineteenth century and one of the first fields to influence cognitive perspectives on SLA when systematic study began in the 1960s.

nominalization: The process of turning entire sentences into fillers for noun phrase positions.

oral (mode): Channel of communication that involves sounds produced by the vocal tract; includes listening and speaking.

orthography: Symbolic writing system.

output: In SLA, the language that learners produce in speech/sign or in writing.

Parallel Distributed Processing (PDP): A connectionist approach to SLA which claims that processing takes place in a network of nodes in the brain that are connected by pathways, and that frequency of input and nature of feedback largely determine language learning.

parameters: Limited options in realization of universal **principles** which account for grammatical variation between languages of the world. Part of Chomsky's theory of **Universal Grammar**.

patterns of activation: Probabilistic associations that develop between nodes in the brain as language learning takes place. Part of the theory of **Parallel Distributed Processing**.

performance: See **linguistic performance**.

phonemes: Speech sounds that contrast in similar contexts and make a difference in meaning.

phonemic coding ability: The capacity to process auditory input and organize it into segments which can be stored and retrieved.

phonology: The sound systems of different languages and the study of such systems generally.

phonotactics: Possible sequences of consonants and vowels for any given language.

plasticity: The capacity of the brain to assume new functions. In early childhood, if one area of the brain is damaged, another area of the brain is able to assume the functions of the damaged area because it retains plasticity.

positive evidence: Actual utterances by other speakers that learners are able to at least partially comprehend.

positive transfer: Appropriate incorporation of an L1 structure or rule in L2 structure.

poverty-of-the- stimulus: The argument that because language input to children is impoverished and they still acquire L1, there must be an **innate capacity** for L1 acquisition.

pragmatic competence: Knowledge that people must have in order to interpret and convey meaning within communicative situations.

pragmatic function: What the use of language can accomplish, such as conveying information, controlling others' behavior, or expressing emotion.

pragmatic mode: A style of expressing meaning which relies heavily on context.

principles: Properties of all languages of the world; part of Chomsky's **Universal Grammar**.

Principles and Parameters (model): The internally focused linguistic framework that followed Chomsky's **Transformational-Generative Grammar**. It revised specifications of what constitutes **innate capacity** to include more abstract notions of general principles and constraints common to human language as part of a **Universal Grammar**.

private speech: The self-talk which many children (in particular) engage in. Vygostky claims that this leads to **inner speech**.

procedural knowledge: Knowledge that requires processing of longer associated units and increasing **automatization** in comparison to **declarative knowledge**. This frees attentional resources for higher-level skills. Proceduralization requires practice.

Processability (theory): A reorientation of the **Multidimensional Model** that extends its concepts of learning and applies them to teaching second languages, with the goal of determining and explaining the sequences in which processing skills develop in relation to language learning.

productive activities: L2 use that involves communicating meaning to others by writing or speaking.

recast: An **indirect correction** that might appear to paraphrase what a learner says but actually corrects an element of language use.

receptive activities: L2 use that involves interpreting the meaning of others by reading or listening.

reduced form: The less complex grammatical structures that typically characterize interlanguage (such as omission of past tense markers).

reduced function: The smaller range of communicative needs that are typically fulfilled by interlanguage in comparison to learners' L1.

registers: Varieties of a language that are used in particular situations.

restructuring: The reorganization of knowledge that takes place in the **central processing** stage of **Information Processing**.

rule-governed behavior: A characterization of language use from the perspective of **mentalism**, which claims that this ability is based on tacit knowledge of a relatively limited set of underlying regularities or rules.

scaffolding: Verbal guidance which an expert provides to help a learner perform any specific task, or the verbal collaboration of peers to perform a task which would be too difficult for any one of them in individual performance.

schemas: Mental structures that map the expected patterns of objects and events.

second language (L2): In its general sense, this term refers to any language that is acquired after the **first language** has been established. In its specific sense, this term typically refers to an additional language which is learned within a context where it is societally dominant and needed for education, employment, and other basic purposes. The more specific sense contrasts with **foreign language, library language, auxiliary language**, and **language for specific purposes**.

Second Language Acquisition (SLA): A term that refers both to the study of individuals and groups who are learning a language subsequent to learning their first one as young children, and to the process of learning that language.

second language learning: The process of acquiring an additional language within the context of a language community which dominantly includes members who speak it natively. This term is also applied more generally to the process of acquiring any L2.

semantics: The linguistic study of meaning.

sequential multilingualism: Ability to use one or more languages that were learned after L1 had already been established.

simultaneous multilingualism: Ability to use more than one language that were acquired during early childhood.

Social Psychology: A societal approach in research and theory that allows exploration of issues such as how identity, status, and values influence L2 outcomes and why. It has disciplinary ties to both psychological and social perspectives.

social strategies: Means for learning an L2 that involve interaction with others.

Sociocultural Theory (SCT): An approach established by Vygotsky which claims that interaction not only facilitates language learning but is a causative force in acquisition. Further, all of learning is seen as essentially a social process which is grounded in sociocultural settings.

speech acts: Utterances that serve to accomplish the speakers' goals, such as requesting, apologizing, promising, denying, expressing emotion, complaining, etc.

S-R-R: stimulus-response-reinforcement: The sequence of factors which account for the learning process according to behaviorism: stimuli from the environment (such as linguistic input), responses to those stimuli, and reinforcement (positive if desirable and negative if not).

stimulus-response theory: A widely held view in the middle of the twentieth century that children learn language by imitation. Refers to two of the factors that are present in the sequence S-R-R.

structural function: The role which elements of language structure in a sentence play, such as a subject or object, or as an actor or goal.

Structuralism: The dominant linguistic model of the 1950s, which emphasized the description of different levels of production in speech.

subject-predicate structure: Grammatical organization at the sentence level with primary constituents being subject and predicate. This organization involves a significant amount of grammatical marking (or inflection) because of the agreement it requires between sentence elements. Contrast with topic-comment structure.

subordinate bilingualism: Organization of two languages in the brain where one linguistic system is accessed through the other. Contrast with compound and coordinate bilingualism.

subtractive bilingualism: The result of SLA in social contexts where members of a minority group learn the dominant language as L2 and are more likely to experience some loss of ethnic identity and attrition of L1 skills.

Sylvian fissure: A cleavage that separates lobes in the brain.

symbolic mediation: A link between a person's current mental state and higher order functions that is provided primarily by language; considered the usual route to learning (of language, and of learning in general). Part of Vygotsky's Sociocultural Theory.

syntactic mode: A style of expressing meaning which relies on formal grammatical elements.

syntax: The linguistic system of grammatical relationships of words within sentences, such as ordering and agreement.

Systemic Linguistics: A model for analyzing language in terms of the interrelated systems of choices that are available for expressing meaning, developed by Halliday in the late 1950s.

target language: The language that is the aim or goal of learning.

tone: Level of pitch as a phonological feature. In some languages (e.g. Chinese), contrasts in tone play an important role in word identification and interpretation.

top-down processing: Achieving interpretation and production of language meaning through prior knowledge of content, context, and culture. This process may allow learners to guess the meanings of words they have not encountered before, and to make some sense out of larger chunks of written and oral text.

topic-comment (structure): Grammatical organization at the sentence level with primary constituents being topic and comment. In this pattern, a topic is stated and then information is given about it. The topic-comment structure does not require the agreement marking that **subject-predicate structure** does.

transactional (purpose): Interpersonal goals in communication that are task-oriented.

transfer: Cross-linguistic influences in language learning: usually the influence of L1 on L2. See **positive transfer** and **negative transfer**.

Transformational-Generative Grammar: The first linguistic framework with an internal focus, which revolutionized linguistic theory and had a profound effect on both the study of first and second languages. Chomsky argued effectively that the behaviorist theory of language acquisition is wrong because it cannot explain the creative aspects of linguistic ability. Instead, humans must have some **innate capacity** for language.

transitional competence: An L2 learner's state of language knowledge that is potentially independent of L1 or L2.

typology: See **Functional Typology**.

ultimate achievement: The "end" result of L2 study.

Universal Grammar (UG): A linguistic framework developed most prominently by Chomsky which claims that L1 acquisition can be accounted for only by innate knowledge that the human species is genetically endowed with. This knowledge includes what all languages have in common.

U-shaped development: A sequence of acquisition for elements of both L1 and L2 where learners use an initially correct form such as plural *feet* (which they first learn as an unanalyzed word), then an incorrect *foots* (which shows they have learned the English plural formation rule of *foot* + -*s*). Finally, learners return to *feet* when they begin to acquire exceptions to the plural inflection rule.

utterance structure: The focus of the **Information Organization** approach to SLA, where emphasis is on "the way in which learners put their words together" (Klein and Perdue 1993:3).

variable: As a defining characteristic of learner language, inconsistency attributed both to developmental changes in what learners know and can produce, and to social context.

variable features: Multiple linguistic forms that are systematically or predictably used by different speakers of a language, or by the same speakers at different times, with the same or very similar meaning or function.

Variation Theory: A microsocial framework applied to SLA that explores systematic differences in learner production which depend on contexts of use.

vocabulary: See **lexicon**.

Wernicke's area: An area of the left frontal lobe of the brain that processes audio input.

written (mode): Channel of communication that involves graphic symbols; includes reading and writing.

Zone of Proximal Development (ZPD): An area of potential development where the learner can only achieve that potential with assistance. Part of Vygotsky's **Sociocultural Theory**.

ZISA: The acronym for a research project titled *Zweitspracherwerb italienischer und spanischer Arbeiter* "Second language development of Italian and Spanish workers."

References

Adamson, H. D. & Regan, V. M. (1991). The acquisition of community speech norms by Asian immigrants learning English as a second language. *Studies in Second Language Acquisition*, 13:1–22.

Anderson, J. R. (1976). *Language, Memory and Thought*. Hillsdale, NJ: Lawrence Erlbaum.

(1983). *The Architecture of Cognition*. Cambridge, MA: Harvard University Press.

Baker, M. (2001). *The Atoms of Language*. New York: Basic Books.

Bates, E. & MacWhinney, B. (1981). Second language acquisition from a functional perspective: pragmatic, semantic and perceptual strategies. In H. Winitz (ed.), *Native Language and Foreign Language Acquisition* (pp. 190–214). New York: New York Academy of Sciences.

Best, C. (1993). Emergence of language-specific constraints in perception of non-native speech: a window on early phonological development. In B. de Boysson-Bardies (ed.), *Developmental Neurocognition: Speech and Face Processing in the First Year of Life* (pp. 289–304). Dordrecht: Kluwer Academic Press.

Bialystok, E. (1990). *Communication Strategies: A Psychological Analysis of Second-Language Use*. Oxford: Blackwell.

(1997). The structure of age: in search of barriers to second language acquisition. *Second Language Research*, 13 (2): 116–37.

Bialystok, E. & Hakuta, K. (1994). *In Other Words: The Science and Psychology of Second-Language Acquisition*. New York: Basic Books.

Biber, D. (1995). *Dimensions of Register Variation: A Cross-Linguistic Comparison*. Cambridge: Cambridge University Press.

Biber, D., Conrad, S. & Reppen, R. (1998). Corpus-based approaches in applied linguistics. *Applied Linguistics*, 15:169–89.

Birdsong, D. (ed.) (1999). *Second Language Acquisition and the Critical Period Hypothesis: Second Language Research and Methodological Issues*. Mahwah, NJ: Lawrence Erlbaum.

Bley-Vroman, R. (1989). What is the logical problem of foreign language learning? In S. Gass & J. Schachter (eds.), *Linguistic Perspectives on Second Language Acquisition* (pp. 41–68). Cambridge: Cambridge University Press.

(2002). Frequency in production, comprehension, and acquisition. *Studies in Second Language Acquisition*, 24 (2):209–13.

Bloomfield, L. (1933). *Language*. New York: Holt, Rinehart & Winston.

Broca, P. (1861). Remarques sur le siège de la faculté du langage articulé suivies d'une observation d'apémie. *Bull. Soc. Anat.*, 6:330.

(1865). Sur le siège de la faculté du langage articulé. *Bull. Soc. D'Anthropologie*, 6:337–93.

Brown, C. (2000). The interrelation between speech perception and phonological acquisition from infant to adult. In J. Archibald (ed.), *Second Language Acquisition and Linguistic Theory* (pp. 4–63). Oxford: Blackwell.

Brown, R. (1973). *A First Language: The Early Stages*. Cambridge, MA: Harvard University Press.

Bruner, J. (1985). Vygotsky: a historical and conceptual perspective. In J. V. Wertsch (ed.), *Cultures, Communication and Cognition: Vygotskyan Perspectives* (pp. 21–34). Cambridge: Cambridge University Press.

Carroll, J. B. (1965). The prediction of success in intensive foreign language training. In R. Glaser (ed.), *Training, Research and Education* (pp. 87–136). New York: Wiley.

Carter, R. & Nunan, D. (eds.) (2001). *The Cambridge Guide to Teaching English to Speakers of Other Languages*. Cambridge: Cambridge University Press.

Celce-Murcia, M. & Olshtain, E. (2000). *Discourse and Context in Language Teaching*. Cambridge: Cambridge University Press.

Chamot, A. (1987). The learning strategies of ESL students. In A. Wenden & J. Rubin (eds.), *Learner Strategies in Language Learning* (pp. 71–83). Englewood Cliffs, NJ: Prentice Hall.

Chapelle, C. & Green, P. (1992). Field independence/dependence in second language acquisition research. *Language Learning*, 42:47–83.

Chomsky, N. (1957). *Syntactic Structures*. The Hague: Mouton.

(1965). *Aspects of the Theory of Syntax*. Cambridge, MA: MIT Press.

(1981). *Lectures on Government and Binding*. Dordrecht: Foris.

(1995). *The Minimalist Program*. Cambridge, MA: MIT Press.

(2002). *On Nature and Language*, ed. A. Belletti, & L. Rizzi. Cambridge: Cambridge University Press.

Chomsky, N. & Halle, M. (1968). *The Sound Pattern of English*. New York: Harper Row.

Clahsen, H. (1984). The acquisition of German word order: a test case for cognitive approaches to L2 development. In R. Andersen (ed.), *Second Language: A Cross Linguistic Perspective* (pp. 219–42). Rowley, MA: Newbury House.

Clahsen, H., Meisel, J. & Pienemann, M. (1983). *Deutsch als Zweitsprachs der Spracherwerb ausländischer Arbeiter*. Tübingen: Gunter Narr.

Cohen, A. D. (1996). Speech Acts. In S. L. McKay & N. H. Hornberger (eds.), *Sociolinguistics and Language Teaching* (pp. 383–420). Cambridge: Cambridge University Press.

Connor, U. (1996). *Contrastive Rhetoric*. Cambridge: Cambridge University Press.

Cook, V. (1988). *Chomsky's Universal Grammar*. Oxford: Blackwell.

(1991). *Second Language Learning and Language Teaching* (Second Edition). London: Arnold.

(1992). Evidence for multicompetence. *Language Learning*, 42 (4): 557–91.

Cook, V. & Newson, M. (1996). *Chomsky's Universal Grammar: An Introduction* (Second Edition). Oxford: Blackwell.

Corder, S. P. (1967). The significance of learners' errors. *International Review of Applied Linguistics*, 5 (4): 161–70. Reprinted in S. P. Corder (1981), *Error Analysis and Interlanguage* (pp. 5–13). Oxford: Oxford University Press.

Crystal, D. (1997a). *Dictionary of Linguistics and Phonetics* (Fourth Edition). Oxford: Blackwell.

(ed.) (1997b). *The Cambridge Encyclopedia of Language* (Second Edition). Cambridge: Cambridge University Press.

Cummins, J. (1981). Age on arrival and immigrant second language learning in Canada: a reassessment. *Applied Linguistics*, 2:132–49.

Curtiss, S. (1977). *Genie*. New York: Academic Press.

de Bot, K. (1996). The psycholinguistics of the Output Hypothesis. *Language Learning*, 46 (3): 529–55.

Diaz, R. M. (1985). The intellectual power of bilingualism. *The Quarterly Newsletter of the Laboratory of Comparative Human Cognition*, 7:16–22.

Diaz, R. M. & Klingler, C. (1991). Towards an explanatory model of the interaction between bilingualism and cognitive development. In E. Bialystok (ed.), *Language Processing in Bilingual Children* (pp. 167–92). Cambridge: Cambridge University Press.

Donato, R. (2000). Sociocultural contributions to understanding the foreign and second language classroom. In J. P. Lantolf (ed.), *Sociocultural Theory and Second Language Learning* (pp. 27–50). Oxford: Oxford University Press.

Donato, R. & McCormick, D. (1994). A sociocultural perspective on language learning strategies: the role of mediation. *Modern Language Journal*, 78 (4)3–64.

Dörnyei, Z. (2001). New themes and approaches in second language motivation research. *Annual Review of Applied Linguistics*, 21:43–59.

Dulay, H. & Burt, M. (1973). Should we teach children syntax? *Language Learning*, 24:245–58.

(1974). A new perspective on the creative construction process in child second language acquisition. *Working Papers on Bilingualism*, 4:71–98.

Eckman, F. R. (1977). Markedness and the contrastive analysis hypothesis. *Language Learning*, 27:315–30.

(1996). A functional typological approach to second language acquisition theory. In W. C. Ritchie & T. K. Bhatia (eds.), *Handbook of Second Language Acquisition* (pp. 195–211). New York: Academic Press.

Ellis, N. C. (2002). Frequency effects in language processing. *Studies in Second Language Acquisition*. 24 (2):143–88.

Ellis, R. (1985). *Understanding Second Language Acquisition*. Oxford: Oxford University Press.

(1994). *The Study of Second Language Acquisition*. Oxford: Oxford University Press.

(1997). *Second Language Acquisition*. Oxford: Oxford University Press.

(1999). Theoretical perspectives on interaction and language learning. In R. Ellis, *Learning a Second Language Through Interaction* (pp. 3–31). Amsterdam: John Benjamin.

Emmorey, K. (2002). *Language, Cognition and the Brain: Insights from Sign Language Research*. Mahwah, NJ: Lawrence Erlbaum.

Ervin, S. M. & Osgood, C. E. (1954). Second language learning and bilingualism. *Journal of Abnormal and Social Psychology*, 58:139–45.

Eubank, L., Selinker, L. & Sharwood Smith, M. (eds.), (1995). *The Current State of Interlanguage*. Amsterdam: John Benjamins.

Fedio, P., August, A., Myatt, C., Kertzman, C., Miletich, R., Snyder, P., Sato, S. & Kafta, C. (1992). Functional localization of languages in a bilingual patient with intracaratid amytal, subdural electrical stimulation, and positron emission topography. Paper presented at the International Neuropsychological Society, San Diego, CA.

Ferguson, C. A. (1971). Absence of copula and the notion of simplicity: a study of normal speech, baby talk, foreigner talk and pidgins. In D. Hymes (ed.), *Pidginization and Creolization of Languages* (pp. 141–50). Cambridge: Cambridge University Press.

Flege, J. (1980). Phonetic approximation in second language acquisition. *Language Learning* 30:117–34.

Flowerdew, J. (ed.) (1994). *Academic Listening: Research Perspectives*. Cambridge: Cambridge University Press.

Floyd, P. & Carrell, P. C. (1987). Effects on ESL reading of teaching cultural content schemata. *Language Learning*, 37:89–108.

Freud, S. (1891). *Zur Auffassung der Aphasien*, translated into English as *On Aphasia* by E. Stengel, 1953. New York, NY: International University Press.

Fries, C. (1945). *Teaching and Learning English as a Foreign Language*. Ann Arbor, MI: University of Michigan Press.

Gardner, R. C. (1985). *Social Psychology and Second Language Learning: The Role of Attitudes and Motivation*. London: Arnold.

(2002). Social psychological perspective on second language acquisition. In R. B. Kaplan (ed.), *The Oxford Handbook of Applied Linguistics* (pp. 160–69). Oxford: Oxford University Press.

Gass, S. (1984). Development of speech perception and speech production abilities in adult second language learners. *Applied Psycholinguistics*, 5 (1):51–74.

(1996). Second language acquisition and linguistic theory: the role of language transfer. In W. C. Ritchie & T. K. Bhatia (eds.), *Handbook of Second Language Acquisition* (pp. 317–45). New York: Academic Press.

Givón, T. (1979). From discourse to syntax: grammar as a processing strategy. In T. Givón (ed.), *Syntax and Semantics 12: Discourse and Syntax* (pp. 81–112). New York: Academic Press.

Glahn, E., Håkansson, G., Hammarberg, B., Holmen, A., Hvenekilde, A. & Lund, K. (2001). Processability in Scandinavian second language acquisition. *Studies in Second Language Acquisition*, 23 (3):389–416.

Gonzalez, L. A. (1986). The effects of first language education on the second language and academic achievement of Mexican immigrant elementary school children in the United States. Ph.D. dissertation, University of Illinois at Urbana-Champaign.

Grabe, W. (1991). Current developments in second language reading research. *TESOL Quarterly*, 25 (3):375–406.

(2002). Reading in a second language. In R. B. Kaplan (ed.), *The Oxford Handbook of Applied Linguistics* (pp. 49–59). Oxford: Oxford University Press.

Gregg, K. R. (1996). The logical and developmental problems of second language acquisition. In W. C. Ritchie & T. K. Bhatia (eds.), *Handbook of Second Language Acquisition* (pp. 50–81). New York: Academic Press.

Grosjean, F. (1982). *Life with Two Languages*. Cambridge, MA: Harvard University Press.

Gumperz, J. J. (1977). Sociocultural knowledge in conversational inference. In M. Saville-Troike (ed.), *Linguistics and Anthropology* (pp. 191–211). Washington, DC: Georgetown University Press.

Halliday, M. A. K. (1973). The functional basis of language. In B. Bernstein (ed.), *Class, Codes and Control*, Volume II (pp. 343–66). London: Routledge and Kegan Paul.

(1975). *Learning How to Mean: Explorations in the Development of Language*. London: Arnold.

Halliday, M. A. K. & Hasan, R. (1976). *Cohesion in English*. London: Longman.

Halpern, D. F. (2000). *Sex Differences in Cognitive Abilities* (Third Edition). Mahwah, NJ: Lawrence Erlbaum.

Haugen, E. (1956). *Bilingualism in the Americas*. The American Dialect Society, University of Alabama.

Healy, A. F. & Bourne, L. E. Jr. (eds.) (1998). *Foreign Language Learning: Psycholinguistic Studies on Training and Retention*. Mahwah, NJ: Lawrence Erlbaum.

Herdina, P. & Jessner, U. (2002). *A Dynamic Model of Multilingualism*. Clevedon: Multilingual Matters.

Herschensohn, J. (2000). *The Second Time Around: Minimalism and L2 Acquisition*. Amsterdam: John Benjamins.

Hinkel, Eli. (ed.) (1999). *Culture in Second Language Teaching and Learning*. Cambridge: Cambridge University Press.

Horwitz, E. K. (2001). Language anxiety and achievement. *Annual Review of Applied Linguistics*, 21:112–26.

Huebner, T., Carroll, M. & Perdue, C. (1992). The acquisition of English. In W. Klein & C. Perdue (eds.), *Utterance Structure* (pp. 61–121). Amsterdam: John Benjamins.

Hymes, Dell. (1966). On communicative competence. Paper presented at the Research Planning Conference on Language Development among Disadvantaged Children, Yeshiva University.

Jackendoff, R. (1997). *The Architecture of the Language Faculty*. Cambridge, MA: MIT Press.

Jakobson, R. (1941). *Child Language, Aphasia, and Phonological Universals*. The Hague: Mouton.

Johns, Ann M. (ed.) (2002). *Genre in the Classroom: Multiple Perspectives*. Mahwah, NJ: Lawrence Erlbaum.

Johnson, K. & Johnson, H. (eds.) (1998). *Encyclopedic Dictionary of Applied Linguistics*. Oxford: Blackwell.

Jones, S. (1998). Learning styles and learning strategies: towards learner independence. *Forum for Modern Language Studies*, 34 (2):114–29.

Kachru, B. B. (1986). *The Alchemy of English: The Spread, Functions and Models of Non-Native Englishes*. Oxford: Pergamon Institute of English.

Kachru, B. B. & Nelson, C. L. (1996). World Englishes. In S. L. McKay & N. H. Hornberger (eds.), *Sociolinguistics*

and Language Teaching (pp. 71–102). Cambridge: Cambridge University Press.

Kaplan, R. B. (ed.) (2002). *The Oxford Handbook of Applied Linguistics*. Oxford: Oxford University Press.

Kasper, G. and Rose, K. R. (2002). *Pragmatic Development in a Second Language*. Oxford: Blackwell.

Kimura, D. (1992, September). Sex differences in the brain. *Scientific American*, 119–25.

Kleifgen, J. (1985). Skilled variation in a kindergarten teacher's use of foreigner talk. In S. M. Gass & C. G. Madden (eds.), *Input in Second Language Acquisition* (pp. 59–68). Rowley, MA: Newbury House.

(1986). Communicative inferencing between classroom teachers and limited English proficient international children. Ph.D. dissertation, University of Illinois at Urbana-Champaign.

Kleifgen, J. & Saville-Troike, M. (1992). Achieving coherence in multilingual interaction. *Discourse Processes*, 15:183–206.

Klein, W. & Perdue, C. (1992). *Utterance Structure: Developing Grammar Again*. Amsterdam: John Benjamins.

(1993). Utterance structures. In C. Perdue (ed.), *Adult Language Acquisition: Cross-Linguistic Perspectives*, Volume II (pp. 3–40). Cambridge: Cambridge University Press.

Krashen, S. (1978). The Monitor Model for second-language acquisition. In R. C. Gingras (ed.), *Second Language Acquisition and Foreign Language Teaching* (pp. 1–26). Arlington, VA: Center for Applied Linguistics.

Kroll, J. F. & Steward, E. (1994). Category Interference in translation and picture naming: evidence for asymmetric connections between bilingual memory representations. *Journal of Memory and Language*, 33:149–74.

Kunt, N. (1997). Anxiety and beliefs about language learning: a study of Turkish-speaking university students learning English in North Cyprus. Ph.D. dissertation, University of Texas at Austin.

Labov, W. (1965). On the mechanisms of linguistic change. *Georgetown University Monographs on Language and Linguistics*, 18:91–114.

Lado, R. (1957). *Linguistics Across Cultures*. Ann Arbor, MI: University of Michigan Press.

Lambert, W. E. (1974). Culture and language as factors in learning and education. In F. E. Aboud & R. D. Meade (eds.), *Cultural Factors in Learning and Education* (pp. 91–122). Bellingham, Washington: Fifth Western Symposium on Learning.

(1991). And then add your two cents' worth. In A. G. Reynolds (ed.), *Bilingualism, Multiculturalism, and Second Language Learning* (pp. 217–49). Hillsdale, NJ: Lawrence Erlbaum.

Lambert, W. E., Hodgson, R. C. Gardner, R. C. & Fillenbaum, S. (1960). Evaluational reactions to spoken languages. *Journal of Abnormal and Social Psychology*, 60:44–51.

Lantolf, J. P. (ed.) (2000). *Sociocultural Theory and Second Language Learning*. Oxford: Oxford University Press.

Leather, J. & James, A. (1996). Second language speech. In W. C. Ritchie & T. K. Bhatia (eds.), *Handbook of Second Language Acquisition* (pp. 269–316). New York: Academic Press.

Leki, I. & Carson, J. (1997). "Completely different world": EAP and the writing experiences of ESL students in university courses. *TESOL Quarterly*, 31:39–69.

Lenneberg, E. (1967). *Biological Foundations of Language*. New York: Wiley and Sons.

Lightbown, Patsy M. & Spada, Nina. (1999). *How Languages are Learned* (Second Edition). Oxford: Oxford University Press.

Liu, J. (2001). *Asian Students' Classroom Communication Patterns in U. S. Universities*. Westport, CN: Ablex.

Long, M. H. (1990). Maturational constraints on language development. *Studies in Second Language Acquisition*, 12:251–85.

(1996). The role of the linguistic environment in second language acquisition. In W. C. Ritchie & T. K. Bhatia (eds.), *Handbook of Second Language Acquisition* (pp. 413–68). New York: Academic Press.

Lynch, T. (1998). Theoretical perspectives on listening. *Annual Review of Applied Linguistics*, 18:3–19.

(2002). Listening. In R. B. Kaplan (ed.), *The Oxford Handbook of Applied Linguistics* (pp. 39–48). Oxford: Oxford University Press.

MacWhinney, B. (2001). The Competition Model: the input, the context, and the brain. In P. R. Robinson (ed.), *Cognition and Second Language Instruction* (pp. 69–90). Cambridge: Cambridge University Press.

MacWhinney, B. & Bates, E. (eds.) (1989). *The Crosslinguistic Study of Sentence Processing*. Cambridge: Cambridge University Press.

McCarthy, M. (2001). *Issues in Applied Linguistics*. Cambridge: Cambridge University Press.

McCarthy, M. & Carter, R. (1997). Written and spoken vocabulary. In N. Schmitt & M. McCarthy (eds.), *Vocabulary: Description, Acquisition and Pedagogy* (pp. 20–30). Cambridge: Cambridge University Press.

McClelland, J. L., Rumelhart, D. E. & Hinton, G. E. (1986). The appeal of Parallel Distributed Processing. In D. E. Rumelhart, J. L. McClelland & the PDP Research Group, *Parallel Distributed Processing*, Volume I (pp. 3–44). Cambridge, MA: MIT Press.

McKay, S. L. & Hornberger, N. H. (eds.) (1996). *Sociolinguistics and Language Teaching*. Cambridge: Cambridge University Press

McLaughlin, B. (1987). *Theories of Second Language Learning*. London: Arnold.

McNeil, D. (1966). Developmental psycholinguistics. In F. Smith & G. A. Miller (eds.), *The Genesis of Language: A Psycholinguistic Approach* (pp. 15–84). Cambridge, MA: MIT Press.

Mack, M. (1992). The relationship between neurolinguistics and applied linguistics. Paper presented at the American Association of Applied Linguistics Conference, Seattle, Washington.

Major, R. C. (2001). *Foreign Accent: The Ontogeny and Phylogeny of Second Language Phonology*. Mahwah, NJ: Lawrence Erlbaum.

Miller, G. A. (1964). The psycholinguists. *Encounter*, 23 (1):29–37.

Miller, J. (2000). Language use, identity, and social interaction: migrant students in Australia. *Research on Language and Social Interaction*, 33 (1):69–100.

Mills, D. L., Coffey-Corina, S. A. & Neville, H. J. (1993). Language acquisition and cerebral specialization in 20 month-old infants. *Journal of Cognitive Neuroscience*, 5:317–34.

Mitchell, R. and Myles, F. (2004). *Second Language Learning Theories* (Second Edition). London: Arnold.

Nagy, W. (1997). On the role of context in first- and second-language vocabulary learning. In N. Schmitt and M. McCarthy (eds.), *Vocabulary Description, Acquisition and Pedagogy* (pp. 64–83). Cambridge: Cambridge University Press.

Nation, I. S. P. (1990). *Teaching and Learning Vocabulary*. New York: Newbury House. Cited in S. M. Gass & L. Selinker, *Second Language Acquisition: An Introductory Course* (p. 374). Mahwah, NJ: Lawrence Erlbaum.

Nation, I. S. P. & Waring, R. (1997). Vocabulary size, text coverage and word lists. In N. Schmitt & M. McCarthy (eds.), *Vocabulary Description, Acquisition and Pedagogy* (pp. 6–19). Cambridge: Cambridge University Press.

Newport, E. (1990). Maturational constraints on language learning. *Cognitive Science, 14*:11–28.

Nida, E. (1953). Selective listening. *Language Learning*, 4 (3–4):92–101.

Novoa, L., Fein, D. & Obler, L. (1988). Talent in foreign languages: a case study. In L. Obler & D. Fein (eds.), *The Exceptional Brain: Neuropsychology of Talent and Special Abilities* (pp. 249–302). New York: Guilford Press.

Obler, L. K. & Gjerlow, K. (1999). *Language and the Brain*. Cambridge: Cambridge University Press.

Obler, L. K. & Hannigan, S. (1996). Neurolinguistics of second language acquisition and use. In W. C. Ritchie & T. K. Bhatia (eds.), *Handbook of Second Language Acquisition* (pp. 509–23). New York: Academic Press.

Ohta, A. S. (2001). *Second Language Acquisition Processes in the Classroom-Learning Japanese*. Mahwah, NJ: Lawrence Erlbaum.

Ojemann, G. A. & Whitaker, H. A. (1978). The bilingual brain. *Archives of Neurology*, 35:490–12.

Oxford, R. L. (1992). Language learning strategies in a nutshell: update and ESL suggestions. *TESOL Journal, 2* (2):18–22.

(1993). Research on second language learning strategies. *Annual Review of Applied Linguistics*, 13:175–87.

Oxford, R. L. & Ehrman, M. (1993). Second language research on individual differences. *Annual Review of Applied Linguistics, 13*:188–205.

Paradis, M. (1987). *The Assessment of Bilingual Aphasia*. Hillsdale, NJ: Lawrence Erlbaum.

Perdue, C. (ed.) (1993). *Adult Language Acquisition. Cross-Linguistic Perspectives*. Cambridge : Cambridge University Press.

(2000). Organizing principles of learner varieties. *Studies in Second Language Acquisition, 22*:299–305.

Piaget, J. (1926). *The Language and Thought of the Child*. London: Kegan Paul, Trench, Truber and Company. (Original work published 1923.)

Pienemann, M. (1998). Developmental dynamics in L1 and L2 acquisition: Processibility Theory and generative entrenchment. *Bilingualism: Language and Cognition*, 1:1–20.

Pienemann, M. & Håkansson, G. (1999). A unified approach toward the development of Swedish as L2: a processability account. *Studies in Second Language Acquisition, 21* (3):383–420.

Piller, I. (2002). Passing for a native speaker: identity and success in second language learning. *Journal of Sociolinguistics, 6* (2):179–206.

Pinker, S. (1994). *The Language Instinct*. New York: William Morrow.

Polanyi, L. (1995). Language learning and living abroad: stories from the field. In B. Freed (ed.), *Second Language Acquisition in a Study Abroad Context* (pp. 271–91). Amsterdam: John Benjamins.

Ramat, A. G. (ed.) (2003). *Typology and Second Language Acquisition*. Berlin: Mouton.

Reid, J. M. (1987). The learning style preference of ESL students. *TESOL Quarterly, 21* (1):87–111.

Robinson, P. (1995). Attention, memory and the "noticing" hypothesis. *Language Learning, 45* (2):283–331.

Rose, K. R. & Kasper, G. (eds.) (2001). *Pragmatics in Language Teaching*. Cambridge: Cambridge University Press.

Rumelhart, D. E. & McClelland, J. L. (1986). On learning the past tenses of English verbs. In D. E. Rumelhart, J. L. McClelland & the PDP Research Group. *Parallel Distributed Processing*, Volume II (pp. 216–71). Cambridge, MA: MIT Press.

Saville-Troike, M. (1984). What <u>really</u> matters in second language learning for academic achievement? *TESOL Quarterly, 18* (2):199–219.

(1988). Private speech: evidence for second language learning during the "silent" period. *Journal of Child Language*, 15:567–90.

(2002). Extending "communicative" concepts in the second language curriculum: a sociolinguistic perspective. In D. L. Lange & R. Michael Paige (eds.), *Culture as the Core: Perspectives in Second Language Education* (pp. 3–17). Greenwich, CT: Information Age Publishing.

(2003). *The Ethnography of Communication: An Introduction* (Third Edition). Oxford: Blackwell.

Saville-Troike, M., McClure, E. & Fritz, M. (1984). Communicative tactics in children's second language acquisition. In F. R. Eckman, K. H. Bell & D. Nelson (eds.), *Universals of Second Language Acquisition* (pp. 60–71). Rowley, MA: Newbury House.

Saville-Troike, M., Pan, J. & Dutkova, L. (1995). Differential effects of L2 on children's L1 development/attrition. *Southwest Journal of Linguistics*, 14 (1–2):125–49.

Scheibman, J. (2002). *Point of View and Grammar: Structural Patterns of Subjectivity in American Conversation*. Amsterdam: John Benjamins.

Schleppegrell, M. J. & Colombi, M. C. (eds.) (2002). *Developing Advanced Literacy in First and Second Languages: Meaning With Power*. Mahwah, NJ: Lawrence Erlbaum.

Schmidt, R. (1990). The role of consciousness in second language learning. *Applied Linguistics*, 11:129–88.

Schmitt, N. and McCarthy, M. (eds.) (1997). *Vocabulary Description, Acquisition and Pedagogy*. Cambridge: Cambridge University Press.

Schumann, J. H. (1978). The Acculturation Model for second language acquisition. In R. C. Gingras (ed.), *Second Language Acquisition and Foreign Language Teaching* (pp. 27–50). Arlington, VA: Center for Applied Linguistics.

(1997). *The Neurobiology of Affect in Language*. Oxford: Blackwell.

(2001). Appraisal psychology, neurobiology, and language. *Annual Review of Applied Linguistics, 21*:23–42.

Scollon, R. & Scollon, S. W. (2001). *Intercultural Communication* (Second Edition). Oxford: Blackwell.

Scovel, T. (2000). A critical review of the critical period research. *Annual Review of Applied Linguistics*, 20:213–23.

Searle, J. R. (1969). *Speech Acts*. Cambridge: Cambridge University Press.

Seliger, H. (1978). Implications of a multiple critical period hypothesis for second language learning. In W. Ritchie (ed.), *Second Language Research: Issues and Implications* (pp. 11–19). New York: Academic Press.

Selinker, L. (1972). Interlanguage. *International Review of Applied Linguistics*, 10:209–31.

(1992). *Rediscovering Interlanguage*. London: Longman.

Shachter, J. (1974). An error in error analysis. *Language Learning*, 27:205–14.

Simpson, R. & Mendis, D. (2003). A corpus based study of idioms in academic speech. *TESOL Quarterly*, 37 (3):419–41.

Singleton, D. (2001). Age and second language acquisition. *Annual Review of Applied Linguistics*, 21:77–89.

Skehan, P. (1989). *Individual Differences in Second Language Learning*. London: Edward Arnold.

(1998). *A Cognitive Approach to Language Learning*. Oxford: Oxford University Press.

Skinner, B. F. (1957). *Verbal Behavior*. New York: Appleton-Century-Crofts.

Spada, N. & Lightbown, P. M. (1999). Instruction, first language influence, and developmental readiness in second language acquisition. *The Modern Language Journal*, 85 (1):1–22.

Swain, M. & Lapkin, S. (1995). Problems in output and the cognitive processes they generate: a step towards second language learning. *Applied Linguistics*, 16 (3):371–91.

Swales, J. M. (1990). *Genre Analysis*. Cambridge: Cambridge University Press.

Swales, J. M. & Feak, C. (1994). *Academic Writing for Graduate Students*. Ann Arbor, MI: University of Michigan Press.

Swan, M. & Smith, B. (eds.) (2001). *Learner English* (Second Edition). Cambridge: Cambridge University Press.

Tarone, E. (1977). *Conscious communication strategies in Interlanguage. On TESOL '77* (pp. 194–203). Washington, DC: Teachers of English to Speakers of Other Languages.

Taylor, G. & Chen, T. (1991). Linguistic, cultural, and subcultural issues in contrastive discourse analysis:

Anglo-American and Chinese scientific texts. *Applied Linguistics, 12* (3):319–36.

Tomlin, R. S. (1990). Functionalism and second language acquisition. *Studies in Second Language Acquisition, 12*:155–77.

Traugott, E. C. & Pratt, M. L. (1980). *Linguistics for Students of Literature*. New York : Harcourt Brace Jovanovich.

Trubetzkoy, N. (1958). *Grundzüge der Phonologie* (Travaux du cercle linguistique de Prague 7). Göttingen : Vandenhoek and Ruprecht. (Original work published 1939.)

Truitt, S. (1995). Anxiety and beliefs about language learning: a study of Korean university students learning English. Ph.D. dissertation, University of Texas at Austin.

Tucker, G. R. (1999). A global perspective on bilingualism and bilingual education. *ERIC Digest*. Washington, DC: ERIC Clearinghouse on Languages and Linguistics.

Vaid, J. (1983). Bilingualism and brain lateraliza-tion. In S. Segalonitz (ed.), *Language Function and Brain Organization* (pp. 315–39). New York: Academic Press.

Vygotsky, L. S. (1962). *Thought and Language*. Cambridge, MA: MIT Press.

(1978). *Mind in Society: The Development of Higher Psychological Processes*. Cambridge, MA: Harvard University Press.

Weinreich, U. (1953). *Languages in Contact*. New York: Linguistic Circle of New York.

Wernicke, C. (1874). *Der aphasische Symptomencomplex*. Breslau, Poland: M. Cohn und Weigert.

White, L. (1996). Universal grammar and second language acquisition: current trends and new directions. In W. C. Ritchie & T. K. Bhatia (eds.), *Handbook of Second Language Acquisition* (pp. 85–120). New York: Academic Press.

(2003). *Second Language Acquisition and Universal Grammar*. Cambridge: Cambridge University Press.

Willett, J. (1995). Becoming first graders in an L2: an ethnographic study of L2 socialization. *TESOL Quarterly, 29* (3):473–503.

Williams, M. & Burden, R. L. (1997). *Psychology for Language Teachers: A Social Constructivist Approach*. Cambridge: Cambridge University Press.

Witkin, H. A., Lewis, H., Hertzman, M., Machover, K., Meissner, P. & Wapner, S. (1954). *Personality Through Perception*. New York: Harper & Brothers.

Wuillemin, D. & Richardson, B. (1994). Right hemisphere involvement in processing later-learned languages in multilinguals. *Brain and Language, 46*:620–36.

Xue, G. & Nation, I. S. P. (1984). A university word list. *Language Learning and Communication, 3*:215–29.

Yaguello, Marina. (1981/1998). *Language through the Looking Glass: Exploring Language and Linguistics*. Oxford: Oxford University Press.

Yang, J. (2002). The acquisition of temporality by adult second language learners of Chinese. Ph.D. dissertation, University of Arizona.

Young, R. (1999). Sociolinguistic approaches to SLA. *Annual Review of Applied Linguistics, 19*:105–32.

Zhu, X. (2001). Chinese Languages: Mandarin. *Facts about the World's Languages* (p. 146). New York: H. W. Wilson.

Index